BRIEF CHRONICLES

BRIEF CHRONICLES

A Survey of the Plays of Shakespeare and the Elizabethans in Actual Performance

by

JAMES AGATE

'. . . the abstracts and brief chronicles
of the time.'
Hamlet, Act II, Sc. 2

BENJAMIN BLOM, INC.

First Published 1943
Reissued 1971 by
Benjamin Blom, Inc., New York 10025

Library of Congress Catalog Card Number 79-92223

Printed in the United States of America

CONTENTS

5

CONTENTS

CONTENTS

7

CONTENTS

CONTENTS

CONTENTS

CONTENTS

11

CONTENTS

CONTENTS

ACKNOWLEDGMENTS

My thanks are due to the Proprietors of the *Sunday Times*, in whose columns all the matter of this book, with the exception of one article, originally appeared, for their courteous permission to reproduce that matter here. For the exception I am indebted to the proprietors of *John o' London's Weekly*.

Also to Messrs. Chapman and Hall (*The Contemporary Theatre, 1924, 1925 and 1926*), Victor Gollancz Ltd. (*More First Nights*), and George G. Harrap & Co. Ltd. (*The Amazing Theatre*).

DEDICATORY LETTER

TO

ALAN DENT

MY DEAR ALAN,

Nobody, I think, will deny that there is one respect in which the soil during the last fifty years has been less generous than in Hazlitt's day, and how poor in the way of criticism surviving in book form it has been from that day to this. If we wanted to know how Shakespeare was acted in the first quarter of the nineteenth century we have Hazlitt, Leigh Hunt and Lamb to tell us. But who was writing, or rather re-printing, in the second quarter of the century? Only G. H. Lewes, John Forster and the last of Hunt. Of the third quarter I know one book by Henry Morley and one by Joseph Knight. In the last, there is that portentous Bulge known as Clement Scott; with the exception of his monument to Irving, *From 'The Bells' to 'King Arthur'*, I know his work but little. In the year 1893 we strike a better period. You will agree that during the last decade of the last century and the first of this, the most authoritative dramatic critics functioning in London were — the order is alphabetical — William Archer, Max Beerbohm, J. T. Grein, Bernard Shaw and A. B. Walkley, all of whom published a selection of their theatrical notices. But Archer, who died in 1924, published nothing that I can find later than 1897: Grein (obiit 1935) nothing later than 1904: Walkley (obiit 1926) nothing in this kind later than 1907. Since the last war the most notable critics, or perhaps I should say the critics who have occupied the most space in the London newspapers, have been Charles Morgan, Ivor Brown, Desmond McCarthy, A. V. Cookman, Herbert Farjeon and — you will permit me to add — myself.

Reasonably rich though the soil has been during the last fifty years, there is one respect in which it has proved less generous

14

than in Hazlitt's day. This is in the treatment of Shakespeare which, in its desultoriness, would seem to have been somewhere between the off-hand and the scurvy. Please remember that I am referring solely to criticisms of the *acted* drama reprinted in book form and so available to the student. I do not say that the critics mentioned neglected to notice the plays of Shakespeare. Such notices were written and appeared; the point is that they occupy a small place in the criticisms their authors have chosen to reprint. For example, I find that of Shakespeare's thirty-seven plays Archer reprinted notices of only seventeen, the most notable omissions being: *The Winter's Tale, King John, Richard II, Henry IV* (Part 2), *Henry V, Julius Caesar, Coriolanus, Macbeth* and *King Lear*; Shaw in *Our Theatres in the Nineties* has articles on twenty-one of Shakespeare's plays, the principal omissions being *The Winter's Tale, King John, Richard II, Henry IV* (Part 2), *Henry V* and *Coriolanus*. In the case of Grein (eight plays) and Max (seven plays) omission is the order of the day. As for that elusive bird Walkley, my shelves contain only the *Pastiche and Prejudice* series which were your Christmas gifts to me. I have never been able to possess myself of *Playhouse Impressions* (1892), *Dramatic Criticism* (1903) or *Drama and Life* (1907).

Conning these matters it has occurred to me that any student wishing to know how Shakespeare fared in the London theatre between the two great wars would be faced with considerable difficulty, only one of the contemporary critics having republished his notices more or less comprehensively — and to say this is not in any way to slight or to wish to appear not to value, enchanting but selective essays by Ivor, Desmond and your brilliant self. For the student to take the Shakespeare out of my twelve volumes covering the plays produced on the London stage during the last twenty years would be an easy job but for the fact that every one of those volumes is out of print. I have therefore decided to bring together my notices of the Shakespeare productions I have seen since I joined the *Sunday Times* in 1923; these cover all the plays, with the exception of *The Two Gentlemen of Verona, The Winter's Tale*, the three parts of *King Henry VI*, and *Pericles*. In addition I have included notices of such of the other Elizabethans and Jacobeans as I have seen. The book is not intended to be an essay in, or contribution to, Shakespearean exegesis. I leave that to those Professors and Commentators who write of the plays as they see them in the study.

Only lately did I sit next to one of these learned scribes. It was on the first night of John Gielgud's latest revival of *King Lear*, and I noted, not without some amusement, that throughout the entire performance Great Authority held the book of the play at nose-length before its face; I am persuaded that it did not catch, or seek to catch, one single glimpse of what was happening on the stage. Now I do not profess to be an eminent interpreter of Shakespeare's inner meanings. What I have done in this book is to record some of the impressions registered not only on my ear but also on my eye, impressions made by the flesh-and-blood actor as he lived and breathed and was, or tried to be, the thing he pretended.

This, then, is the book I dedicate to you, my dear Alan, in gratitude for the help you gave me throughout the years during which it was first written. Beggar that I am, I hope you will not hold me poor in thanks.

JAMES AGATE

Villa Volpone
10 Fairfax Road
N.W.6
1943

SHAKESPEARE'S COMEDIES

THE TEMPEST
(Sadler's Wells)

MR. LAUGHTON AND MISS LANCHESTER

SIR ARTHUR QUILLER-COUCH said that this play and *A Midsummer Night's Dream* require to be acted by amateurs: 'The professional mummer has never made any hand with either play; nor, I think, ever will.' Not having seen any masterly rendering by the Uxbridge Strollers or the Chingford Thespians, I shall boldly declare *The Tempest* to be one of my unfavourite plays of Shakespeare. Regarded, that is, not as poetry but as acting piece, which difference I take to be that between fowl and boiling fowl. One agrees with Sir Arthur in so far as one has seen some professional mummers act Prospero. Mr. Ainley played that endless chunnerer — Miranda says: 'The *strangeness* of your story put heaviness in me' when she really means 'length'! — Mr. Ainley played the old codger like a toastmaster celebrating his golden wedding, while another famous actor reminded me of a conjurer in decreasing demand at Masonic banquets. As for the Benson troupe, their distinguished chief used to hang by his toes from the tops of poplars, leaving Prospero to be played by the stick engaged for Duncan and anybody else over eighty. I never heard of Irving playing Prospero. Presumably he had more sense. Postage stamps may be saved by readers desiring to tell me that the opinion set down above is uniquely crass. *Je m'en fiche.* In an article entitled *Enchanting Bores* an earlier critic wrote: 'Prospero fears that at times he must be boring Miranda, and therein, I think, reveals Shakespeare's own fear that he must be boring his public. At the last revival of the play, Mr. Henry Ainley spoke

17

and played Prospero beautifully — I cannot imagine a better performance — but I was glad when it was over. Not even this accomplished actor could hide from us the fact that Prospero is sometimes a bore.' I am content to be crass in the company of Arthur Bingham Walkley.

Let me run over one or two things which couldn't be anybody's reasons for liking this production. Certainly not the scenery, which consisted of an almost bare stage sparsely furnished with logs constructed out of pink Edinburgh rock, an igloo or wigwam made out of raffia as used by Miss Cicely Courtneidge for her production numbers, and three screens similarly fringed. Nor yet the costumes, since Prospero's magic robes would have shamed the Queen of Carnival at that town obviously hinted at in the lines:

> The approaching tide
> Will shortly fill the reasonable shore,
> That now lies foul and muddy.

To wit, Southend. Could it have been the music? Or some of it? Mr. Herbert Menges is not to be blamed because his island noises are Mr. Norman O'Neill's all over again. They are virtually as good, because they are virtually the same; probably in them we hear the song the sirens sang. But the songs Mr. Dennis Arundell makes Ariel sing are another matter. Pedantry may have some excuse in holding that Arne isn't old-fashioned enough, and in insisting upon Jacobean melodies played upon shawms and sackbuts and other strange serpents. But to insist upon steel-furniture ditties for Ariel is modernity at its worst.

But I very much liked Mr. Arundell's masque in the classical style; for Purcell could do no wrong, and to my ear spoof Purcell is better than spoof Delius. I do not, however, believe that everything that Iris and Ceres and Juno say should be sung. Taking the Cambridge Shakespeare as guide, I find that Iris has to enter to 'soft music', which means that the musicians should play and Iris talk through them. Iris and Ceres have a long dialogue to which Juno adds three lines before the stage-direction 'They sing' occurs. Which singing should, I think, end after twelve lines, when

Ferdinand compliments the artists with the words: 'This is a most majestic vision and Harmonious charmingly.'

One knows that stage-directions are late impositions. The point is that Shakespeare never wrote a lyric to be sung except in short lines, such as Juno's:

> Honour, riches, marriage-blessing,
> Long continuance, and increasing.
> Hourly joys be still upon you!
> Juno sings her blessings on you.

It is as inconceivable that Shakespeare meant Juno to speak this as that he intended Iris to sing:

> You nymphs, call'd Naiads, of the windring brooks,
> With your sedg'd crowns and ever-harmless looks,
> Leave your crisp channels, and on this green land
> Answer your summons; Juno does command.

The difference in the quality of the verse indicates that Shakespeare knew which would be covered up by music and which would not.

Mr. Laughton, having been told that he couldn't play Pickwick, was apparently determined to give us a Prospero incurring no charge of a second failure in benignity. There is some justification for this kindly view; the necromancer had his enemies where he wanted them and let them off with a minimum of revenge. Mr. Laughton, by the aid of taking thought and some first-class wiggery, composed a Prospero deriving snowily from Blake, Devrient's Lear, Michael Angelo's Noah, M. Boverio's Noë, possibly Noah himself, and certainly Father Christmas. But, alas, he made the old boy perform his hocus-pocus with a naughty little twinkle in his eye, and never for one moment suggested 'the potent wizard brooding in gloomy abstraction over the secrets of his art'! In a word, this was not Prospero but some good-natured spiritual ancestor of Mr. Maskelyne. But obviously the power to terrify must be at least latent in the character; how else could the old josser keep the whip-hand over Caliban?

All great actors have their kinks, and always at the wrong time. Bernhardt — I will *not* be muzzled — told me that she cooed and gurgled throughout Hugo's play because she held that Lucrezia Borgia, apart from that trifle of poisoning, was the most dove-like of her sex. The result was a performance almost as appallingly wrong as Mme. Pitoëff's Joan. Similarly Mr. Laughton seems to have decided that Prospero is a creature out of Dendy Sadler's Wells, I mean world, only too anxious to pass the port, but with a face cherubically set against spirits which may turn out to be evil. Mr. Laughton's failure is, however, more respectworthy than Sarah's. She was merely following her stock-line of personal fascination, while he purposely discards familiar face-pulling, mowing and gibbering in order to add to his range. This is extremely good for Mr. Laughton, but hard lines on Prospero.

May I be forgiven for saying that until Miss Elsa Lanchester the part of Ariel has never been acted? Ariel fails if there is the least suggestion of girl dressed up as boy, or even of boy. One must be able to say: 'Hail to thee, blithe spirit! Boy thou never wert!' and continue, if our memory is good enough:

> What objects are the fountains
> Of thy happy strain?
> What fields, or waves, or mountains?
> What shapes of sky or plain?
> What love of thine own kind? what ignorance of pain?

Now couple this with:

ARIEL   Your charm so strongly works 'em,
        That if you now beheld them your affections
        Would become tender.
PROSP   Dost thou think so, spirit?
ARIEL   Mine would, sir, were I human.

Yet though this clever actress invincibly suggests that Ariel belongs to his own kind, we who pretend to set forth what that kind is like are still bound, being mortal, to mortal visions for our parallels. One way of defining a thing is to say what it is not like, and therefore let it be set down that this Ariel bears no resemblance to the portico'd notion of that spirit cherished at Broadcasting House. In the matter of direct comparison he is a mixture of Nijinsky's Faun and Gilbert's Eros, the latter because he too is silvered from head to foot, with the addition of a touch of lovely colour in the red, tiny wings and cape. But this alone would not give us an Ariel beyond the reach of a competent mime or dancer. Miss Lanchester has added lightness, or better, taken away weight; she is imponderable, has no mass, and is as little felt by the island's earth as she is seen by its inhabitants. So impalpable to sight is this Ariel that his body seems to offer nothing to human glances. You see through him. He has a radiance that cannot be explained, and by an ingenious, unwearied, yet unwearisome movement of the arms suggests kinship with that insect creation which, quivering in the sun, puts to shame the helicopter of human invention. This Ariel speaks in a voice that is both shrill and soft and in my view sings as well as Ariel should, since there is no excuse for a coloratura soprano with full bosom and empty head. In short, it is a lovely performance of exquisite invention.

Next we come to Mr. Roger Livesey's Caliban, a delicious monster compounded of Frankenstein and Petrouchka. There is too much cause to bewail the absence of versatility, so let it be noted that in Mr. Livesey we have an actor who in a few months has played the French peasant in *Martine*, the Duke in *Measure for Measure*, Pishtchik and Caliban — all equally well. A little time ago we talked of this young player in terms of promise; the terms must now be those of achievement. Trinculo and Stephano are not too well done, and that dismal sextet which is Alonso, Sebastian, Antonio, Gonzalo, Adrian and Francisco would defeat any actors who ever lived. Incidentally I cannot understand why Prospero should be some four times as old as his brother. As Ferdinand and Miranda, Mr. Clifford Evans and Miss Ursula Jeans do nicely, and as Iris, Ceres and Juno, Mesdames Margaret Field-Hyde, Flora Robson and Evelyn Allen look like goddesses from the Forest of Elizabeth Arden.

First Nights: January 8, 1934

MERRY WIVES
(King's, Hammersmith)

How modern this play is! Mr. Caradoc Evans would not disown Sir Hugh, whose 'If I be drunk, I'll be drunk with those that have the fear of God' has the very accent of Capel Sion. And at the Welshman's 'Your wife is as honest a woman as I will desire among five thousand, and five hundred too' we realize how little three hundred years means in terms of national character and expression. The rough-and-tumble between Evans and Caius went off with the same quality of boisterous success which used to attend the efforts of Mr. Fred Karno's comedians. The audience laughed out of the fulness of their present breasts, and not because it was decorous to imitate their forefathers. Sir John himself is as much alive to-day as ever he was, and yields not an ounce of modern melancholy to the hero of *Le Martyr de l'Obèse*, that French study of fatness which won the Prix Goncourt last year. Even that amazing compendium contains nothing more tragical than Falstaff's abhorrence of death by drowning — 'for the water swells a man; and what a thing should I have been when I had been swelled!'

Mr. Baliol Holloway is a fine actor and has fatness in his very bones. His Falstaff is the mob's intellectual master, as he should be, though he is never called upon to prove it. You divine it in the cock of his eye. He comes on to the stage á great man in full sail, trimming with infinite condescension his course to the mean necessities of his purse. Whenever, noting a really magnificent Shakespearean performance by an actor whom I do not recognize, I feverishly consult my programme for the name of the new star, it always turns out to be Mr. Frank Cellier. His Ford is quite perfect, never merely peevish or irascible, and stopping short of excess. It is, as it ought to be, a first study for Othello. Mr.

THE MERRY WIVES OF WINDSOR

Cellier has presence, gesture, and, above all, voice; and every one of his ringing exits brings down the house in the old-fashioned way. The Mistress Page of Miss Olga Katzin is a witty, fragrant, and graceful performance. This actress looks well, walks well, and talks well, and takes the stage with a distinction unknown to the pinchbeck *ingénues* of the West End. Miss Dorothy Green's more staid Mistress Ford is an admirable foil.

June 4, 1923

MERRY WIVES

(Lyric, Hammersmith)

MR. BYFORD'S FALSTAFF

MR. ROY BYFORD, as Falstaff, is the round peg in the round hole, but he will forgive me if I say that he is still not round enough. Mr. Byford is of a full and generous habit; Falstaff was of a gormandizing and hoggish exterior. Does he not walk before his Page like a sow that hath overwhelmed all her litter but one? Falstaff's enormity turns his thoughts to being rendered down drop by drop to 'liquor fishermen's boots' — marvellous image! Mr. Byford's Falstaff is not so stout as all that comes to, but it is getting on.

There should be a spiritual fatness about the old man, a lethargy and a somnolence, a *ruminativity* from which he wakes to unholiness. He should be a patriarch taken in a fever. Mr. Byford represents him as in eager, tireless pursuit of mischief, like that old fribble, Hulot, in *La Cousine Bette*, or Nucingen in *Splendeurs et Misères des Courtisanes*. I want to make a remark here, which is that whenever I devote considerable space to saying in what way a performance falls short of perfection this means that perfection is within sight. *De minimis non curat lex*. Or, in good plain English, the critic does not bother about bad performances.

23

The reader is a greenhorn who has not gathered that Mr. Byford's Falstaff is a piece of work of the very highest class. His face lights up as though he had not only supped with the Devil, but swallowed him.

Miss Edith Evans's Mistress Page is a masterpiece of mockery, and I would rise from a bed of influenza and make the journey to Hammersmith simply to hear her read the letter and emit that mirthless 'Ha, ha!' Miss Dorothy Green claps on all sail as Mistress Ford, and the two ride the stage like frigates before a stiff breeze. I did not think that Mr. Frank Cellier's Ford could be bettered. It cannot. But Mr. Randle Ayrton showed that it could be equalled. A wonderful piece of acting! The Mistress Quickly of Miss Elsie French is a thing of strident beauty. Never was cackle so hag-like and infectious. The whole show is a gorgeous success.

December 27, 1923

TWELFTH NIGHT
(New)

MISS FORBES-ROBERTSON'S VIOLA

THE modern critic holds, or is taught, that it is his business to go behind the achievement of the artist and conduct searching inquiries along the line of intention. It is not enough, he is told, to say that Mozart wrote a pretty tune; it is his job to declare why nobody else but Mozart could have written it, and to discover what thing it was in Mozart that forced him to write that particular combination of notes and no other. He may not even decline the gambit as Mozart himself declined it when he announced the method of his Muse to be as much beyond his control as the shape of his nose. Now, either this last is nonsense, or Mozart is as much or as little of an artist as a linnet, a waterfall under moonlight, or any other beautiful and helpless thing. Applying this to Miss Forbes-Robertson's performance, we have to ask ourselves whether it is effortless and hit upon not by accident but by that fatalism which marks the inability to do a thing in any other way. To what extent is this Viola the outcome of some desperate battle like that which Keats waged with the famous line about 'perilous seas'? How often has the actress tried different renderings of a passage and weighed this excellence against that? How far is that exquisite immaturity of youngest green unfolding to the light the result of conscious artifice? Can what ought to be art in this actress's performance be no more than the result of her chiselled inheritance, a poise and a profile which, before she has spoken, bring a lump to the spectator's throat?

Perhaps to inquire why a thing is, is to waste time which could be more usefully spent in affirming what it is. I will not say that this is the one and only perfect Viola, for there have been others, Ellen Terry's for example, in which fun and tenderness were contrasted like sunshine and the shade of some woodland pool. Nothing is contrasted in this Viola, where the sauciness alluded to by Olivia is no bubble of unreflecting gaiety but the considered candour of an uncompromising little realist old beyond her years. If one could think that anything in this performance is deliberate one would cite an avoidance of points which any fussy, competent actress would be ashamed to miss. Miss Forbes-Robertson's opening:

> And what should I do in Illyria?
> My brother he is in Elysium —

followed by 'Perchance he is not drown'd' and this, again, by 'What think you, sailors?' had no more emotion than would be used by someone arriving at St. Martin's Lane after looking for the New Theatre in the Charing Cross Road, hoping the curtain is not up, and asking whether the commissionaire thinks it is. Then take the passage:

> I am all the daughters of my father's house,
> And all the brothers too: and yet I know not.
> Sir, shall I to this lady?

Miss Forbes-Robertson speaks this on one level note, though surely there are three tones here — the witty evasion, the little pang, and the starting of a fresh topic, the last of these being accentuated by the Duke who, having had enough of Viola's affairs and wanting to get back to his own, says: 'Ay, that's the theme!'

But the point about Miss Forbes-Robertson's performance, though one may fault it here and there, is that its sum is absolute and flawless perfection however attained. It is possible, and even probable, that the smallest addition of any art, artifice, or conscious thought would destroy it. Viola's steel-true and blade-straight quality, her sticking to the spirit as well as the letter of Orsino's instructions, can never have been conveyed better. One spectator, who has seen this performance three times, is always at Viola's first entry brought to the verge of tears, with the rest a mere blur. What other tribute would any Viola have? If Montague had lived we should have had some phrase to immortalize this grave baby; as it is, I can only salute and call attention to a perfect and perhaps unintentional thing.

Up other streets are the blazingly competent and brilliantly professional performances of everybody else. There is Miss Phyllis Neilson-Terry, who brings to that wilting bloom, Olivia, all the colour and perfume of a Botanical Garden, with a hint of Queen Elizabeth thrown in. There is Mr. Robert Atkins, who as Sir Toby, acts the drunken scene very well indeed, but does not 'play' Sir Andrew as deliberately as he might. So long as Mr. Norman Forbes cares to act the part of Aguecheek it is, of course, his for the asking, and to Malvolio Mr. Arthur Wontner brings an inner life which helps to make credible the savagery of the prison scene. The rest of the cast is so-so, except that Mr. Godfrey Kenton manages to get some emotion into the not good part of Sebastian. The mounting is elegant, and Mr. Herman Finck has devised the incidental music with exceptional tact and helpfulness. The piece is well produced by Mr. Robert Atkins, except that the last verse of the concluding lyric is taken away from the Clown and given to Olivia. This is an unwarrantable and damaging mutilation of Shakespeare's pattern, which I must believe to have been thrust upon Mr. Atkins. It would be no defence if Miss Neilson-Terry sang like Jenny Lind, Patti and Melba put together, which she very nearly does. If Shakespeare had wanted Olivia to wind up this play he would, not being inarticulate, have said so.

First Nights: May 25, 1932

MEASURE FOR MEASURE
(The Fellowship of Players)

MR. MILTON'S ANGELO

WHAT a delight your 'advanced' playwright would have taken in pointing out the evils which result when a virtue is pushed beyond reason. Chastity is a blessing, he would say, but not as this lady conceived it. Isabella, chastity's spokeswoman, is too much the 'thing ensky'd and sainted'; she has no place by the fireside. It was an early critic who first pointed out that we do not feel the same confidence in the virtue that is sublimely good at another's expense as if it had been put to some less disinterested trial. There is no more to be said, except, perhaps, that we feel that Shakespeare would not necessarily have drawn a less elevating moral if he had given his working out a radical twist and called the play *The Magnanimous Virgin*. Later writers have done this, and have been absolved from the charge of corruption. As it is, Shakespeare leaves Isabella between the devil and the deep sea. If she be ice-cold we class her as a prig and take no further interest in her; if she warm to any semblance of humanity we resent her failure to live up, at the critical moment, to humanity and sisterhood. We have got to believe in Isabella and dislike her, or take some sort of liking and then not believe in her. Probably we should attach importance to the play's date. It belongs to the *Lear* period, when the dramatist brooded most sombrely over the

27

dark passions and dilemmas of the world; and it may be that he was not bent upon creating a 'sympathetic' heroine. The speech beginning:

> O you beast!
> O faithless coward! O dishonest wretch!
> Wilt thou be made a man out of my vice?

is of the same mood and temper as Lear's:

> Thou shalt not die; die for adultery! No.

although, superficially, they appear to be the flattest of contradictions. Both are frenzied with the scorn of humanity's baser aspects; both show what has been called the 'tormented unreticence of the very pure'.

Add to this most difficult of heroines a hero who is also the play's villain, and unpopularity is assured. Angelo is a great part, though no actor can make him entirely convincing. The trouble is not that we cannot 'see' him as amorist, but that we do not believe in his precedent rigour. Claudio is not a 'nice' person, though his naturalness has never been questioned. The Duke is an imbecile — a chairman who deserts his post to see how 'Mr. Vice' will get through the toasts. His excuse about a stricter administration of justice since baby has taken to beating the nurse is merely a device — and a senseless one — for getting the play going. There is an enormous humbugging power in great acting. When Courtenay Thorpe played the Duke, he enwrapped the silly fellow in such semblance of flesh and blood that he became credible, and hung upon his shoulders a mantle of so much dignity and grace that the speech 'Be absolute for death' rose above its poetry and became sense. The argument is as specious as any you shall hear at the Old Bailey; it is many years since I heard this actor deliver it, and I have not forgotten a single intonation. On Sunday the part was not well played, and one missed the humbugging. The play came to an end where it must always do — with Isabella's rending of Claudio. Magnificent up to this part, it peters out. Angelo makes no more appearances

that matter, and we spend the rest of the evening in watching
Shakespeare's efforts to weave tragic issues to some stuff of comedy.
The broad and sweeping lines of the play are now broken up into
petty plots about loose-livers whose heads are supposed to be off,
and loose-thinkers whose heads are never properly on. Does the
Duke look for happiness in Isabella? We should like to take him
on one side and read him Cayley Drummle's description of the
first Mrs. Tanqueray. 'Marble arms and black velvet' hits off
Isabella exactly. Angelo is to marry for a penance, but we do not
envy Mariana. Neither do we pity her; Ninny's tomb would
have become her well. Lucio, too, is in for an unquiet house; and
we do not know enough about Juliet to discuss Claudio's future
ménage. What a fuss they made in those days about forms and
ceremonies! What a confounding of morality and 'lines'.

Exception has often been taken to the more admittedly comic
characters. There, again, the matter is largely one of acting. Mr.
Andrew Leigh took all the offensiveness out of Pompey, and played
him with a charity which stimulated the house to equal generosity
of understanding. How human he made the rogue, a jackanapes
not to be utterly condemned! Mr. Baliol Holloway's fantasy is
not on a par with his heavy tragedy, and I will not insist that his
Lucio was a great success. Messrs. J. Leslie Frith, Wallace,
Evennett, Shayle Gardner, and Colin Ashdown gave what it is
usual to call satisfactory accounts of Froth, Elbow, Abhorson, and
Barnardine. Claudio, entrusted to Mr. Duncan Yarrow, lacked
youthfulness and charm. He should be just from school if he is to
win our sympathy; and to play him carefully and conscientiously is
not enough. The Escalus of Mr. Cecil Brooking was good, though
hardly attaining to the high dignity which Alfred Brydone used to
impose on that part. Miss Grizelda Hervey played Isabella with
considerable skill. She rose finely to the denunciation of Angelo,
but was less good in her rounding upon Claudio; the rounding
was there, but her previous tenderness to her brother made it
improbable. Perhaps there is only one actress in England who
would not fall between these two stools, and that is Miss Thorndike. The hardness which does not go with Imogen, and the

implication of moral grandeur which was so sovereignly suited to Beatrice in *The Cenci*, would be inestimable here. Isabella is not a person but an emanation, with thin lips like a mouse-trap. Can an emanation have lips? Yes, when Miss Thorndike wills. But Miss Hervey was good in a human, breathing way. Mr. Ernest Milton's Angelo was an extremely fine and subtle performance, of great fire and vigour, satisfying to eye, ear and brain. He put into each line some of Irving's intensity of perception, and collectors of pieces of acting will be glad to have bagged this. The commotion was in the brain, where it ought to be.

The Contemporary Theatre, 1924: April 20, 1924

MEASURE FOR MEASURE
(The Old Vic)

MR. LAUGHTON'S ANGELO

Measure for Measure has always been an unpopular play, and for a job lot of reasons. It is not 'pleasant'. Its subject contravenes the rule of the sentimental English that the way of a man with a maid shall begin with the eyes and stop at the chin. It pours scorn upon every man in the audience who, if he be not a liar, would ask his sister to render him what in comparison with death is a trifling service. One has not died, and one is not a convent novice. But one is sufficient of a mathematician to weigh annihilation, which is total loss, against the shedding of a single virtue, and sufficient of a realist to know that to lose a virtue against one's will is not to lose it at all. In plain English, if Isabella had yielded to Claudio's request she would not only have been more ensky'd and sainted than ever, but proved herself a decent sort as well. What Elizabethan audiences thought of this aspect of the play it is difficult for us to guess, since encrusted upon those notions must be the inherited layers of Restoration raillery, Victorian prudery, and neo-

Georgian flippancy. Plus, or course, that general degradation of ideas and values which is Hollywood's awful responsibility. Put Claudio's demand to any blonde nitwit of the screen and she will reply: 'Sure! I'm no angel. Tell Angelo to come up and see me!' Is not this the world's masterpiece of irony? For three hundred years the best English consciences have conspired to persuade us that Isabella was right, while what every man and woman who is honest with himself or herself knows to be the truth comes to us at last through the vulgar mind of Hollywood.

One takes it that the academic objection to this play is represented by something Keats wrote: 'The excellence of every art is its intensity, capable of making all disagreeables evaporate from their being in close relationship with beauty and truth . . . But in this picture [by West] we have unpleasantness without any momentous depth of speculation excited, in which to bury its repulsiveness.' My own objections to the play are simple. The first is that the Duke in the long speech, 'Be absolute for death,' talks the most absolute bosh that ever fell from human lips. 'Thy best of rest is sleep, And that thou oft provokest; yet grossly fear'st Thy death, which is no more,' is on the intellectual level of Miss Seward's: 'Annihilation is only a pleasing sleep without a dream.' Dr. Johnson, as will be remembered, at once blasted this with his: 'Annihilation is neither pleasing, nor sleep; it is nothing!' The rest of the Duke's speech, considered otherwise than as music, is beneath modern contempt! It is significant that Johnson, who must have hated this play's preoccupation with death, in his notes to it makes no allusion to the main theme. He holds, on the other hand, that 'the light or comic part is very natural', though how Johnson came to be a judge of the naturalness of Viennese brothels is obscure. My second objection is that the piece is broken-backed. This is not academic fudge. I hold that the interest definitely stops with the Duke's recommendation at the end of Act III, Scene 1: 'Haste you speedily to Angelo: if for this night he entreat you to his bed, give him promise of satisfaction!' and Isabella's: 'I thank you for this comfort. Fare you well, good father.' Why did Shakespeare funk that scene of excellent dissembling in which Isabella promised Angelo satisfaction? The drama cries aloud for it. Can it be that Shakespeare had this play on the stocks for some time and when he came back to it was in another mood? Or that the people at the theatre asked him to lighten it? The fact remains that at this point Angelo goes out of the play except for his final discomfiture, and that with Angelo out the play is out, too. Here Mariana steps in, sad pastry for an audience consisting even of Barbauld, More, Edgeworth, Hemans, Wollstonecraft, Martineau, Yonge, Procter, and Ward! And there is nothing left for the sophisticated playgoer except the final touches to that picture of unglossed vice which shows that Shakespeare when he wrote Sonnet CXXIX knew what he was talking about.

Continuing his back-door attacks upon the Shakespearean drama, Mr. Laughton has now promoted himself to that side-entrance which is Angelo. Granted a certain modernity of feeling and that Mr. Laughton's voice has not yet acquired the full resonance for blank verse, it would be difficult to imagine a finer performance. Garbed in black watered silk Angelo takes the stage like some distressful eagle — for he never quite descends to vulture — and expresses his indecision in perambulation. The hands are folded in a semi-austerity which is only half counterfeit, and in that well-fleshed mask the combat is unceasing. But it is in the continual pacings to and fro that the chiefest dread resides, and whenever this soul comes to anchor to deliver his soliloquies of torment the house falls into a hush the like of which is rarely sensed in our theatre. This performance whets the appetite which, after once more tantalizing it with that dreary codger, Prospero, Mr. Laughton promises presently to satisfy with his first attack upon the real stuff — Macbeth. That good actor, Mr. Roger Livesey, tackles the Duke with a will, and his is the kind of success achieved by a wicket-keeper who unexpectedly scores a century. The fact that the Duke is an arrant *poseur* and dilettante, much more interested in himself than in Viennese morals, puts Mr. Livesey's sincerity out of court. And perhaps only those who remember how the late Courtenay Thorpe used to say: 'Look, the unfolding star calls up the shepherd!' know how this beautifully cadenced rôle should be spoken.

Admiration of Miss Flora Robson has been so often and so freely expressed in this column that one has no hesitation in saying that Isabella is the last Shakespearean part for which one would cast her. Isabella's lineaments should be, as Gautier might put it, *gardiens du contour pur*; it is this and her sexlessness for which Angelo falls. But warring bronze rather than white and marble wonder bespeaks this actress, whose forte is sensuality in tempestuous restraint. And as Claudio was obviously a well-behaved young gentleman, the great scene between them rather went as if it were Isabella who had come to ask him to redeem some peccadillo of hers, though this, of course, would have necessitated turning Angelo into a mediaeval Mrs. Ormiston Chant! And do beings ensky'd and sainted cuff and slap under any provocation? At the line 'I will proclaim thee, Angelo; look for't', Isabella fell upon Angelo as Mrs. Nupkins's cook fell upon Mr. Job Trotter and 'tore and buffeted his large flat face with an energy peculiar to excited females'. Indeed, the cook appeared to have the daintier sense, since, 'being a lady of very excitable and delicate feelings, she instantly fell under the dresser and fainted away'. Miss Robson, of course, has the excuse that the formalized setting at the Vic does not permit of a dresser. According to the learned Miss Macnamara the Duke's marriage with Isabella allegorically presents Shakespeare's remedy for a corrupt Court; the ordinary playgoer will reflect that handsome is as handsome does, and that with more tantrums in the offing the Duke is getting more than he bargains for.

Mr. Dennis Arundell is admirable as Lucio, that fantastic whom Mrs. Amanda Ros would doubtless have apostrophized as 'Student of Ephebism!' The minor parts are all well filled, but it is no discourtesy to the highly distinguished team of players to say that the best members of the cast on this occasion are Mr. Tyrone Guthrie, the producer, Mr. Herbert Menges, who has composed the music, and Mr. John Armstrong, who has beautified the scene with unimaginably lovely costumes. Since what obviously sets out to be a tragedy peters out half-way through the evening, the resolution has been wisely taken to turn the rest of it into the best kind of Cochran revue.

First Nights: December 4, 1933

MUCH ADO ABOUT NOTHING
(The Old Vic)

MR. CASS'S SCENERY

A COBWEBBY steeple from the top of which sombrely gibed a stringy, featherless fowl, the bird of night complaining to a bored moon, an odd, inaccurate constellation or two, and perhaps the suggestion that the whole thing was conceived in Bloomsbury during a hang-over. Having taken in this sad scenic joke, one promptly forgot all about it. Which suggests a line of what may be inquiry for some, though I have long made up my mind about it. I hold that getting itself immediately forgotten is the first function of all scenery in plays that speak to the mind. In my view the proper way to stage *Œdipus Rex* is to throw a couple of pillars and a staircase together, while the right way with *Hamlet* is to fish out any battlement, any palace scene, and fix up Gertrude's bedroom with any pair of red curtains. Shakespeare wrote for the Elizabethan stage. Good! Some of us find that dull, and think that with to-day's resources he would not have rejected more elaborate settings. Good again! The great point is to decide which settings, given the present day's mechanical facilities, would have been acceptable to Shakespeare's mind. I believe that the author of *The Tempest* would have turned down any model showing Prospero in the garb of a Regius Professor, and Ariel in the buttons of a modern page-boy, and have accepted without hesitation Mr. Selfridge's Father Christmas and any fairy from the Lyceum pantomime. I believe that he would have thrown under foot and trampled on the choicest designs of Messrs. Craig, Komisarjevsky,

34

Bakst, and Picasso. I utterly decline to believe that he would have approved a crazy night on a geometrical heath with Lear on a spiral staircase defying an algebraical sky. Not for William any gyring and gimbling in that wabe! Shakespeare's choice of modern setting would, I am convinced, have been strictly representational, and the nearest possible approach to historical accuracy. He would have elected for Romans and Britons as they looked to each other, and not to-day's 'amusing' counterparts. He would have had everything to do with realism, and nothing to do with stylizing. He would have made Macbeth's soldiers carry actual firs and real larches from Birnam to Dunsinane. He would have insisted upon an authentic wood for his midsummer night's dream. He would have been of the school of Tree. I do not believe that a mind completely filled with one thing can have room for any other thing, and Euclid would agree with me. The mind which requires frescoes and statues by contemporary artists to hang and stand in the Senate while Caesar is being murdered is not wholly filled by Shakespeare's thoughts on the murder of Caesar. That unwise spectator who wants to hear the spoutings of Coriolanus with Beethoven's Coriolan Overture as incidental music is lending less than his whole ear to Shakespeare's orchestra. Lear's rumblings fill the mind as an organ fills a cathedral, and to the extenuation of lesser tinklings. Only in slight plays like *The Two Gentlemen of Verona* have mind and ear their leisure moments.

Hear, now, the conclusion of the matter. There are plays of Shakespeare which do not take up all of our attention, and may therefore be lawfully treated as masques. *Much Ado About Nothing* is possibly one of them. Some may like the play done as Mr. Poel would do it; I happen to like it done in the Lyceum manner of 1882, with a fully choral service for Hero's wedding; Mr. Cass likes it fantasticated, and my complaint is that he has not fantasticated enough. He made a very good beginning when a quattrocento Benedick made love to a Beatrice wearing the clothes and hat in which Mrs. Siddons sat to Gainsborough. But surely in the comic scenes the producer has let I dare not wait upon I would?

For example, the First Watch used with great effect at his first entry the tituppy walk that Herr Werner Krauss used for Spring-heel Jack in the film of *Waxworks*. But why was he allowed to drop it half-way through? Why wasn't the whole fantastication carried out like an oil-and-colourman's nightmare? Where were the pools of ochre and the lakes of crimson? My colleagues have dubbed this production mad; I could have wished it madder!

That it is too late to embark upon exhaustive analysis of the acting saves me from the old pitfall of grumbling that Benedick and Beatrice were not played by Fred and Ellen Terry. But that brother and sister will not occur again. Sufficient to say that Mr. Evans and Miss Newcombe gave us of the best Evans and New-combe vintage, that Mr. Cecil Trouncer's Leonato was delight-fully testy, and that Mr. Alan Webb made an agreeable Claudio. Mr. Morland Graham chose to play Dogberry as a dry rather than an unctuous constable. And as Hero Miss Nancy Hornsby acquitted herself with as much distinction as a cricketer who should have to field long-stop to Ames. That is to say, she had nothing to do, and did it charmingly.

November 8, 1934

A MIDSUMMER NIGHT'S DREAM
(Kingsway)

MR. HOLLOWAY'S BOTTOM

Is it possible that simplified scenery is being overdone? That this play does not go well with a setting simple as Noah's Ark was the chief impression produced upon me by Mr. Calthrop's revival. But, of course, to make these fantastic mortals and common-sensical immortals convincing on the stage is a problem which has ever baffled solution. Hazlitt, we remember, suggested that the play would do admirably as a Christmas after-piece, and proposed Kean for Bottom! 'What an opportunity for processions,

for the sound of trumpets, and glittering of spears! What a flutter-
ing of urchins' painted wings; what a delightful profusion of gauze
clouds, and airy spirits floating on them!' Well, they took his
advice and two months later, early in the New Year of 1816, the
Dream was done at Covent Garden. Hazlitt, after the perverse way
of critics, at once declared the thing unactable, and begged everybody's pardon for a recommendation which had converted a delightful poem into a dull pantomime. He hoped he had not been
guilty of murder! All that was fine in the play was lost in the
representation. Yet Hazlitt stuck to his guns in the matter of the·
scenery. The genius was fled, but the spectacle had been fine.
'Oh, ye scene-shifters, ye scene-painters, ye machinists and dress-
makers, ye manufacturers of moon and stars that give no light,
ye musical composers, ye men in the orchestra, fiddlers and
trumpeters and players on the double drum and loud bassoon,
rejoice! This is your triumph; it is not ours.'

I am afraid that Kingsway performance is not anybody's
triumph, with the exception of Peter Quince. There is hardly
any scenery — none at all in the old-fashioned sense of the word —
and no more than a modicum of music. We miss the leafy sense,
and the tinkle of fairies. The plain truth of the matter is that our
material faculties are starved; and even outraged, upon occasion.
It may be that Lysander and Demetrius, Hermia and Helena
cannot be humanized, in which case the thing to do is to formalize
these characters and bid the actors ravish eye and ear with gesture
and tone. If these actors have been instructed so, they have dis-
obeyed. I do not remember ever having known such ungainly
motion and harsh sound as proceeded from this quartet. Miss
Viola Tree wailed and moaned, and threw her arms about as
though they were 'branch-charméd by the earnest stars'. Miss
Joyce Carey's voice is entirely unapt for poetry, and I do not think
that Shakespeare is her playwright. Neither is he Mr. S. T.
Warmington's. Mr. Bruce Belfrage is better. I take this young
actor to be a beginner with not very much knowledge of the stage.
But at least he knows nothing wrong, and does not overlay the
poetry of his part with the prose of yesterday's melodrama.

Remain the clowns and the fairies. He would be blind who failed to recognize in Quince a great Shakespearean actor. Mr. Cellier is unrivalled in our time as Henry IV, unequalled as Cassio, a raging lion as Ford, and as Quince the very shell of a man. We have heard of the mastery of mind over matter; Mr. Cellier achieves this in terms of his own body. Set this actor in a heroic part and he will grow before our eyes. We know now what Tennyson meant when he wrote:

> And I myself, who sat apart,
> And watched them, waxed in every limb;
> I felt the thews of Anakim,
> The pulses of a Titan's heart.

Cast this actor for pantaloon, and the flesh falls from him till there is nothing left save the husk of the dotard. Garrick, we are told, could subdue his piercing eye to the lack-lustre of a dead fish, or come on as a deaf man so that his audience knew of his infirmity by merely looking at him. Mr. Cellier has something of this power. You divine Quince's lack of wit and weak hams. His eyes purge amber and plum-tree gum as, conning his play-book, he gathers together the remnants of his weak mind. A riotous spectacle, yet somehow pathetic; you would say a noble goose havering in the wilderness. Though somewhat overshadowed, Mr. Baliol Hollo-way's Bottom is a good performance. It may perhaps err on the side of being too intellectual a performance. Nick is too crafty; his egotism, one thinks, should be more naïve. The best in this line was Benson's old actor, Weir, whose tongue not only dropped fatness, in the Falstaffian sense, but licked up, as it were unconsciously, the fat in other men's parts. Mr. Holloway's Weaver would play the tyrant and the lover, the lady and the lion out of the desire to put himself forward rather than the innocent conviction of superiority. Bottom is a child who must have all the cakes on the platter. One may doubt whether Mr. Holloway's egoist would have won the nickname 'Bully'. This aspect apart, Bottom is admirable.

Only the clowns in this play are real. The mortals are impossible; the fairies, though they show some approach to humanity, must be neither man nor woman. Mr. Nicholas Hannen's Oberon may definitely claim to have joined the 'empire of the butterflies'. This was a performance of distinction. So, too, was Miss Athene Seyler's Titania, though this actress has hardly the physical qualifications for the part. Her queenly sense, however, and her beautiful diction between them made ample rescue. I am grieved to say that the Puck of Mr. George Howe was not good; the intention was admirable, but not fulfilled. For one thing, this sprite gabbled as though the girdle which he would put round the earth in forty minutes had been an electric one. If I had not known Puck's lines I do not think I should have been able to make out a single word of them. Titania's dark-clad train was a little like some troop of deep-sea girl-guides. I prefer my fairies to be blond.

To go back to the starting-point, there was not in this production enough of feasting for the eye. Is it too reactionary to suggest that bad realistic scenery were better? It is certain that real trees, real water, and real grass, with perhaps a real lamb trained to caper strictly à la Botticelli — it is certain that the old-fashoned method of presentation would do this play less harm than the modern sort achieves. One harks back to that French prose-poem in which the hero insists that his mistress's robe shall be of handsomest velvet or brocade, her throat plastered with diamonds, her fingers stiff with jewels. 'Je ne lui ferais pas grâce d'un anneau ou d'un bracelet.' I find it difficult to dispense with the least of those sumptuosities which it has been customary to lavish upon this play, or to forgive Mr. Calthrop one single note of the Mendelssohn which he withheld.

The Contemporary Theatre, 1923: November 18, 1923

SHAKESPEARE'S COMEDIES

A MIDSUMMER NIGHT'S DREAM
(Theatre Royal, Drury Lane)

MR. PETRIE'S PUCK

It is not easy to discover from what cause the acrimony of a scholiast can naturally proceed . . . The different readings of copies, and different interpretations of a passage seem to be questions that might exercise the wit without engaging the passions. — SAMUEL JOHNSON

As of a single passage, so, too, of a whole play. There is nothing in this very handsome execution of a most intricate job to beget either acrimony or temper. Think of the engaging difficulties! To begin with, there is the play itself – a tripartite affair of romantics, gossamer, and clowning, all pulling against one another like the players at cut-throat bridge. Or you might say that the broadest humours to which Shakespeare ever descended — or ascended — are embedded and enjellied, like the lark and leveret in Tennyson's pie, in the richest of his verse. The first thing for any producer of *The Dream* to aim at is a kind of unity. Nothing is feasible in this play, but at least the three infeasible sections must synchronize in time, and, if one may say so, in space also. It is a great triumph on Mr. Dean's part to have achieved one story rather than three. Theseus, Oberon, and Quince's Amateur Dramatic Society all meet in the same wood and in the same century — impossible, if you like, but always the same kind of impossibility. Then think of the size of the theatre. Some recent editors of the play would have it presented as taking place within a large Elizabethan hall with a huge staircase, beneath which is a cavity with sliding doors. These, being opened, are to reveal a secondary stage, for the use of the fairies. At the end, when the bridal couples are gone up the great staircase, Puck and his friends are to swarm down the balusters into the now darkened hall, reciting in hushed voices:

A MIDSUMMER NIGHT'S DREAM

Through the house give glimmering light,
By the dead and drowsy fire . . .

The play was probably done like this in 1598. It is an enchanting idea, but one demanding a small theatre. At Drury Lane there can be little intimacy, and Mr. Dean certainly did the right thing in going in for a 'slap-up' production, even at the risk of flamboyance. Up to the end of the first part all went well. The dream-sense was preserved, and if Puck had asked if we believed in fairies we should undoubtedly have clapped our hands. But the second part was less successful. We began to think that M. Fokine's perfect ballets were perhaps not devised in the same age as Mendelssohn's perfect music. There was a slight jarring of notes here, and then the scenery took a definitely plain turn. After all, Shakespeare insists upon his wood, and the mossy carpet was obviously rock. Warwickshire seemed very definitely to have yielded to Provence, and that part of Provence, all stunted trees and scrub, in which is Daudet's Windmill. The Palace of Theseus, in the third part, was a garish affair, like Alma-Tadema at his best — or worst; and one would not have been altogether surprised to see Cinderella and her Prince with the Brothers This and That descend the stairs to claim their deserts. Yet there are many enchanting things in this production. The fairies are always there, peeping at you out of crannies, or with their chins resting on the level of the rocks. One, who is a butterfly, will flutter to a tree and hang there motionless. The ballets are finely invented and carried out, though if the piece, which runs some three and three-quarter hours, is to be cut, it is on the dances that this operation should be performed. And possibly the curtain might go up at once on the second and third parts. The *entr'actes* show Mendelssohn in a mood something penitential.

The outstanding performance in a great cast was Mr. Hay Petrie's Puck. This was the actor's first triumph in the West End, and must surely have set the seal on the great reputation he has made at the Old Vic. This shaggy sprite of Mr. Petrie's — half satyr and half elf — dominated the tale, as indeed he should, so much so that a Frenchman might now take the piece to Paris and produce it there under the title of *La Soirée d'un Faune*. And a faun wholly mischievous and wholly kindly, with a hidden store of philosophy laid up for the winter. Mr. Robert Harris gave the lines of Oberon their full music, and the Titania of Miss Ffrangcon-Davies was an enchantment both to eye and ear; she looked most amazingly like the early portraits of Queen Victoria. The lovers' quartet was of super-excellence. The Hermia of Miss Athene Seyler was a little Tartar of delicate perceptions, while Miss Edith Evans gave to Helena five-foot-ten, or thereabouts, of clucking, hen-witted gaby floundering for a shoulder upon which to lay her distracted head. Lysander and Demetrius are perhaps not more dissimilar than Rosencrantz and Guildenstern, but as two handsome peas in a pod Messrs. Leon Quartermaine and Frank Vosper were all that could be desired. Messrs. Allan Jeayes and Brember Wills — stars of the first magnitude in any sky — did all that was possible with Theseus and Egeus. Mr. Cellier's Quince was too recently described to need recapitulating. It is the same masterly shell of a man as before. Messrs. Clifford Mollison, Miles Malleson, Alfred Clark and H. O. Nicholson make up as rich a company of mechanicals as you shall find on the stage, or in the study by the fireside. Remains the Bottom of Mr. Wilfred Walter, and of this I think I must say that it is as good a performance as any actor, who has no positive genius for the unctuous, could encompass. Humour is superimposed upon Mr. Walter's personality; it does not ooze through the actor like butter through a keg. And I imagine that we were not given all that lies behind the lines: 'Not a word of me. All that I will tell you is, that the Duke hath dined.' What Bottom means is that his vision is too rare to be imparted to those rude and, since they have no share in the vision, henceforward and for ever inferior minds. And Mr. Walter did not quite give us the wonder and pathos of his translation. But elsewhere he was excellent. Let me offer Mr. Dean the warmest congratulations on his actors. 'I hope here is a play fitted', he may say with Peter Quince.

The Contemporary Theatre, 1924: December 28, 1924

A MIDSUMMER NIGHT'S DREAM
(The Old Vic)

MENDELSSOHN'S MUSIC

THERE are nine-and-sixty ways of constructing tribal lays, wrote Mr. Kipling, proceeding to remark that every single one of them is right. There are probably as many right ways of producing *A Midsummer Night's Dream*. I, personally, hanker after a real wood such as the scene-painters of my youth, Conrad Tritschler and Hawes Craven, knew so well how to devise, and such as, if left to themselves, Messrs. Joseph and Phil Harker will still devise. Then I must have Mendelssohn's music, since in this connection all is dross that is not Bartholdy. I do not say that this is the only right way to produce the fairy comedy; what I do say is that it is the right and only way for me, and that any other way is to take the piece out of the region of fairyland and dump it into a Tom Tiddler's Ground of other and even unwelcome beauty.

There is, one supposes, no particular reason why a German Jew writing in the early and middle nineteenth century should have fitted music to this sixteenth-century Warwickshire play with a greater cunning than wig or boot-maker ever used to fit head or foot. Yet the miracle is. Nor is it a good argument that the theatre in Shakespeare's day knew nothing of the modern orchestra, or that to a Shakespearean audience prim and formal little tunes conjured up the lawless fairies. We who go to the play to-day are going in our own time and listening with our own ears, and to pretend that the late Cecil Sharp's or anybody else's arrangements of old folk-tunes have any fairy quality is the very pedantry of archaism. It may be that as time moves on, future composers will accomplish for the children of the next age what Mendelssohn did for the children of the Victorian age. It is possible that the twenty-first century will find Mendelssohn as hopelessly unfairylike as I find Cecil Sharp's prosaic assertions.

43

Even to-day one could conceive a stage-setting by M. Picasso and a musical setting by Herr Hindemith which would occasion much joy to the Picassites and Hindemithians. There cannot, I think, be any logical objection to an age expressing fairydom, or anything else, and eking out Shakespeare's expression of fairydom, or anything else, according to the means that age thinks best. If Hindemith and Co. can do better than Mendelssohn and Co. — and by better I mean better help the contemporary imagination — then hurrah for Hindemith and Co.! But to pretend that sober, four-square Christmas Carols conjure up a midsummer night better than Mendelssohn's Scherzo because they were written in Shakespeare's day is like pretending that we should put on greater receptivity if we rebuilt the old Globe Theatre and adopted the rushes and rude benches of the time. There are people to whom all music sounds alike; these will naturally join the pedants on behalf of some fantastic 'accuracy'. But both kinds together are as small in number as the people who demand that Puck shall be shaped like a rhomboid and dance atonally. Nine-tenths of playgoers are, in my computation, still essentially Victorian as far as this play is concerned. Mendelssohn's music, to their and my mind, heightens the play; the folk-tunes by their dullness — dullness in the theatre as distinct from the chimney-corner — detract from it. Nevertheless I steel myself to the opinion that the way in which nine-tenths of us desire this play to be produced is still only one way, and that sixty-eight other good and correct ways remain.

In the matter of costumes I am less sensitive, probably because after the first shock it really doesn't very much matter what sort of costumes plays are acted in or what sort of scenery they are acted before. Having once taken in scene and dresses, which takes about a minute, the normal playgoer thinks no more on them, whereas the music is a continuous imaginative aid or let. Then again, the Athens of this play had better be a Warwickshire town, since the clowns are obviously Warwickshire yokels. Shakespeare never quite decided where this play was happening; it is we who have settled upon Warwickshire, and to dress it all in Warwick-

shire fashion is to give it more unity and so knit the play's outer
edges closer to the fairy-ring which is its core. But the rightness
of this has nothing whatever to do with the wholly extraneous
and unimportant fact that in Shakespeare's time Elizabethan
costumes must have been used. I shall be obstinate, then, only
in the matter of the music; the costumes and the half-indoor,
half-outdoor staircase on which the play happens at the Old Vic
are well enough. The present method of production has one
aspect in which it is undoubtedly right — that of cheapness. The
old-fashioned representational setting must always be expensive,
and Mendelssohn calls for a full orchestra. To make a virtue of
necessity is an excellent thing, and any repertory company
does better to do this play the justice of a handsome, stylized
setting and an adequate accompaniment of drones and chirps
rather than let it down with scamped grandeurs and an orchestra,
let us say, fifty per cent below strength.

Take it for all in all, the present Old Vic production is extraordinarily effective, and before the end converted me in every
.respect save the musical one. It was good to listen to the exquisite
diction of Mr. John Gielgud, who delivered the passage:

> But we are spirits of another sort:
> I with the morning's love have oft made sport;
> And, like a forester the groves may tread,
> Even till the eastern gate, all fiery red,
> Opening on Neptune with fair blessèd beams,
> Turns into yellow gold his salt green streams —

as though he realized the kinship here with that other lovely image:

> Kissing with golden face the meadows green,
> Gilding pale streams with heavenly alchemy.

This Oberon belonged, too, to an age when it was manly to
recite poetry; Mr. Leslie French's Puck was honest, straightforward, and pleasingly boyish; and Miss Adèle Dixon did all for
Titania that extreme prettiness and good accompanying discretion
may do. As Helena Miss Martita Hunt spoke beautifully and

looked graciously, than which nothing more can be demanded; the rest of the quartet got through reasonably enough, which again is all that can be asked. Mr. Gyles Isham played Bottom probably as well as any actor may who is without one ounce of natural drollery in his composition. Bottom is a working man whom Shakespeare probably met in the skittle-alley; Mr. Isham is a cultivated gentleman who admires and unconsciously imitates the conscientious bucolics of the school of Mr. Jay Laurier. But he is not and can never be Bottom, just as Mr. Brember Wills convinces us that he must have infinite difficulty in being anybody other than the havering, doddering, and altogether delightful Peter Quince. On the whole a very good show, received on Thursday afternoon by a house crowded from floor to ceiling with keenly perceptive fifth-form boys and girls and rapt, englamoured tots.

December 9, 1929

LOVE'S LABOUR'S LOST
(The Old Vic)

MR. PETRIE'S COSTARD

OF *Love's Labour's Lost* Hazlitt pronounces that if we were to part with any of the comedies it should be this. He is probably speaking from his reading only; I can find no record of his having seen the play on the stage. Comparing this earliest of the comedies, as given at the Old Vic, with *Cymbeline*, as performed at the New Theatre, I, personally, would prefer to discard the later play. But perhaps Hazlitt would have called *Cymbeline* a History. One would not set up 'When daisies pied and violets blue' against 'Fear no more the heat o' the sun', for the reason that to attempt to prove the excellence of any Shakespearean play by its lyrics would be to resemble the pedant who, when he offered his house for sale, carried a brick in his pocket as a specimen. The lyrics are not integral to the Shakespearean fabric; say, rather, bits of stained glass from hall and staircase. And if neither play is a palace, it can at least be said of the early piece that it is not the mud-hovel of *Cymbeline* prettified by a master-decorator. *Love's Labour's Lost* is a pleasant retreat, an arbour set in a garden of playful fancy. A Watteau, to change the figure, of charm and that significance in ordered beauty which unity alone can give, rather than a sprawling cartoon with one ear and one hand by the master, and the rest by a pupil of no particular talent. It is this unity which so offended Hazlitt, because he found it a unity of tedium. Modern fashion, looking round for excuses on this play's behalf, postulates for it a certain 'revue-interest' in the days when John Lyly aired his fantastical style, and Italian grandees and Russian nobles walked our streets, all apt for mockery. But literary piety is a poor reason for visiting the theatre, and if *Love's Labour's Lost* were really dull, I should not recommend anybody to see it on account of its historical interest, nor yet because its production is the penultimate lap in the Old Vic's really tremendous feat of producing the whole of Shakespeare.

In this production the eye is pleasantly rested, the ear is enchanted, and now and again a line will roll and break upon a familiar shore, and remind the hearer of the tide which was just beginning to flow. Surely we must know the surge of poetry's incoming sea in some such passage as:

> For valour, is not Love a Hercules,
> Still climbing trees in the Hesperides?
> Subtle as Sphinx; as sweet and musical
> As bright Apollo's lute, strung with his hair;
> And when Love speaks, the voice of all the gods
> Makes heaven drowsy with the harmony.

Mr. Ion Swinley delivered these lines with great beauty, and spoke the whole of his long part 'with good accent and good discretion', as a Nestor of criticism once remarked. Mr. Swinley is probably the best romantic actor in England to-day. He knows that to put on grace it is not necessary to put off virility, and his admirable

47

and poetic diction is well matched by his mastery of gesture. Everybody who saw this actor's Giovanni in Ford's play will realize that the Old Vic has made a great acquisition. The Don Adriano of Mr. George Hayes contained an almost feline quality of felicity. The actor made sleek little dabs at all the fun in his part, and must have amused even those who had never heard of *Euphues*. Excellent, too, was Mr. Walter's Holofernes. There is not much, perhaps, to be done with the rest of the *précieux ridicules*. Those deflators of preciosity, the ladies, were good; and Miss Florence Saunders lived up to the line which enjoins that she shall have 'a velvet brow, with two pitch-balls stuck in her face for eyes'.

But the great performance of the evening was Mr. Hay Petrie's Costard. There was no mere antiquarian interest here. Costard breathed the very spirit of the numskulls of Elizabethan England, yet he contrived to be as amusing, and amusing in as modern a way as, say, Mr. Bert Coote in revue. As Pompion the Great in the masquerade he was singularly like Mr. Billy Merson in Roman toils. Withal he had that quality which alone your truly great comedian possesses — the suggestion, beneath lunatic disguise, of the descent from God. Costard was an innocent. He would stare at a gallant or a great lady as at some thing outside and beyond his mental reach. For some time yet his brain would remain a dark, unlighted chamber, and then, as Lamb says of Dodd, you would see the first dawn of apprehension steal slowly over his countenance — a painful process resulting at the end in no more than a twilight conception. Then the poor fellow would tire, and let his attention wander — though his gaze remained fixed — and withdraw into a mood for which 'contemplative' is too significant a word. He would ruminate, and come back to this planet with a start. Yet despite the vacant eye and the mind elsewhere you felt that the fellow had a soul. He was lovable, and you knew that to his creation the actor had put the same kind of passion that Lauder expends upon Doughie the Baker. Mr. Petrie does not imitate any other actor, and these comparisons are not meant to be more than finger-posts in the direction of his kind of excellence. Let me say that this Costard is one of the greatest pieces of comic acting that I have ever seen. It is all in one piece, and human.

The Contemporary Theatre, 1923: September 30, 1923

L O V E ' S   L A B O U R ' S   L O S T
(Westminster)

MR. SOFAER'S BIRON

My distinguished colleague of *The Times* has held that 'fortunately it is a little late in the day to discuss the substantial merits of this strange essay in, or satire on, the euphuistic convention'. Why not call the thing a tedious masterpiece? Of course there are lovely bits in it, and the man who denies the poetry ought never to be allowed another look at the Sonnets. But does that poetry improve when (a) it is set to music, or (b) when it is recited? In the first matter the man who thinks that Bach and Wagner and Sullivan and Mr. Roger Quilter, having co-opted Schubert and Hugo Wolf to help them, are going to add to the emotion which comes from reading 'When daisies pied and violets blue', or even reproduce it — such a man is an ass! Shakespeare's worst fault was his mock-modesty, because without this quality he must have wound up his play by saying: 'The words of Mercury make nonsense of the music of Apollo!' Does the poetry improve when it is recited? This is difficult to answer in the affirmative unless one is prepared to say that one wants the Sonnets mouthed. The actor who in this revival plays Biron has a musical voice and a good Shakespearean manner, but, alas! his lineaments are not romantic for reasons which Cyrano de Bergerac has sufficiently explained. It is appropriate to comment here upon the modern tendency to ignore physical qualities in the actor. To those of us who call attention to these there always comes the parrot-retort: 'You complain when there is casting to

type, and you complain when there is casting against type.'
But surely there is a middle way which insists that Romeo shall
be acted by the player with his body and not by moral intention
alone? Sarah Bernhardt, in her manual on acting, put the matter
in a nut-shell when she wrote: 'An actor who is too short has no
future.' And again: 'There is a fitness of things intellectual, and a
fitness of things physical, and the latter should receive as much
attention as the former . . . Renounce the stage if you are unfit by
nature, or accept only those parts which you are able to play,
and which your physical characteristics and your appearance do
not enjoin you to refuse.' Mr. Sofaer is going to be one of our best
character actors, but he must not play romantic parts.

What, then, is there left since it is equally a little late in the
day to make the point that the play has no action? Well, there is
the bright fooling, a little of which with most playgoers goes a
considerable distance. There is the business of Costard and Dull,
which reminds all remaining playgoers how much better Shakespeare was to do the same kind of thing later on. There is opportunity for bird-comings and bird-goings on the part of graceful
ladies twittering on upland lawns, all behaving like Beatrices in
embryo with the skirts fully grown and the wit not yet arrived.
There is pleasant occasion for a designer of costume, for a scene-
setter, and for a highbrow producer to come on afterwards and
tell us what a wildly exciting play it is, how in it Shakespeare's
genius stands revealed, and, by implication, what donkeys those
of us are who hold the interest in the play to be purely academic.
Schlegel talks about the 'lavish superfluity of labour in this play's
execution', and I cannot help suggesting that for some there is
lavish superfluity of labour in listening to it. Perhaps the piece
is not held together as it was when the Old Vic did it. There is not
in Mr. Eugene Leahy's entire personality one single pennyweight
of fantastication, of which quality Don Adriano is wholly composed, and one gets a little tired of listening to Sir Nathaniel
when he is played like a castrato from the Italian Opera. I have
praised Mr. Richard Goolden often enough to suggest that the
silly quality in Costard — the quality which Coleridge meant

when he called the buckets 'silly' — does not lie in his composition, as it did with Mr. Petrie. Mr. Evan John's Holofernes is perhaps the best of the fun. Among pleasant ladies Miss Vera Poliakoff's Princess is tall, moves with dignity, and possesses the singular attribute of appearing to enunciate better the further you are from the stage.

Unstinting praise should, however, be given to the audience which brought to what has been well called 'this strange ghostly play' learning and all the sympathies of learning. Industriously in the intervals they pointed out to one how in this early comedy Shakespeare was doing for the playgoers of his day what a few years ago Mr. Noel Coward did for the playgoers of our day. They bade one remark the quaint seriousness which overtakes the piece at the end just as that quality overtook Mr. Coward in the matter of his piece about the war. They adjured one to think Shakespeareanly, and were altogether very pleased with the playwright and with themselves. In fact the audience behaved exactly as we read that it did when the comedy was produced at Stratford twenty-five years ago: 'When the play grew very dull and no ingenuities of the actors could save us from what might have been critical moments, there was no impatience, but only the nervous attention of agitated friends. We all breathed freely again when Mr. Benson turned a somersault or made some other exhilarating diversion.' But times have changed, and on Wednesday night somersaults were strictly out of fashion.

July 6, 1932

THE MERCHANT OF VENICE
(The Old Vic)

MR. PETRIE'S SHYLOCK

YOU have seen those 'Protean' artists of the music hall who, by putting on another shape of hat pretend to be Ignatius Loyola, Savonarola, Swedenborg, and all the time remain plain Mr.

Roscius Jones. I do not mean that there were no differences between Irving's Shylock, Wolsey, and Becket. Of course there were differences, but you felt that they were superficial, and that each character had only just, by the merest accident, missed being Mr. Gladstone. Perforce Irving was tremendously pathetic as the Jew. Perforce he made touching business with Shylock's return to his empty house — of which Shakespeare says never a word — concluding with a terrific show of injured innocence in the matter of his apostasy.

Probably all that the old Lyceum audience knew of Shylock's race was the accounts they had read of the hucksters of the East End and the accounts they had kept with their brethren in the West End. But the audience which assembles in the Waterloo Road is not so simple. Half of it remembers *Potash and Perlmutter*; the other half knows their originals. All of it realizes, at least subconsciously, that the Jews are one of the greatest races which have ever peopled the earth, and the richest of all in intellect and what theatre-folk call 'character'. Irving's Shylock had the brains but lacked the characteristic temperament. He was not noticeably Jewish; or perhaps I should say that he had the grandeur, the mysticism, the austerity and poetry of the race, but lacked the familiar touches which make for recognition. It was a magnanimous and heroic portrait which entirely burst the play, turning it into a tragedy with an irrelevant epilogue tacked on at the end.

Mr. Petrie's Shylock restores the play's balance, and brings it back into the region of comedy. There is pathos in his final exit. But the sun has not gone out for ever, and there is what the film people call 'continuity' in the moon-gazing of Lorenzo and Jessica. This is a Shylock *intime*, Potash's neighbour, the wealthy relative of the stall-holders in the New Cut near by, the tree whose sprigs enliven our West End on Saturday nights, the friend whose interest may be purchased. He has as much pathos as may become the central figure in a comedy, sufficient dignity, and a nicely controlled amount of power. This Shylock is not a Lear uprooting oaks and leaving them lying around; the storm passes, and we are ready to bask in the sun again. The actor was extraordinarily good in the scene with Solanio and Salarino, which he began with a kind of whirling, backward entrance, like a Dervish converted to Judaism. It was obvious which of his losses was the considerable one, and 'I know not what's spent in the search' went to the heart. Grief for Jessica ranked third; second in injury was the affront put upon *his house*. This, I submit, was right. It was clearly linked up with the solicitude of

> But stop my house's ears, I mean my casements:
> Let not the sound of shallow foppery enter
> My sober house.

and the later

> Nay, take my life and all; pardon not that:
> You take my house, when you do take the prop
> That doth sustain my house.

The sense has changed here, but it is significant that the old man should, in his extremity, turn for a metaphor to his fixed idea of the house. For the house is the family, and that, in turn, means the race. The proof, even of a Jewish pudding, must be in the eating; and it is to be recorded that the audience exhibited a delightful apprehension of a familiar and heightened intimacy. To my mind this was the Jew of Shakespeare's imagining — half-way between the pre-Macklin buffoon and the high priest of Irving.

The play's remaining characters, all excellently played in this revival, are a poor lot. Antonio confesses himself a sheep; Bassanio is a spendthrift who pledges his friend's life that he may give routs and go a-wooing; Gratiano has the mentality of a medical student engaged in a rag; Lorenzo is a receiver of stolen goods, Morocco a windbag, and Arragon a Turveydrop Junior. Jessica is unworthy of her race. Hazlitt makes the silly remark that he should like Lorenzo better if he had not married a Jewess; it should have been the other way round. Nerissa is nobody. Remains Portia, who, saving everybody's reverence, isn't a person at all but a part for a leading lady. Ellen Terry made her delightful, not because she was like Portia, but because Portia was like Ellen Terry. Miss Florence Saunders did very well indeed, but a little of even the very best in this character goes a long way. I feel about Portia's pleadings, subterfuges, and skittishness as Mr. Bennet did about Mary's singing — 'That will do extremely well, child. You have delighted us long enough.' And when is somebody going to pluck up courage and declare the 'quality of mercy' speech to be excellent copybook ethics but negligible poetry?

The Contemporary Theatre, 1924: April 13, 1924

THE MERCHANT OF VENICE
(Alhambra)

MR. GRANVILLE-BARKER'S VIEWS

The general opinion of Bassanio is unflattering. I don't. know why he is considered such a poor specimen of manhood. My impression is that he has great charm.
— *Four Lectures*: ELLEN TERRY

MR. GRANVILLE-BARKER thinks little of this piece, judging from the fact that in the second series of his *Prefaces to Shakespeare* he allots it only 43 pages as against 122 to *Antony and Cleopatra* and 110 to poor old *Cymbeline*. Nevertheless, he makes a sufficiently formidable catalogue of the play's merits and says as little as may be about its demerits — the neurasthenic Antonio, the good-for-nothing Bassanio, the conscienceless and most un-Jewish Jessica, and those crashing bores, the Gobbos. In regard to these last one wonders that the creator of Dogberry and Verges could ever have thought to entertain us with a theme of sand-blindness, until we remember that it is not we but Elizabethan groundlings who are supposed to be entertained. Mr. Granville-Barker holds

Shylock to be real, and I suppose that he is real in the sense that he might have stepped out of one of Michael Angelo's cartoons. But I do not find him Jewish, since he lacks the great and constant Jewish virtue — humour. But, of course, only a Jewish author can do justice to the Jewish race, and to expect Shakespeare to find jokes for Shylock is perhaps equivalent to inviting Dean Inge to write for the Marx Brothers.

It is interesting to note that Mr. Granville-Barker devotes several pages to showing that Portia and Bassanio are also 'real' characters consistent with themselves throughout. We are told that she is at once a great lady and a slip of a girl, while he, 'a painfully poor figure by the gospel according to Samuel Smiles', is sound at heart because of the contrition which he shows on receiving Antonio's letter. But consider what a howling cad Bassanio is! He approaches Antonio, from whom he has already borrowed many a time and oft, with a verbiage which adds insult to the proposed further injury: ''Tis not unknown to you.' These are the first words of an elaborate and long-winded scheme for borrowing fresh money to repay the old. Antonio's obvious and proper reply is that he has heard that tale before. But let it not be thought that I am carping at Shakespeare's plot; the play has to be got going somehow and that is why Antonio cannot turn his friend down. Now see how much or how little Bassanio protests against Shylock's proposal:

> You shall not seal to such a bond for me:
> I'll rather dwell in my necessity.

Those who know anything of the mentality of borrowers will not expect Bassanio to say more, though the perfunctoriness of his protest establishes him as a pretty mean hound.

Then comes the scene of the caskets and all that talk about 'gaudy gold, hard food for Midas, I'll none of thee'. Why should this Bad Egg, having borrowed as much of Antonio's gold as he can get hold of, suddenly start canting and sermonizing like Chadband and Pecksniff put together? Then comes Antonio's letter followed by his friend's:

O sweet Portia
Here are a few of the unpleasant'st words
That ever blotted paper!

Mr. Granville-Barker's comment is: 'Shakespeare shows us Bassanio, his heart's desire won, agonized with grief and remorse at the news of Antonio's danger. Such moments do test a man and show him for what he is; and this one, set in bright light and made the scene's turning-point, counts for more in the effect the character makes on us than all the gentlemanly graces of his conventional equipment . . . Here speaks Shakespeare's Bassanio; and it is by this, and all that will belong to it, that he is meant to live in our minds.'

But do not the words 'O sweet Portia' show that Bassanio is already preparing to borrow from his lady the wherewithal to pay his friend's debts, which further loan he effectively pulls off in less than three minutes? Here in my view speaks the real Bassanio, who lives in my mind as the complete and perfect parasite. There are hints that Shakespeare strove against this; probably if Molière had written this play he would have called it *Le Gigolo Malgré Lui*. What I am driving at is the old folly of imagining that Shakespeare's characters have any reality apart from that which is given them by the text. Walkley was very sound and sane about this when he said that *Hamlet* is not 'a play of real life, led by people who have independent lives outside it', but that, on the contrary, it is 'a work of art contrived by a certain man at a certain time under certain influences and with certain objects'. In other words Professor Bradley's 'some precedent *état d'âme* in Hamlet himself' is bunkum. A whole book could be written on the Walkley-versus-Bradley theme which I shall not pursue here except to say that which ever view be held of Portia must also be held of Bassanio. When Portia says: 'Since you are dear bought, I will love you dear' she is no better than one of Ned Lathom's heroines. But would Mr. Granville-Barker permit us to judge Portia on this single aspect of her? Why, then, must we judge Bassanio by his one decent sentiment, which, when you

56

look at it closely, is only the cover to further borrowing exploits? He talks of his friend's 'gaping wound issuing life-blood'. This appeals to the woman in Portia, and as Bassanio knows her to be a great lady, he reinforces the picture with the cunning touch about Antonio's ancient Roman honour. This does the trick, and when Portia asks what sum Antonio owes, Bassanio is ready with his: 'For me three thousand ducats', after which he shuts up like a knife. Whereby we realize that Shakespeare knew brevity to be the soul not only of wit but also of sponging. Now let me disclaim any wish to insist on this portrait of Bassanio. This for the reason that I do not believe that Bassanio exists at all, except as a projection on paper of a personage whose mental, moral and all other qualities veer and shift as the necessities of the plot determine.

To the foregoing is to be added the old point about the wholesale miscarriage of the moral in this play, in which Shakespeare asks us to condemn Jewish spleen, which has reason behind it, and applaud Christian malignity, which has none. Add all these things up, and really I do not see how to avoid the conclusion that this is a pretty poor play about a Jew who has the minimum of Jewish characteristics, a hero who may or may not be a cad, and a great lady who at one moment is prepared to buy her lover and at another desires only to stand high in his account.

> Yet, for you
> I would be trebled twenty times myself;
> A thousand times more fair, ten thousand times more rich.

The wretch has need to be! There remains, of course, this play's poetry which, by dint of being knocked into me at school, was knocked out of me for ever. If anybody throws a stone at me for this I shall reply with a massive boulder from Sir Arthur Quiller-Couch: 'I came first to this play as a schoolboy, and though I got it by heart I could not love it.'

The principal characters are nicely taken by Mr. Franklin Dyall, Miss Marie Ney, and Mr. Jack Livesey, and two of these more than nicely. For the rest Mr. Basil Gill as Antonio plays up to Bassanio's Roman line, Mr. Leslie Holland works at Launcelot like a cohort of Trojans, and as Balthasar Mr. John Sullivan has a terrific success with his single line: 'Madam, I go with all convenient speed.' On the night I attended the line was delivered with such solemnity and grandeur that the house rose at Mr. Sullivan. But it quickly sat down again to resume contemplation of a set of stage-pictures which would have warmed the hearts of Alma-Tadema, Herkomer and Fildes. Mr. Stanley Bell's production carries us back to the barmy days of British scene-painting, and I for one am not disconcerted. I hold it quite right that old Gobbo should nearly fall into that waterless canal on whose bare bed gondolas are groggily propelled. And I hold it even more than right that the end of the comedy should find Antonio reading in a bird-sanctuary the happy news that his argosies are still A 1 at Lloyd's.

First Nights: March 15, 1934

AS YOU LIKE IT
(The Old Vic)

MISS EVANS'S ROSALIND

THE company at the 'Old Vic' gave a very spirited performance of this comedy, which Théophile Gautier chose to illustrate the peculiar enchantment of the English poet. To do this he took up some fifty pages of *Mademoiselle de Maupin*, and failed handsomely. That is to say, he failed for us, though he may have succeeded for the poor foreigner. To read *Comme il vous plaira* may make a Frenchman feel as if in the course of a country walk he should turn a corner in the road and meet the shade of a forgotten mistress. But this association of ideas is, one suggests, equally foreign and repugnant to English taste. The Forest of Arden may be peopled with lovers, but at least their affairs are eternal and have to do with love, self-sacrifice and remembrance, rather than passion, sacrificing the other person, and forgetting.

But Gautier thought he knew all about Shakespeare, and went so far as to translate a bit here and there. And again he made a mess of it. Take that little speech of Rosalind to Orlando after the wrestling match. She says simply:

> Gentleman,
> Wear this for me, one out of suits with fortune,
> That would give more, but that her hand lacks means,
> Shall we go, coz?

This is not great poetry, yet it has a smack of something which is not of the everyday world. Now mark what Gautier does with it. According to him Rosalind says: 'Brave cavalier, portez ceci en souvenir de moi, d'une jeune fille qui vous donnerait plus si elle avait plus à vous offrir.' Which is exactly what the midinette might say to the coiffeur round the corner. Perhaps it is the little word 'coz' which baffled him. What hope, then, have they to make something of the mighty things in Shakespeare who cannot cope with the most trifling of his ornaments?

The company, I repeat, do it very well. It may be that for some ten minutes or so what you might call the pictorial aspect of Miss Edith Evans's transformed Rosalind does not quite satisfy. But you soon forget that in the bubbling seas of Renaissance wit on which this gracious artist launches you, and which she herself rides like some fair frigate out of the Book of Romance. She does it all so buoyantly, carelessly, understandingly, and rightly. There is just the proper note of mischief and the exact love-lorn *nuance*. Mr. Frank Vosper makes a handsome Orlando, Mr. Duncan Yarrow gives us a thin, intellectual Touchstone, who, one feels, would regale Audrey in the evening with readings aloud from Proust, Mr. Baliol Holloway is a duly adequate Jaques, reciting with gusto that piece which might easily be the winner in a competition as to Shakespeare's Worst Bit, and Mr. John Wyse endowes Sylvius with that accent which people who have never been to Oxford mistakenly attribute to her children.

March 1, 1926

AS YOU LIKE IT
(The Old Vic)

MISS ASHCROFT'S ROSALIND

THERE are many ways of producing this comedy. You can say it with matting to represent grass, lashings of leaves, real running water, real goats, conies, and other fauna, and a live producer to come on at the end and bow his acknowledgments. Or you can say it with curtains. Or with doublets of japanned leather and tin-foil eyebrows. (This is foolish, but the highbrows like it.) You can produce it after the manner of *The Insect Play*, or among Expressionist scaffolding, or in the black-and-white manner with Celia and Rosalind making a duet of the epilogue because both actresses have singing voices. All these have something to recommend them. But there is nothing, I think, to be said for a method which presents the Forest of Arden as a bare, wind-swept plateau without hint of vegetation. I do not suppose that this is really Mr. Harcourt Williams's notion of the Forest of Arden. He may even plead that the Old Vic's poverty but not his will consents. Even so, Mr. Williams was not guiltless of some oddity in casting when he invited Mr. Geoffrey Wincott to give us a Touchstone slender, sprightly, and apparently in the twenties. Every line in this part presumes ripe age, and there is the further point about Touchstone that his prodigious unfunniness demands the portly aspect. Then how about Phebe, that embodiment of 'the red glow of scorn and proud disdain'? Let anybody read that first speech beginning: 'I would not be thy executioner,' and tell me whether this does not conjure up some regal gipsy. And if this does not convince, what about Rosalind's:

> 'Tis not your inky brows, your black silk hair,
> Your bugle eyeballs, nor your cheek of cream . . .

Properly cast, Phebe can be a glorious little part. In the present hands she could only be a schoolroom chit. To compensate us, Mr. Charles Hickman as Silvius spoke his few lines admirably; this actor and Mr. Malcolm Keen, who played Jaques, reminded us of Shakespeare oftener than anybody else. Mr. William Fox is too young to play Orlando, another part which, when it is whipper-snapperish, becomes nothing. Years ago Sir Frank Benson did it fine, and I have never seen anybody else get near it. Miss Peggy Ashcroft was the Rosalind, and that young lady gave us all that is left after taking away the poetry, the depth of feeling, and what I should like to call the lineage of the part. Rosalind is sister to Beatrice, and in other ages would be Millamant and Clara Middleton. In plain words, she must have style. Miss Ashcroft made her a nice little girl in a wood.

November 3, 1932

A L L ' S   W E L L   T H A T   E N D S   W E L L
(Arts)

MISS   IRIS   BAKER'S   HELENA

I CAME away from this little-performed play with no idea in my head except that it was Shakespeare botching and bungling at his worst. This, I said, will never do for Sunday, and began to look round for that wherewith to buttress this column. Wasn't there an old article by William Archer? There was. In it Archer makes a confession which throws an astonishing light upon the state of the London stage in 1895 and that of his own experience. Archer only goes to this play, which is being given by amateurs, that he may 'bag a new Shakespeare' and reduce the number of Shakespeare plays unseen by his erudite self. There are nine of these including *The Tempest, Coriolanus, Richard II*, and the Second Part of *Henry IV*. The last omission is staggering, and equally staggering are the admissions that he has only seen the First Part played by amateurs, *Cymbeline* in the provinces, *King John* at the Crystal

Palace, and *Julius Caesar* by a German company. In the matter of Shakespearean acting, whaur's your Wullie Archer noo?

It was even more amusing to collate what Mr. Shaw wrote on the same occasion: 'I should not like to see another such performance of *All's Well* or any other play that is equally rooted in my deeper affections.' 'Deeper affections' are the operative words here, and it was with a chuckle that, turning back to Archer, I found: 'The thing is a fairy-tale, and as a fairy-tale it pleases the imagination, on its sensual rather than its spiritual side. On the plane of real life, Shakespearolatry alone can find the fable edifying or attractive'. Fancy pinning sensual delight on to Mr. Shaw, and accusing him of Shakespearolatry! Beards must have wagged that day, and among them a red one!

Opinion has wobbled more disconcertingly concerning Helena than about any other Shakespearean heroine. Coleridge thought her the flower of them all. In our own day Professor Allardyce Nicoll says: 'The story is nauseous and disgusting. The thought of a noble woman's so debasing herself as to capture a husband by the means presented here is so degrading that few can take any pleasure in the reading of the play'. He goes on to call Helena 'one of the most characterless of Shakespeare's heroines', which I take to be plain nonsense. The young woman who could propose to slake a romantic passion at the Court of France by trumping up the most prosaic of reasons for visiting it was at least not without wit. Mr. Shaw found Helena's 'sovereign charm' in the fact that she anticipated Ibsen's Nora, and Archer talked of that 'sincere and noble mind' which drove her to 'methods which, if used by a man towards a woman, would brand him as a villain of the deepest dye, and earn him the execrations of every gallery in Christendom'. In Archer's view what is saucy in the gander is not saucy in the goose, and Mr. Shaw agreed to the extent of creating in Ann Whitefield a heroine who, if she had been born three hundred years earlier, would undoubtedly have used Helena's method of compelling a husband.

None of these eminent critics, however, has tackled the real problem of this play, which is the reason for the supineness of

Master Bertram. If the plot had been Shakespeare's own invention one might think that he had begun the comedy in the mood of the earlier sonnets and diverted its course at a later date; the ear suggests that the break took place half-way through the third act. One might further think that, since 'present fears are less than horrible imaginings', Warwickshire discretion overcame Freudian valour. Otherwise how could Shakespeare have refrained from his favourite device of dressing up Helena as he did Rosalind, Viola, Imogen, Julia, in which case we should have had another *As You Like It*, only as the age wasn't prepared to like it?

However we dispute about this, the fact remains that until the break in the middle of the play the soldier Bertram is utterly null, and what the Germans would call a Männchen in uniform. But, alas for speculation, the plot was not Shakespeare's invention but Boccaccio's, and our William was perfectly capable of taking his bad where he found it and leaving that bad alone. Perhaps Boccaccio was not so slipshod a story-teller as those surmise who only know him in a prudish translation. In any case further probing must wait an idler hour. One insists, however, that the early part of the play is youthful Shakespeare. Being required to mention the day after to-morrow, Helena says:

> Ere twice the horses of the sun shall bring
> Their fiery torcher his diurnal ring;
> Ere twice in murk and occidental damp
> Moist Hespersus hath quench'd his sleepy lamp;
> Or four and twenty times the pilot's glass
> Hath told the thievish minutes how they pass . . .

If 'thievish minutes' is not Shakespeare's early music, any Chinese bandit can have my ears!

The play stands or falls by Helena, whose tenderness Miss Iris Baker conveyed extremely well. But Helena is more than soft and clinging, and this young actress failed to give the glint which should be in the eye of this peripatetic puss. As Bertram Mr. Walter Hudd was cheerfully null, though his accent was a 'traifle' too Bayswatery. Mr. Ralph Truman invested the King of France, temporarily *hors de combat*, with the melancholy proper to England's fourth Henry. This was a lovely performance, and so too was Mr. Andrew Leigh's Clown and also Mr. Frederick Culley's Lafeu. The Countess of Roussillon is said by Mr. Shaw to be 'the most beautiful old woman's part ever written', and Miss Martita Hunt very nearly made us believe this, though she looked too young for the part, like lamb dressed mutton-fashion. Mr. John Laurie's playing always seems to me too light in body, and that perhaps is why I cannot think he carried quite enough comic guns for Parolles.

To conclude, I do not see why I should not now pose as a Shakespearean commentator. Has anybody else noticed that when the Countess says to the Clown inviting her to guess his riddle: 'I will be a fool in question, hoping to be the wiser by your answer,' she is merely indulging in the Elizabethan for: 'All right; I'll buy it'?

November 29, 1932

THE TAMING OF THE SHREW
(New)

MISS EVANS'S KATHARINE

I IMAGINE that at the dress-rehearsal Mr. Gurney, the producer, addressed the assembled company something as follows: 'My young friends, I will not let you alone. And why? Because I am a toiler and a moiler, because you are delivered over untoe me, and are become as precious instruments in my hands. My friends, may I so employ these instruments as to use them toe your advantage, toe your profit, toe your gain, toe your welfare, toe your enrichment! — I say that this tedious and doubtful Shakespearean farce is like a young man devoid of parents, devoid of relations, devoid of flocks and herds, devoid of gold, of silver, and of precious stones, and devoid of the light of Terewth! Of Terewth, gentlemen, say not to me that it is not the lamp of lamps. I say to you, it is! I say to you that I will produce this unworthy play of Shakespeare's in the light of my Terewth. I say to you that if you rear yourselves against it, you shall fall, you shall be bruised, you shall be battered, you shall be flawed, you shall be smashed. In other words I am going to produce this play as I like, and you are going to like it.'

Mr. Gurney has been better than his alleged promise. Miss Doris Zinkeisen's settings and costumes are witty and charming. It is obviously Easter Sunday and everybody in Padua has got a new mantua. If these *agréments* distract one from the play all the better, and they have this additional advantage, that when the revival is over the whole lot can be offered to Sadler's Wells for their next production of *The Barber of Seville*. There is at least one hat which any Don Basilio might be proud to have on his head when he bids the company, 'Buona sera!' If it is a good evening for everybody, which it is, the credit is almost entirely due to Mr. Gurney, and in less measure to the young gentlemen who distribute furniture with a wholly Renaissance grace, and to the young ladies who come unto these yellow sands, take hands, curtsey, and do all the things Ariel mentioned in his entirely unintelligible lyric, plus a bit of Websterian spookery. Nor must we forget in this entablature of the evening's irrelevances the music of Mr. Richard Addinsell, who at one point contrives something reeking of Albéniz and the Seville of happier days.

It is always said that sequels are never so good as that which they follow. But surely the best of *The Shrew* lies in the end which has never yet been told? Human nature does not change, and feminine nature is more changeless still. Who does not realize that this shrew's better manners are but skin deep, and that she will grow a new skin within the year? Yes, there could be a very pretty sequel on the lines of Mr. St. John Ervine's *The Lady of Belmont*, showing Petruchio wheeling a perambulator through Verona or wherever Kate decided to bring up her child.

Johnson said 'The whole play is very popular and diverting.' May I put it that it is much too popular and does not divert me? Why on earth Miss Evans wanted to play Kate I have no notion, except it be to show that a course of round, swingeing abuse can convert a sullen scold into a model for Sir Peter Lely. I did not believe this, and I doubt if Miss Evans believes it either. But, all the same, it was very nearly worth while going to the theatre to hear her say 'Young budding virgin!' to the aged Vincentio. That was the true Evans. Christopher Sly being restored, the part was played by Mr. Arthur Sinclair, and I can only say that Mr. Sinclair bereft of an Irish play is a state of affairs almost as melancholy as an Irish play bereft of Mr. Sinclair. Mr. Leslie Banks made a good Petruchio, except that he was not physically big enough or sufficiently full of voice; Kate could and would have shouted down this bantam. Mr. George Howe as Baptista made senility far more enchanting than, I am beginning to think, it actually is, and a great many elegant and agreeable young gentlemen, including Mr. Alec Clunes, Mr. Anthony Ireland, and Mr. Ronald Simpson, cluttered and uncluttered the stage according as Terewth and the lamp of lamps demanded.

March 23, 1937

THE COMEDY OF ERRORS
(Strand)

The Comedy of Errors always strikes me as the most excruciatingly boring farce ever devised by a man of genius. Preliminary announcements had said nothing about a double bill, and the curtain was up before I had time to examine my programme. I was justified, therefore, in taking the scene, a kind of minor throne-room, to represent the Hall in the Duke's Palace, and a bowed and grief-stricken figure for that of the Merchant of Syracusa, condemned to death in the cause of Free Trade. Strange to say, the seeming Merchant wore an Abbess's gown and the features of Miss Sybil Thorndike; and though that lady has in her time played some extraordinary parts, one had hardly reckoned upon Ægeon as a likely incarnation. Still, there she was. As soon,

however, as an actor, who, despite his beard, was obviously Mr.
Lewis Casson, had asked, 'How does your Grace?' and the figure
had replied, 'O Griffith, sick to death!' I realized that the evening
was not going to be so very boring after all, that there was at least
a *bonne bouche* to begin with in the shape of Queen Katharine's
Death Scene from *Henry VIII*.

The part suits Miss Thorndike really well, is neither too sweet
nor too melancholy, and permits just that dash of astringency which
is her greatest asset. Katharine had both spirit and character, and
bore her woes womanfully. Shakespeare must, indeed, have been
grateful to Henry for allowing her to die a natural death; otherwise he must have been to the expense of some nonsense about
laying her head on the block 'as meek as 'twere my pillow', and so
done violence to a virtuous, yet unhysterical, lady. Miss Thorndike played the scene with a very sure touch and considerable
pathos, fretting and fussing not at all. She made us realize, quite
in Mrs. Alving's vein, what a nuisance to a thoroughly bad man is
a persistently good wife, the unhappiness of the conjunction being
feelingly conveyed in the line:

> Say his long trouble now is passing
> Out of this world . . .

Mr. Casson, too, was good, and spoke his estimate of Wolsey like a
human being, and not in his more familiar manner of a professor
elucidating some problem in economics. The poor Queen had
hardly breathed her last before the orchestra struck up, with
ludicrous inappositeness, a jig from Edward German. One
doesn't expect musicians to have brains; but temperament alone
should have told them that to join hands in a frolic round the bier
of the dead Queen was in poor taste.

Pedants may talk of *The Comedy of Errors* as a lyrical farce
blending elegiac beauty with comic effect. *Tot homines, quot* funny-
bones; and, personally, I find five acts of twin-Antipholuses and
twin-Dromios intolerably dull. Dryden, on the same subject, is
also boring, which hardly surprises us; it is more significant that
Molière should strike less than his usual wit out of his two

Amphitryons. No, these buffoons are almost as unplayable as their masters, and I shall wait for a happier occasion to discuss the excellences of those two capital Shakespeareans, Messrs. Andrew Leigh and Hay Petrie. When the French want a synonym for boredom they have recourse to the famous Récit de Théramène from *Phèdre*. I suggest that Ægeon's opening solemnities might serve the same purpose over here. Was there ever such a driveller? The Duke scented him from afar, as he would nose a club bore. 'Well, Syracusian, say in brief . . .' he commands, and the old boy's brevity runs to exactly 105 lines of the blankest verse that ever Shakespeare turned out, winding up with the dreadfullest couplet in all the plays:

> Hopeless, and helpless, doth Ægeon wend
> But to procrastinate his lifeless end.

June 17, 1923

ELIZABETHAN COMEDIES

THE SHOEMAKER'S HOLIDAY

BY THOMAS DEKKER

(The Old Vic)

'BUT for that wireless favourite, "Drink to Me Only", Jonson and all his works had passed into the limbo of forgotten things.' Thus a recent gossip-monger's paragraph. Next day I discovered Dekker in a crossword puzzle. So, you see, Time brings in his revenges. There is a kind of poetic inevitability in this return to the age of Elizabeth. The maddest motorist has only to career England long enough to strike Stratford in the end.

Comparatively little is known about Thomas Dekker except that he was a hack-writer of whom Jonson, Webster, Ford, and others made use. Nearly all that has come down of him is taken from Henslowe's *Diary*, in which there are allusions to advances made on account of work to be done. Dekker is described by one authority as 'possessing all the thriftlessness and pecuniary shamelessness of Micawber'. But at least he did the work for which he had been paid! *The Shoemaker's Holiday* proves that, like Dickens, Dekker possessed the common touch. Here again are the humour and the pathos, the relish for absurdity and the vein of sentiment. Both had the eye for the odd character and both took delight in showing good-nature peeping through the holes in rascality's blanket. Dickens's scullions may have more brains, but Firk, the journeyman shoemaker, has the root of their grey matter. The play is really all about caste. A king is introduced to do honour to a master-craftsman, and the son of the rich merchant makes honourable amends to a common soldier. 'Who'd 'ave thought the long swell 'ad it in 'im?' is written on the countenance of Firk, new-enlightened after the manner of Sam Gerridge. We can imagine how all this must have pleased Elizabethan groundlings, and we must recognize that the theme of this comedy is equally near to the general heart to-day. Subservience in the matter of the touched wage and forelock — the conspiracy of social inferiority may still be part of labour's mental make-up. Recent years have re-taught the world, if indeed the world had ever forgotten, that Jack is as good as his master in such things as dying for his country, or hating to find his woman another's. As good, too, in the minor matter of untutored wit. Note honest Firk's retort when the Lord Mayor takes him for a knave — 'No knave, sir, but Firk, the shoemaker, lusty Roger's chief lusty journeyman, hoping your worship is in good health as I was at the making of these shoes, I bid you farewell, yours, Firk.' This is not only Sam Gerridge but Sam Weller, and the rapturous delight with which the sally was received by the Old Vic audience proved its kinship with the enduring wit of London streets. Cockaigne is a country which never changes, and Firk is a constant feature in its landscape. In this character Dekker owes nothing to any other dramatist, and it is obvious that for it he went straight to life. One feels a little differently about Simon Eyre, the mad shoemaker, who is a hurly-burly of a man compounded in equal parts of Falstaff and Pistol. The play was published about the same time as *The Merry Wives of Windsor*, and it is impossible not to think that for his principal character Dekker went a-borrowing.

The piece was put on as well as need be, and was capitally played. First there was the Simon Eyre of Mr. Baliol Holloway, who gave us all there is in the part. This actor's Falstaff is a banquet, but this was at least a sufficient meal. Then Mr. Horace Sequeira played Firk with a great deal of ingenuity; this is a comedian of promise. Mr. John Garside was good as Hodge; and Mr. Neil Porter as Ralph, the wounded soldier, put extraordinary passion into the scene in which he rediscovered his wife by means of her old shoe. But throughout the whole play Mr. Porter contrived to wear that shining look with which St. Dunstan's and other hospitals have made us familiar, and to suggest, in his voice, trials bravely endured. 'Are we downhearted?' is a cry as old as Agincourt. As Henry V Mr. William Monk bore himself royally and well, but would perhaps do even better if he did not appear to be quite so greatly tickled by his part.

Remains Miss Evans, who found Margery Eyre a sketch of a part, and turned her into a complete woman. One would describe the versatility of this actress as amazing if it were not that one has become entirely unamazed at it. Miss Evans has this characteristic of all good acting — that she takes hold of her dramatist's conception, absorbs it, and then gives it out again re-created in terms of her own personality and delighted imagination, so that you get the twofold joy of one fine talent superimposed upon another. 'How shall I look in a hood?' asks the new-enriched dame, to be answered, 'Like a cat in the pillory.' Whereupon Margery has the astonishing, irrelevant, 'Indeed, all flesh is grass'. Hear Miss Evans say this, mark the relish with which she passes absurdity under your nose in the manner of a connoisseur extolling old brandy — note this, and you reflect, first, that Dekker was a good playwright, and, second, that the best wit in the world gains when it is delivered by a witty actress.

It is not pretended that the audience at this theatre is composed of anything but simple, middle-class people. Well, here is the play for them. Watching it, and noting how the wage-earning spirit of the late sixteenth century called to the wage-earning spirit of the early twentieth, one realized that there is an unchanging England which does not know serfdom and ignores plutocracy. We cannot tell what the curled gallants and scented ladies of Dekker's day thought about this piece. Perhaps, taking a leaf out of the modern book, they didn't visit it.

The Contemporary Theatre, 1926: March 28, 1926

THE SHOEMAKER'S HOLIDAY

BY THOMAS DEKKER

(The Playhouse)

'WHO was this Dekker anyhow?' said a young man of recognized intellectual attainment when I suggested to him that he might do worse than go to see Miss Nancy Price's revival of *The Shoemaker's Holiday*. I hope to confine myself here to saying who Dekker was, and to refrain right to the end of the article from expressing any view about this generation's unconcern. Since fogeydom seems to impend, I must take a tip from Heywood, another delightful Elizabethan, and adopt as motto and maxim:

> I am sudden, and not superfluous;
> I am quarrelsome, and not seditious;
> I am peaceable, and not contentious;
> I am brief, and not compendious.

Dekker's Christian name was Thomas, and the little that is known about his life is taken from the Diary of Henslowe, who was part-manager of the Fortune Theatre in the closing years of the sixteenth century. The first entry is dated January 8th, 1597, and refers to the sum of twenty shillings, 'lent unto Thomas Dowton to buy the book of a play by a certain Mr. Dickers'. Spelling being wholly arbitrary at this period, this playwright's name is to be found in half a dozen different forms. The second entry is still promising. It shows a further sum of four pounds paid to Dekker for what was doubtless another instalment of his play. But the third entry is less good. It reads: 'Lent unto the company, the 4th February, 1598, to discharge Mr. Dicker out of the counter in the Poultry the sum of forty shillings.' In other words, young Dekker had been in prison for debt. This proves one of two things, though I am not quite sure which — that either men of genius never have any money, or men of money never have any genius.

We do not know the date of Dekker's birth and death, but we know that he was married before 1594, and had already won fame as a playwright in 1597. Mr. Ernest Rhys's admirable account in the 'Mermaid Series' puts the date of Dekker's birth at 1569 or possibly a few years earlier. Shakespeare, as even some of to-day's young men may have heard, was born in 1564, so that the two playwrights at any rate grew up together. Marlowe, of course, was of the same period, and of all the dramatists of the time Marlowe and Shakespeare are the only two who do not seem to have called in Dekker as collaborator. Playwriting then was a much more go-as-you-please business than it is to-day, and no Elizabethan dramatist who was short of a comic scene, and did not feel in a funny mood himself, thought it beneath his dignity to apply to somebody else to invent such a scene for him. And if it was a comic playwright who wanted a dramatic scene filling in, he also had no compunction in the matter. Dekker was a hack-writer of extraordinary adaptability. He was collaborator with Webster in writing *Westward Ho*, *Northward Ho*, and *Sir Thomas Wyat*, with Middleton in *The Roaring Girl*, with Ford in *The Sun's Darling*, with Rowley and Ford in *The Witch of Edmonton*, and with Massinger in *The Virgin Martyr*. It is from the plays which Dekker wrote single-handed that we can best estimate the share which he had in the plays of other men. Literary criticism is largely made up of putting two and two together, and it is easy to connect Dekker's incarceration with the blithe and sunny spirit of *The Shoe-maker's Holiday*. Your mean-spirited scribe never gets imprisoned for debt because he never has any debts to be put in prison for. 'Debt', said Balzac, some centuries later, 'is a flight of poetic imagination which no creditor can understand.' We may take it that Dekker was a hard worker and boon companion, careless and happy-go-lucky, with an immense zest and taste for life, and above all an understanding of the lives of common people. He was endowed with a sunny disposition and the gift of poetry. If this be so, then we may assume that it is the passages of natural obser-vation and of human as distinct from sublime poetry that Dekker contributed to the plays bearing his name jointly with those of other writers. Swinburne talks of Dekker as having an intimate and familiar sense of wretchedness, a great and gentle spirit of compassion for the poor and suffering with whom his own lot in life was so often cast, in prison and out. And Lamb says simply: 'As for Dekker, why, he had poetry enough for anything.'

In case it should be any incentive to visit the present revival, let me state that there is less poetry in *The Shoemaker's Holiday* than in this writer's other original plays; in the enchanting *Old Fortunatus*; in that magnificent double play, *The Honest Whore*, which Mr.

Clifford Bax would like to revive if anybody would let him; and even in that shrewd knock at Ben Jonson called *Satiromastix*, which you might think a mere pasquinade until you open it and find astonishing things like this:

> Suppose who enters now,
> A king whose eyes are set in silver; one'
> That blusheth gold, speaks music, dancing walks,
> Now gathers nearer, takes thee by the hand,
> When straight thou thinkst the very orb of heaven
> Moves round about thy fingers . . .

The Dekker play now to be seen has nothing in this vein, for it is a lusty, rollicking comedy about the ordinary workaday people of Shakespeare's time, the groundlings. It has some of the flavour of Chaucer and more than a dash of Dickens. 'Honest labour bears a lovely face,' and what is more to the point, a jolly face, and the language is the rich round stuff that seems, to my old-fashioned taste, to be the next best thing to poetry in the literature of the stage. Hear Simon Eyre, that hurly-burly of a man, that shoemaker turned Lord Mayor, berating his wife, Margery:

> Peace, Maggy, a fig for gravity! When I go to Guildhall in my scarlet gown, I'll look as demurely as a saint, and speak as gravely as a justice of the peace; but now I am here at Old Ford, at my good lord mayor's house, let it go by, vanish, Maggy, I'll be merry; away with flip-flap, these fooleries, these gulleries. What, honey? Prince am I none, yet am I princely born.

A brief breathing-space to allow of a song that recalls the mad blackbird hidden in the wet beech-tree, a song with the refrain:

> O the month of May, the merry month of May,
> So frolick, so gay, and so green, so green, so green.

And then Simon is off again, and all the better for his lyrical refreshment:

Be ruled, sweet Rose: th'art ripe for a man. Marry not with a boy that has no more hair on his face than thou hast on thy cheeks. A courtier, wash, go by, stand not upon pishery-pashery: those silken fellows are but painted images, outsides, outsides, Rose; their inner linings are torn. No, my fine mouse, marry me with a gentleman grocer like my lord mayor, your father; a grocer is a sweet trade: plums, plums. Had I a son or daughter should marry out of the generation and blood of the shoemakers, he should pack; what, the Gentle Trade is a living for a man through Europe, through the world.

This is the stuff for an actor, and Mr. Edmund Willard is the actor for it. He is half Pistol and half Falstaff, which is exactly right. If my readers prefer the flip-flap, not to say the pishery-pashery, of current comedy, they must go to it; I am going again to *The Shoemaker's Holiday*. The production is fresh and gay, among the subordinates Mr. Harold Warrender, Mr. Hedley Briggs, and Miss Mabel Constanduros have the proper spirit, and Miss Price is once again to be congratulated on her temerity and her faith.

November 18, 1938

THE KNIGHT OF THE BURNING PESTLE
BY BEAUMONT AND FLETCHER
(The Old Vic)

THE other night at the Old Vic one found oneself enjoying this enchanting piece in half a dozen ways. One began by taking it as the good-natured, easy thing it is, a panorama of the joy of being alive, shot here and there with something of that beauty and pain which plagued every Elizabethan. This brought one back to the sense of period and set one, as these old plays always do, to the making out of a profit-and-loss account. What do we lose? Well, not to be too pedantic or exhaustive, we lose something of what might be called correspondency. Our wealthy grocers and their ladies still patronize art and artists, though not in the simple way of this play's Citizen and Wife. We still must launch into the world our young fortune-seekers whom we call go-getters. But with care and art and insinuation, and not after Merrythought's way of counting ten shillings into Jasper's hand and singing him down the wind. And what of Merrythought himself, the unrepentant spendthrift reduced to forty shillings but who has never yet come into his dining-room without finding excellent meat and drink on the table, or worn out a suit without prevailing on his tailor for a new one? 'Without question it will be so ever; use makes perfectness. If all should fail, it is but a little straining myself extraordinary, and laugh myself to death.'

Perhaps the economic sense is sharper than it was; we do not look so kindly upon Harold Skimpole. But then Skimpole could not have said: 'All I have to do in this world is to be merry; which I shall, if the ground be not taken from me; and if it be, (*Sings*)

> When earth and seas from me are reft,
> The skies aloft for me are left.'

Then, too, just as Beaumont and Fletcher's audience must have recognized their characters as skits upon familiar types, so the whole play must have been a burlesque of the romances of the period. Perhaps that is the reason why the play when it was first produced was a complete failure, for if human nature does not change neither do theatre audiences, and we know that even to-day no burlesque succeeds which is at the expense of that to which the public is genuinely if sentimentally attached. As the seventeenth century advanced, the taste for sixteenth-century romances presumably declined, whereby one would expect a burlesque of them to become more popular; in any case, it is significant that Beaumont and Fletcher's play, which failed in 1611, was a great success in 1635.

We lose the immediate sense of Michael's: 'Is not all the world Mile End, mother?' and his mother's reply: 'No, Michael, not all the world, boy; but I can assure thee, Michael, Mile End is a

goodly matter.' We lose, too, the contemporary excitement of
hearing Ralph spout:

> By Heavens, methinks, it were an easy leap
> To pluck bright honour from the pale-faced moon —

and the immediate joy of detecting that he goes on to misquote
and make a mess of a passage from a current masterpiece. But
that is enough of our losses. What we gain is something that
Henry James, talking of old pictures, called 'the tone of time'.
Perhaps no old masters looked in their own day as lovely as they
do in ours; an unintended mellowness has come upon them. But
there is more in it than this, for we look upon old beauty by the
light of newer lamps, and it is difficult to believe that late Elizabethans saw in this piece the naïveté that we do. Sitting at it I
found myself wondering whether our attitude to the stage has not
changed more greatly than we suspect. May not the Elizabethans
have regarded a play as something beginning and ending with its
performance? At the end of Beaumont's piece the Citizen says:
'Come, Nell, shall we go? The play's done.' To-day we regard
Hamlet as something existing, so to speak, outside Shakespeare's
page; so definitely are we persuaded of this that we indulge in
theories and speculations about the character apart from Shakespeare's words. Hamlet and his world have become so real to us
that any stage presentation of the play is only a *translation* of that
world to the boards instead of being the whole of it. I agree that
this is wrong. Wrong or right, that sense was completely absent
the other night.

One asked oneself, too, exactly how impressionable were late
Elizabethan and early Jacobean audiences, and whether the dis-
carding of the platform stage and the substitution of the picture
frame has not increased impressionableness. When Ralph cannot
pay his reckoning at the inn the Citizen jumps on to the stage and
produces the money, and when Michael has chilblains the
Citizen's Wife is extremely forthcoming as to their cure. But the
actors who are performing for the benefit of the Citizen and his
Wife do not seem particularly put out by the interruptions which

go on throughout the play. In fact, they *are* the play, for Ralph, the grocer's apprentice, who' clambers over the footlights, turns himself into the play's hero, again without incommoding the company. When in the old melodrama the sailor leaped on to the stage it was because he was over-convinced by what G. H. Lewes called the *optique du théâtre*. One wonders how much of the *optique du théâtre* existed in Beaumont and Fletcher's day. I was persuaded the other night of one of two things. Either this piece is the most sophisticated, Pirandellish thing that ever existed, since Citizen, Wife, and Apprentice are three 'characters' in search of a play, in which case the audience of the time must have been highly sophisticated. Or else it was always a wild farrago of reasonless absurdity which might well have been called *It's a Grocer!*

With the blazing exception of Miss Thorndike and the careful one of Mr. George Zucco the piece is not too well acted. To the part of the Wife Miss Thorndike brings all that warm-heartedness which she has at command equally with Greek austerity. She must often have felt the need, in Rachel's phrase, to 'disenduchess' herself, and she seizes the present occasion with gusto even to the importation of a Lancashire accent. As the Citizen, Mr. Zucco gives a more than agreeable performance. But surely Mr. Richardson is miscast? His stolid, inexpressive mien, altogether admirable in Bottom and in all delineations of the downright, and his general suggestion of the tongue-tied do not belong to the volatile, mercurial Apprentice who has been an amateur actor and spills the loquacity of which he is full. Histrionics should tumble out of Ralph because he cannot help it, and to invite Mr. Richardson to do this is like asking a stonewaller to play one of Macartney's innings. Mr. Richard Ainley was this company's actor for the part, but he is young and his turn is not yet. A still more unfortunate piece of casting was the choice of Mr. Frank M. Clark to play Merrythought, for Merrythought has innumerable snatches to troll, and Mr. Clark has no voice to troll with. Nor, I submit, should the part be made so wholly pantaloon, for the merriment is that of the round and not the shrunken belly. Mr. Robert

EPICŒNE

Harris spoke Jasper's lines beautifully, and delightful music was discoursed throughout. The play's reception was most enthusiastic.

First Nights: January 4, 1932

EPICŒNE; or, THE SILENT WOMAN

BY BEN JONSON

(Phoenix Society)

Is it shameful not to have enormously liked this old play? One went to it with good-will, which remained at full stretch until the clowning scene between doctor and parson at the end relieved the tension. That was capital fun, and straightway the author put on the likeness of a human being. For the rest of the comedy he was all schoolmaster, even pedant. Praise must always be given to old Ben for his power of observation and his industry in recording the results of that observation. But he possessed also, and to the maximum degree, the defects of his qualities. He observed down to that which was least worthy of observation, and, like some fanatic of the microscope, attributed value according as the object had escaped the notice of others. Shakespeare's genius consisted in decking out afresh that which all men knew, whereas Jonson's talent lay in discovering what no man before him had thought worthy to lay bare. And then the pertinacity of the fellow! Having made acquaintance with some landlord who called his drinking-cups his Bull, his Bear, and his Horse, Jonson must needs invent a Captain Otter to exploit a joke which is not a good one to begin with, and ends by being insufferably tedious.

Hazlitt says that Jonson is like a dull man with a disagreeable subject from which he cannot be turned. His characters are invariably low, and entirely lacking in that humanity which makes Shakespeare's boors more agreeable company than any other dramatist's gods. His humour is, 'as it were, confined in a leaden cistern, where it stagnates and corrupts'. His wit is good, but there is a complete absence of poetry, and, in this play at

79

least, not once is there any preoccupation with beauty. There is no air round Ben Jonson's personages. His plots are poor. That a man should be so hateful of noise that he must marry a dumb wife is not matter for three hours' exploiting. Or not in Jonson's hands. The characters are ill differentiated, and there is not a ha'porth of individuality about Dauphine, Clerimont or True-Wit.

Sir Amorous la Foole is a frank copy, and the scene between him and Sir John Daw is filched from *Twelfth Night*, and not improved in the filching. The dénouement is taken from the *Merry Wives*. Mesdames Haughty, Mavis, and Trusty, the 'Ladies of the College', baffle modern inquiry as to the constitution of that assembly. They are unintelligent blue-stockings without a word to say in their own defence or anybody else's attack. But the parody of pedantry at the end is magnificent, and this and some animadversions upon the use of lip-stick applicable to our own day are nearly all that can be said for this very dull play.

Remains the character of Morose, in which part one Benjamin Jonson is said to have given a tremendous exhibition of comic distress. Unfortunately, Mr. Cedric Hardwicke gave us a character-study utterly barren of comedy. Indeed, it was hardly a study; the actor composed and then presented a mask of misery, and was content to leave it at that. I can imagine that Mr. Petrie or Mr. Cellier would have been very fine, but, then, these actors cannot always be playing everything. Epicœne was discreetly played by Mr. Godfrey Winn, who looked well in the part. This should always be played by a man, though Mrs. Siddons, who had the Kemble delusion about comedy, is said to have seen herself *en travesti*. Mr. Harold Scott's Sir Amorous would have been excellent but for one bad, and purely mechanical, defect. Every time the actor took breath he did so with a kind of hoarse gulp, which after a time became distressing. Mr. Scott is much too good an artist not to remedy this at once.

November 18, 1924

VOLPONE; or, THE FOX
BY BEN JONSON
(Westminster)

DE gustibus and so on. Speaking for myself, I had as lief see this comedy by Ben Jonson as any by Shakespeare. Perhaps liefer, though the unfamiliarity of the one and the over-familiarity of the other may have something to do with it. But then I would sooner live surrounded by Hogarths than by Watteaus, since to me the English painter, despite the grossness of his subject, is warm and alive, while the Frenchman, despite the elegance of his, is cold and not so alive. And there the not very good analogy must end. Still holding each to his own taste, I submit that it is possible to prove Hazlitt all wrong about this play. Consider Volpone's speech, which begins: 'Why droops my Celia?' and goes on:

> See, behold
> What thou art queen of; not in expectation,
> As I feed others, but possess'd and crown'd.
> See here a rope of pearl, and each more orient
> Than that the brave Ægyptian Queen carous'd;
> Dissolve, and drink them. See, a carbuncle,
> May put out both the eyes of our St. Mark;
> A diamond would have bought Lollia Paulina,
> When she came in like star-light, hid with jewels
> That were the spoils of provinces; take these,
> And wear, and lose 'em. Yet remains an ear-ring
> To purchase them again, and this whole state.

Look over the exquisite passage beginning:

> Thy baths shall be the juice of July flowers,
> Spirits of roses, and of violets,

The milk of unicorns, and panthers' breath,
Gather'd in bags, and mix'd with Cretan wines;
Our drink shall be prepared gold and amber,
Which we will take until my roof whirl round
With the vertigo . . .

It seems to me that Faustus himself would not have disdained

When she came in like star-light, hid with jewels,

and that Perdita would have been at home with

The milk of unicorns, and panthers' breath.

Yet Hazlitt's adjectives for Johson's verse are 'dry', 'literal', and 'meagre'. The point is that the great essayist is a sentimentalist and will take no pleasure in a play unless he can find in it some nice person with whom to identify himself: 'There is almost a total want of variety, fancy, relief, and of those delightful transitions which abound, for instance, in Shakespeare's tragi-comedy. In Ben Jonson, we find ourselves generally in low company, and we see no hope of getting out of it. He is like a person who fastens upon a disagreeable subject and cannot be persuaded to leave it.' But, in heaven's name, who wants anybody to leave a disagreeable subject if he can make it more interesting than an agreeable one?

Hazlitt thinks that the trouble with Jonson's comedy is that it is mean. This is palpably absurd, since one of the concomitants of meanness is littleness. I would rather call Jonson's comedy riotous, and his humanity of the cartoonist's size. Volpone bestrides his world as Valmont bestrides that of Choderlos de Laclos and Vautrin that of Balzac; the lesser rogues have still something Michael-Angelesque about them. Hazlitt denies Jonson gusto because he does not like the things the gusto is about, and because, like every sentimental playgoer, he wants to warm himself at the spectacle of good men routing bad ones, and sees no fun in villains destroying one another. It dismays him that Volpone should be undone by Mosca, and that both should be punished by a bench of zanies. He dislikes the caperings of Volpone's minions because he would not have them behaving so in his own drawing-room. To sum up, Hazlitt desires that comedy should make him think better of mankind, whereas I demand of comedy only that it shall make me think. So long as the comic dramatist is writing well and not ill I am indifferent whether his characters behave well or ill. 'Jonson had a keen sense of what was true and false, but not of the difference between the agreeable and disagreeable.' This proves my case against any playgoer demanding that the things shown him in the theatre shall be agreeable rather than that they shall be true. Judged by the West-End standard of popularity, *Volpone* is 'cross-grained', 'prolix', 'improbable', 'repulsive', and even 'revolting'. Yet in a critic as good as Hazlitt the critical habit dies hard, and he cannot help saying that 'this best play' of Jonson 'is written *con amore*'. This sentence clinches my argument. It is all very well for its author to attempt to recover by saying that the play 'is made up of cheats and dupes, and the author is at home among them'. The gibe comes too late; *the piece is written* con amore!

In the revival at the Westminster the boundless spirit is at large. Mr. Michael MacOwen has given their heads to Mr. Peter Goffin and Mr. Edmund Rubbra, and, thus encouraged, Mr. Goffin responds with a gold-encrusted Jacobean tableau which Mr. Sickert ought to paint, and Mr. Rubbra, meeting his producer more than half-way, conjures from the throats of clarinet, oboe, and bassoon a concourse of sounds even more obnoxious, in a Hazlittean sense, than the scenes they accompany. This spirit extends to the players. Mr. Donald Wolfit makes a splendid mouthful of the Fox; he is right in presence, and he speaks the verse as the actor of Jonson's day must have spoken it. There must be many ways of playing Mosca, and Mr. Alan Wheatley has chosen to be a silk thread among the hempen villainy. Mr. Mark Dignam is the vulture-lawyer of all time, and Mr. Stanley Lathbury a most pointed, witless crow. As I wish this revival immensely well, and as at this point the praise of the acting must get thinner, I stop.

The Amazing Theatre: January 30, 1938

ELIZABETHAN COMEDIES

THE FAITHFUL SHEPHERDESS
BY JOHN FLETCHER
(Phoenix Society)

UNDENIABLY the best actor at this revival was Sir Thomas Beecham. Admirably patterned though the Overture was, I am not to be persuaded that it had quite so much point as Sir Thomas pretended; his baton appeared to be whole dramas in folio. But on the musical side of the affair I must be dumb, lest I encroach upon a colleague's province. Yet let me say that it was very amusing to listen to the guessing-competition disguised in a learned bandying of composers' names. Sir Thomas, declining to let all of his musical cats out of their obscure bags, sate serene, mysterious, Olympian, like some king of the tribe of *Felidae*. Méhul, Grétry, Paisiello were hazarded, and once during an exquisite *pianissimo* I heard 'Mozart, for a dollar!'

What maggot, I wonder, was in Fletcher's brain when he wrote this distraught paean to chastity? J'ever see such a prig — as my Lord Castlewood might have said — as the holy shepherdess Clorin, whose attitude towards natural and healthy ardour was that of the writers of stories for girls in the early part of the last century? (The wench is something too disinfectant; Clorin-of-lime should be her name.) J'ever see such a wooer as Thenot, who was in love with his mistress's fidelity to a dead swain, and fled her so soon as she returned his passion? Not even the Germans have invented a name for so self-immolatory a disease. Perigot and Amoret are a little better, but not much — they are a pair of gabies; and perhaps we do not get into touch with humanity at all until we come to Chloe, a 'wanton shepherdess', and Amarillis who has fire, or at least blood, in her veins.

This pastoral is, by virtue of its poetry, an exquisite thing to read. The setting was lovely, the music such as seldom ravishes the ears of English theatre-goers, the acting sufficient — yet it remained a poor thing to see. What gluttons Elizabethan audiences

84

must have been! Personally I could desire to join a Society for cutting certain of the Phoenix programmes in half. Three hours and a quarter of Fletcher is too much of a middling dramatist. When Goethe's 'Egmont' was produced in Paris a French critic wrote, 'Musique de Beethoven? Hélas, pourquoi y en a-t-il si peu?' Alas, there was too little of Beecham and too much of the poet. It is no use pretending that a marriage can be arranged between music and the spoken word. It can't. Anyhow, not in Fletcher's case. Just as Shakespeare's lyrics can be too good for almost any setting, so almost any setting is too good for Fletcher.

The acting was adequate. Miss Cathleen Nesbitt spoke her lines with beautiful discretion; Miss Mary Merrall invested her foolish virgin with the naked simplicity of a blanch'd almond. As a kind of Druid, Mr. Ben Webster was imposing in a bonnet which Mrs. Skewton might have envied. But the best piece of acting seemed to me to be Mr. Harold Scott's Satyr, full of grace and compassion.

July 1, 1923

SHAKESPEARE'S HISTORIES

KING JOHN
(Fellowship Players)

MR. MILTON

ONE does not pretend that the play has no good bits. There are one or two exquisite bits. And there is some good declamatory stuff in it, made up of single lines which seldom flow into each other. This gives a disjointed, halting effect, and the resulting sum is not poetry. Such lines as:

> Which now the manage of two kingdoms must
> With fearful bloody issue arbitrate

might almost be parody, the second line being the perfect echo of Peter Quince. There is that affecting schoolboy stuff — the scene between Arthur and Hubert — but both the story and the total gesture of this play are poor. King John is a character at once odious and weak, and the worst kind of rogue — the vacillating sort. He would murder Arthur, and then he would not. His villain's blood is not thick enough, the compunctious visitings of nature are too many for him. Shakespeare, we must think, had little taste for the spineless, and therefore wrote this play, not about, but round King John, whom he leaves mum in the middle of the stage whilst everybody else, including that old bore, Pandulph, talks his head off. And when John does talk it is all wind.

One of the reasons why this play is so seldom acted is the difficulty of doing much with the title-rôle. Beerbohm Tree's bearded make-up for the part was exactly like the picture in *Little Arthur's History of England*, entitled 'King John granting Magna Charta'. But Mr. Milton wore no beard, and gave the character the air, not of a King of England, but of some hang-dog second murderer. Did anybody ever really sympathize with Constance? After all, people who lived in the Middle Ages ought to have known the danger of being too near the throne, and ordered their lives accordingly. Why didn't Constance withdraw Arthur to Wales or Scotland or some other inaccessible spot? However, she is a good enough railer, and with those old crones in *Richard III* is the authentic pre-Dickensian Mrs. Gummidge. Miss Esmé Beringer gave a first-class exposition of Constance's grief and snobbery. ('Thy word is but the vain breath of a common man.') But one could not have pitied this Constance. She was twice as hard as nails and *felt* no grief, or did not persuade us that she did, though Miss Beringer spoke the lines magnificently. Faulconbridge the Bastard is the one first-class character in the play, and Mr. Norman V. Norman played him with great gusto and humour. This was a miracle of casting, and the part can never have been better done.

November 9, 1924

KING JOHN
(Sadler's Wells)

MR. SPEAIGHT

Not much good has ever come out of compliments, and none out of idle ones. As a well-wisher to the Old Vic and a fanatic for Shakespeare on the stage as well as in the study, I am compelled to say that if the cast of *King John* reveals the full playing strength for the new season it is not enough. In Mr. Gielgud and Miss Green the company has lost two extremely accomplished players, and there is none to succeed them. This may seem to weigh a little hardly on Mr. Robert Speaight and Miss Phyllis Thomas, and since it is possible that the monotony of Constance is not a fair test of all that may be in an actress, I will, for the moment, reserve observations on the feminine side of the cast.

But King John is a good enough part to show what an actor is made of intellectually, emotionally, and spiritually, and how he is made up physically. Now, the first thing to be laid down, and all actors must accept it, is that in acting the physical half comes first. No amount of interpretative power will save an opera-singer who sings out of tune, and the Shakespearean actor is in the same case, for his body must be in tune. All the critics, from Hazlitt onwards, have insisted upon this, and about every new actor the first question has always been not Can he feel? but Has he presence, and Is his countenance noble? Garrick and Kean lacked the inches, but again the first thing criticism had to say about them was that their genius concealed the lack of inches. There was, you might say, that in both countenances which made the spectator indifferent as to how many feet they were above the floor.

Of Mr. Speaight one would say that he has none of the physical attributes necessary for the great rôles in Shakespeare, and that while he has imagination, brains, and perception, the sum of these qualities does not yield sufficient magnetism to compensate for the physical deficiencies. Whatever King John's actual measurements may have been he must not, in Shakespeare's play, look puny or mean of countenance. Above all, he must look like a man of a certain age, whereas Mr. Speaight makes him look like a schoolboy with a beard tacked on for speech-day. Faulconbridge is a man, and something more than a weakling is necessary to explain that allegiance. Yet, that Mr. Speaight can act is proved by his admirable soliciting of Hubert, and again by the death-scene. Nature having designed this actor for secondary parts, it is up to Miss Baylis to find a player with the graces necessary to cope with the well-graced rôles. Looking round the company one recommends the rapid promotion of Mr. Richard Riddle, if only for the fact that here is a young player with all the physical attributes out of which a fine actor may be made. In this piece he plays the Earl of Salisbury, and though the part is not big the playing of it is invested with great quality. Mr. Riddle has the height and the looks and the voice, and continually the eye seeks him out, which is in itself significant. Mr. Ralph

KING JOHN

Richardson, who a year or two ago was good in a shambling sort
of way, has discarded loutishness and an oafish gait and trans-
muted these into the sterling of forthrightness and honesty. His
Kent was superb, and his Faulconbridge is as good. He has a
direct and manly pathos and can fill any rôle that needs vitality
and command. Once more Mr. Harcourt Williams brought his
very nice pictorial sense to the solution of this play's many pro-
blems. The single Norman-Nondescript scene — for presumably
the Plantagenets had to live somewhere till they started building
for themselves! — drew the early parts of the play together and
gave them an interest which only the priggish will contend that
they possess. The battle-scenes were infinitely more realistic than
the normal clash of ironmongery, and the compressed tableau of
John hardly able to breathe for Barons not only recalled the wood-
cuts to Gardiner's *English History* and so revived the schoolboy's
sense of period, but gave a very fair image of the time's political
pressure.

September ·5, 1931

KING JOHN
(New)

MR. MILTON

WHAT a bad play this is! All about a war in which it is not
possible to take the slightest interest. No critic has ever had much
to say for *King John*, which is beautifully summed up by Hazlitt
when he says: 'The same exposure of the policy of courts and
camps, of kings, nobles, priests, and cardinals, takes place here
as in the other plays we have gone through, and we shall not go
into a disgusting repetition.' And what a wretched lot of characters! John himself doesn't start living till he starts dying, and
while it is the ambition of every robustious actor to make us think

the Bastard a good fellow, he can never hide the fact that at heart he is a noisy braggart. Constance, with her apostrophes to stenches that are 'odoriferous' and rottennesses that are 'sound', and Queen Elinor, who only wants a chance to give back as good as she gets — here are two of the least bearable of Shakespeare's scolds. The fact that Arthur is invariably played by a buxom young woman suggests that after the war there should be a more diligent rummaging in musical drawers and cupboards. Somewhere, I am sure, will be found a score entitled *Il Rè Giovanni*, dramma lirica de Guglielmo Shakespeare e Guiseppi Verdi, with a second act curtain falling on a duet between Arturo and Oberto. One evening, on some Sussex sward . . . But I divagate.

Mr. Tyrone Guthrie and Mr. Lewis Casson, calling in Mr. Frederick Crooke to design the scenery and costumes, made the play beautiful to look at. There is nothing to be done with the principal character, which is the reason, perhaps, why Mr. Milton could not do very much. He wore a really wonderful wig apparently made out of a discarded tea-cosy, and later a crown like the business part of a permanent-wave machine. And he had great fun throughout, suggesting that the monarch was always on the verge of incredible misbehaviour, while the soliciting of Hubert was a wonderful piece of egging-on. As was to be expected, Mr. Milton got all the poetry out of the part, and I suspect him of having put some of it in! Incidentally Mr. Ernest Hare gave a beautiful performance of that sensitive clod, Hubert, who normally behaves as if he had called to cut off the electric light. As Constance Dame Sybil Thorndike went into top speed the moment the flag fell and kept it up till the finish. As Queen Elinor Miss Esmé Church growled like distant thunder. Miss Renee Ascherson did very nicely with Blanche, and as Arthur Miss Ann Casson acted very well but looked like Robin Hood in a Christmas pantomime. And why must Prince Henry be given to a young woman? There were lots of young men on the stage. Mr. Lewis Casson made Pandulph an old fox, silver with age and sophistry; the combination of cracked voice and sound brain was irresistible. Was Mr. George Hagan a trifle light as the Bastard?

Anyhow, it is not every actor's part, and the one really good
Bastard that I have seen was never superlatively good in anything
else.

July 7, 1941

KING RICHARD II
(The Old Vic)

MR. GIELGUD

Richard II has never been a popular play with actors. Down to
the middle of last century it was performed, with one exception
only, in the euphemistical phrase 'as altered by' Tate, by Theobald,
and by Wroughton. Vandenhoff, Macready, Charles Kean, and
one Finch each had a cut at the unfortunate monarch, while in
our own time the only performances one remembers have been
those of Benson, Tree, and Leslie Faber. Edmund Kean performed Wroughton's version. But Garrick, Kemble, Cooke, and
Irving would have nothing to do with the part, and perhaps it was
left to the last month of the last year of the last century to find
that in the play which not only the great actors but the great
critics had not up till then discovered. Benson first played
Richard in London in March 1900, having in the previous
December given the provinces a taste of what one must believe
to have been the play's new quality. Montague, writing of this
performance, said that the actor brought out admirably that half
of the character which criticism seemed almost always to have
taken pains to obscure, that half of Richard which is self-conscious
artist. Is it possible that the words 'almost always' were mere
modesty on this great critic's part? For Montague went on to
point out how Professor Dowden misconstrued the character
'with a quite choice and pointed infelicity', and how criticism in
general had failed to point out that: 'Shakespeare meant to draw,
in Richard, not only a rake and muff on a throne and falling off

91

it, but, in the same person, an exquisite poet; to show with one hand how kingdoms are lost and with the other how the creative imagination goes about its work; to fill the same man with the attributes of a feckless wastrel in high place and with the quite distinct but not incompatible attributes of a typical, a consummate artist.' Is it possible, one asks again, that this was the first discovery not only of what Shakespeare was really at, but of the one quality in the part which prevents it from being a rather monotonous essay in the melancholy of retribution?

I suggest that the date of Montague's criticism is all-important. The world had just passed through the 'nineties, in which period it was first fashionable for artists in this country not only to be self-conscious but to prate about that self-consciousness. Up till that time heroes were heroes and villains villains, and a man who was a bit of both was something of an oddity; people did not go about publicly tasting their heroism, villainy, or what not. Charles Lamb had said that it was worth while being robbed to get the 'idea of' a thief; but one has not heard that thieves, when hanging for theft was the fashion, went to Tyburn prattling about the 'idea of' being hanged.

The 'nineties, however, had changed all that; Wilde could not tire of chattering about the beauty of failure and the ugliness of success. The world, then, was ready to receive the notion that a man who had made an unholy mess of his career might, as to half of him, weep for all he had lost, and as to the other half exult at the richness of experience gained. In 1899 the time was ripe for Montague's discovery of the new Richard; before that year any critic happening upon the 'artist notion' would probably have dismissed it as an unhealthy trick of his own brain. The play is stiff with sign-posts to what is now plain as a pike-staff. Since Montague wrote, the major signs have become the common property of criticism, so that there is no longer need to insist upon the significance of: 'That sweet way I was in to despair,' the passage in which Richard at saturation-point bids his enemy: 'Say that again!' and that still more famous passage in which the defeated king tries to read some pattern of philosophy on his prison-wall. But the sign-posts are so many that one wonders how the road ever came to be missed. One wonders whether it is possible that not all of them have been discovered, though to suggest discovery of a new one is rather like a half-day Cairo excursionist preening himself upon finding something overlooked by generations of learned Egyptologists. Perhaps the point I have in mind is so obviously significant that nobody has thought it worth while to draw attention to it? It is concerned with a peculiarly glaring example in Act III, Scene III, of Richard's mania for crossing disastrous bridges before he is within hail of them. Bolingbroke has sent Northumberland to parley, and his 'coming hither' has 'no further scope' than the repeal of Bolingbroke's banishment and the restoration of his inheritance. These granted, 'his glittering arms he will commend to rust', and so on. The offer is fair-sounding, with, at the moment, nothing behind it except Richard's fears. But Richard conquers these sufficiently to send Northumberland back with a fair answer, after which *and without waiting for Bolingbroke's reply* he straightway embraces the idea of deposition, and in the soliloquy: 'What must the king do now? Must he submit?' plunges his nose with zest into the bouquet of humiliation. I suggest that there is more than cowardice here. Richard has put up a bluff, and even the most cowardly gamester waits for his bluff to be called before throwing in his hand. Richard, then, does more than court disaster: he weds it, and with the passion of a bridegroom.

Any performance of the character must stand or fall by the actor's delivery of this passage, which should be done deliriously and with growing ardour, so that each successive humiliation is held to the light like a jewel, sniffed like a wine, and rolled over the tongue with gusto. The thing is a kind of descending riot. First Richard will lose the name of king. Then the king's mind runs over the material things he must surrender. He is to become an almsman, and enumeration of what an almsman may yet possess brings Richard to the carved saints for which he has exchanged his subjects. The mention of subjects calls up again the 'large kingdom' which he is now willing to barter against the 'little grave'. Now note how Richard's fancy eggs him on. A little grave is not enough; it must be 'a little, little grave', and better still 'an obscure grave'. But even that is not the end. Richard must be buried in the king's highway, 'some way of common trade', so that his body may be literally trampled upon by the feet which now figuratively trample on his heart. Primed by Montague I suggest that the note of all this should be *relish*. Richard is not only absolute for misery, but determined to get the most out of misery, and, in so far as he is an artist, exhibit the beautiful pattern he is making out of misery. Mrs. Gummidge, we remember, felt things more than anybody else. Richard is conscious not only of feeling deposition more than any other monarch, but of phrasing that feeling better than it has been done before. Or rather, half of Richard is so occupied. The other half is facing disaster as apprehensively and with as sincere an apprehension as the old-time highwayman who felt the rope about his neck and did not care what sort of dangling spectacle he was to make for the Tyburn windows.

Mr. Gielgud gives us almost nothing of the artist-half of Richard, though he does complete and perfect justice to what I should like to call the elegiac-half. The great soliloquy which I have attempted to analyse was spoken beautifully, but without the least suggestion of revelling in the woes anticipated. Yet Richard *knows* that he is talking out of something other than a full heart. 'Would not this ill do well?' he demands, mightily contented at the pretty image of the two kinsmen who dig their graves with weeping eyes. He adds: 'Well, well, I see I talk but idly, and you laugh at me.' Mr. Gielgud missed completely the first indication of the dual nature of his subject. This occurs when Scroop throws out the hint that health and happiness are not the message of his 'care-tuned tongue'. At once Richard wants to know whether his kingdom is lost, and he follows this up by saying: 'Why, 'twas my care; And what loss is it to be rid of care?' Here is the first hint to the audience that Richard is a taster of his own sorrows. The line is no more than a grace-note; yet in my view it is immensely important, and the audience should be made aware of its importance. Mr. Gielgud took the line in his stride, and so warned us that the essential half of Richard was not to be created. There can be no doubt that Richard is the most subtle of all Shakespeare's characters, and it may be that to cope with the shadowy artist-half a special technique must be invented. Whether Benson did invent such a technique or whether one read it into his performance I have never been able to determine. But my recollection is, and the impression he made on me at the time was, that as each artist-passage came along a special glint leaped to the actor's eye, and a warning, distinguishable note crept into his voice. Montague goes so far as to say that Benson, after uttering Richard's dying lines as any ordinary man might utter them, 'half rises from the ground with a brightened face and repeats the two last words with a sudden return of animation and interest, the eager spirit leaping up, with a last flicker before it goes quite out, to seize on this new "idea of" the death of the body'.

It was in this last scene that Mr. Gielgud principally failed. The last soliloquy, 'I have been studying how I may compare', with its dramatic challenge to the attention followed by an intricate quasi-metaphysical argument, is a teaser anyhow, and perhaps this actor is not to be greatly blamed for not making it impressive. But the whole of his failure — if failure it was — concerned only half the character; the other half, the weakling, understandable half, was beautifully presented, with a command of noble pose and gesture, a gracious melancholy mien, and a lovely handling of the language to which one would not refuse the highest admiration. Mr. Gielgud, alas! was not sufficiently supported. Mr. Brember Wills, as John of Gaunt, had too little voice, and the great 'sceptred isle' speech went for nothing. Mr. Gyles Isham's Bolingbroke was not nearly full-blooded enough; there should be the clatter of armour about this personage and something of Mr. Edmund Willard's trumpetings. The minor personages with which this play swarms had not even tentative merit, and the famous garden scene was ruined by a little boy in a beard. Miss Martita Hunt's Queen Isabella and Mr. Donald

Wolfit's Bishop of Carlisle made some amends, and one liked very much the costumes and settings of Mr. Owen P. Smythe. Mr. Harcourt Williams produced capitally. But not even the best producer can conjure up acting talent where no talent is.

November 18, 1929

KING RICHARD II
(The Old Vic)

MR. EVANS

EITHER one is becoming a more attentive playgoer or the method of Shakespearean production is getting more lucid. Or was it that in the old days the star-actor appeared, did his bit, and went off to have a breather but allowing no more of the business of the play than was necessary for him to recover breath? There was a time when Shakespearean playgoers who gathered their Shakespeare entirely from the stage could hardly know what any play was about. The production of *Richard II* at the Old Vic is admirable in this respect. So much of the play is left that one can even gather whose son Richard is! The staging is excellent, the return from Ireland being indicated by a single mast and sail quite breath-taking in assurance, and very nearly as good as the cromlech in the Westminster production of *King Lear*. The mind once being satisfied, everything that the characters say will be granted them. 'Barkloughly Castle call they this at hand?' says Richard looking up at the upper box on the O.P. side, and Barkloughly Castle that upper box promptly becomes. 'My lords of England,' says York, and now that we are in the mood the very supers become noblemen and the ground they stand on is England.

One of the best jokes of this production is the miscasting of Miss Mary Newcombe for the Duchess of York. Or perhaps I should say Miss Newcombe's refusal to cast herself properly. The Duchess is wife to the Duke — so much even the cantankerous

96

will not gainsay. York is brother to John of Gaunt, notoriously in his dotage, and it is sufficiently plain that York himself is a doddering old fool. Whence it follows that the Duchess is no chicken. 'Have we more sons?' she says. 'Or are we like to have? Is not my teeming date drunk up with time?' There is no doubt that the Duke and Duchess are this play's two comics, for, if they were not, Shakespeare would have found some other two. Whence it follows that if York is, as the text dictates, a garrulous time-server and cackling old idiot, his Duchess must be at the beldam stage with her knees creaking with rheumatism. In the face of all this Miss Newcombe, coming to plead for her son Aumerle's pardon, makes skimming entry like a swallow down wind or a seagull lighting on a pier — virtuosity in motion of which any dancer in the Russian Ballet would be proud. Whereat Boling-broke, who is thirty-three, the gentleman of the period, and solicitous for the old lady, has to say: 'Good aunt, stand up!' Mr. Abraham Sofaer's Bolingbroke is a rich, resonant, and finely controlled performance; here is the man who is master not only of England but of himself. Mr. David Horne gives weight and authority to Northumberland, and I dissociate myself from those who appear to think that Mr. Horne is not a good Shakespearean actor. He lends weight to a company which is inclined to be on the young side. After all, even in the jimp and modish dawn of the Renaissance some of the men must have been full grown.

Mr. Maurice Evans is faced with one of the most difficult of all Shakespearean rôles. It was Benson who first discovered Shake-speare's Richard. Or perhaps it would be better to say that it was Montague who discovered what Sir Frank had discovered in the part, since which time we have all gone on re-discovering Mon-tague. The whole of this great piece of criticism hangs upon Benson's repetition of Richard's last two words — 'to die'. Mr. Evans restores the balance by leaving them out! But he must be said to do remarkably well in view of the fact that he is the last person one would cast for Richard. The first and last pitfall of the acting profession is for the actor to think that by imagination, cerebration, or sheer acting he can play *any* part. This is just not true. Henry Irving could no more pretend to be a bluff, gormandizing hearty than Ellen Terry could 'get away with' malevolence. Mr. Evans is of the Hotspur type. His body and mind are wiry, quick to active decision, and hence the very opposite of Richard's luxury and indolence. Whether Richard is conceived as conscious artist or minor poet uttering a good deal of major verse makes no difference to our acceptance of this Richard, which is just not forthcoming. The whole performance, then, is, as it were, surrounded by a thin circumference of disbelief. Yet Mr. Evans is so good an actor that, given the rim of non-acceptance, we unhesitatingly believe everything within the circle. That which should be petulance becomes genuine passion, and as passion is very fine indeed; this Richard would not say these things in this way, but we realize that Mr. Evans is saying them very well. His speech beginning: 'We are amazed' is a magnificent piece of declamation, and he renders the metaphysics of the last soliloquy with greater cogency than anybody I have seen. Where this clever young actor is most at home is in the early scenes, in which he achieves a glittering impertinence. The serious half of the play, though not lying within his physical scope, is at least as well done as the handicap permits.

More First Nights: October 15, 1934

KING HENRY IV, PART I
(His Majesty's)

MR. ROBEY'S FALSTAFF

So much preluding and fanfaring, so much use of tucket answered by sennet prompted my neighbour to ask me whether I thought Mr. Sydney Carroll intended to turn the play into an opera. I said it was quite possible, my revered colleague being, like Habbakuk, *capable de tout*. Presently, however, the cheerful din, elegantly assembled for the occasion by Mr. Ernest Irving, subsided, and the curtain went up to reveal a highly Plantagenet London exceedingly unlike Regent's Park. It was an interesting experience to hear the King's opening speech unpunctuated by the sough of cedars, the twitter of robins, and the cry of 'love-fifteen' from the neighbouring lawn-tennis courts. That this was very much an indoor performance was proved by the vagaries of the limelight man, who, less sure of himself than Nature's luminary, kept trying to marry his colleague's amber with various shades of blue. Perhaps this was intended to be deepening twilight or the drawing-on of early afternoon? Apart from this Mr. Carroll did grandly, in equal measure of valour and discretion.

It would be easy to fault Mr. John Drinkwater for lack of exhilaration in the title rôle if one did not remember that whoever plays the part must take his cue from the opening line: 'So shaken as we are, so wan with care.' One did, however, think that the actor overdid the part's sobriety; after all, this was once Henry Bolingbroke and the fire should still be there though it has burned low, whereas Mr. Drinkwater gave one the impression of being a personage who had become extinct without ever having been a volcano. In any case he had a deal of history to get off the royal chest, and the extent to which any given spectator found His Majesty long-winded must have been governed by that spectator's degree of liking for Shakespearean history. For myself,

Shakespearean history is like beer; some is better than other some, but none is bad. I could sit for hours and listen entranced to such cataloguing as:

> The Earl of Douglas is discomfited:
> Ten thousand bold Scots, two and twenty knights,
> Balk'd in their own blood did Sir Walter see
> On Holmedon's plains. Of prisoners, Hotspur took
> Mordake the Earl of Fife, and eldest son
> To beaten Douglas; and the Earl of Athol,
> Of Murray, Angus and Menteith . . .

Hotspur was valiantly played by Mr. Edmund Willard, always given that while the part is one for a silver trumpet the note of Mr. Willard is Coleridge's loud bassoon. And surely the text calls for the impetuosity of youth and not the morose pugnacity of middle-age? I very much liked Mr. Lewis Casson's Owen Glendower who, having conjured up musicians to accompany his daughter, listened to her singing with his arms held in the air and the ferocious, rapt expression of a Chief Bard at an Eisteddfod; he only wanted a wreath of mistletoe to be the spit and image of the Celtic, intarissable bore. Mr. Patrick Waddington was inclined to over-accentuate the priggish aspect of the Prince. If there is a more revolting passage in Shakespeare than that which begins: 'Yet herein will I imitate the sun,' I have still to read it. The gorge of Pecksniff himself must have risen at the hypocrisy of:

> And like bright metal on a sullen ground,
> My reformation, glittering o'er my fault,
> Shall show more goodly and attract more eyes
> Than that which hath no foil to set it off.
> I'll so offend, to make offence a skill;
> Redeeming time when men think least I will.

Sir Arthur Quiller-Couch says that this speech, if we accept it, poisons all of Harry that follows: 'Most of us can forgive youth, hot blood, riot: but a prig of a rake, rioting on a calculated scale, confessing that he does it coldly, intellectually, and that he proposes to desert his comrades at the right moment to better his own repute — *that* kind of rake surely all honest men abhor.' The lines are obviously Shakespeare's. 'Who doth permit the base contagious clouds To smother up his beauty from the world' must be by the same hand that wrote the sonnet lines: 'Anon permit the basest clouds to ride With ugly rack on his celestial face.' Sir Arthur tries to avoid holding that the priggishness is not Harry's but Shakespeare's — which, of course, it must be, *vide* Walkley's denial of the precedent *état d'âme* theory which I have quoted too often to need more than reference here — by suggesting that Burbage or somebody came to the poet and said at a later date: 'Look here, they (meaning the audience) are not going to stand for a rapscallion turned Sunday-school teacher. You've got to get them right about him in the beginning!' Whereupon, according to Sir Arthur, Shakespeare went back and obediently inserted the miserable stuff. I am afraid that this argument won't wash, and that Shakespeare himself had the priggish strain. Are there not other lines of the immortal bard which, according to Mr. Shaw, in their 'canting, snivelling, hypocritical unctuousness perfectly catch the atmosphere of the rented pew?' And then Burbage's case was no case at all, since at the end of Part I Harry has already become reasonably noble; indeed his parleyings with and about Hotspur are in the very best temper of the king he afterwards became. The high-placed ragtag and bobtail, who in the histories lay plots, get executed for them, and spend their entire time splitting on one another, were very well acted by Messrs. Leslie Frith, Henry Oscar, Cecil Ramage, George Skillan, W. E. Holloway, and John Laurie.

This brings me to the comedians, and probably not too soon, since I believe the whole of the foregoing has been so much wasted effort. Just as nobody would have dreamed of going to see this play at His Majesty's without Mr. Robey — which was Mr. Carroll's legitimate reason for this extraordinary casting — so I do not believe that any reader wants to bother with anything about the present production, or the play, or the poet, or anything at all except how Mr. Robey acquitted himself, and whether he left the theatre without a stain on his artistic integrity. In my view it would be more to the purpose to ask *how the audience acquitted themselves*, and whether they helped or hindered Mr. Robey in the very difficult task of shedding one kind of glory to take up another. The answer is a good deal of Yes and a little of No. Whenever the actor relaxed an inch, the audience took an ell. It came about in this way. Mr. Robey walked on to the stage with the disciplined intention of playing the part and not clowning it, of moving in Shakespeare's world and not in that which he has made so gloriously his own. But, alas, he was not word-perfect! Now there are two ways in which an actor can be so handicapped; the part may come to him in rushes culminating in stops, or he may lag just that painstaking fraction of a second behind which is so distressing to him and to everybody else. Mr. Robey is too good an artist not to have known that he must cover up his difficulty, and that the obvious way was to hold the audience with his eye and so gain time for the next line to percolate into memory. But the effect of that basilisk stare produced reaction beyond the audience-victim's control; it laughed willy-nilly, whether there was anything to laugh at or not. Action and reaction being equal and opposite, not the Robey eyebrows but the places where they were wont to be would go up, and the actor find himself climbing into a meridian of nonsense not in Shakespeare's contemplation. And, I repeat, the audience took advantage of the relapses into Robeydom.

Then there is another thing. Many a time and oft Mr. Robey has made great play with archaic methods of pronunciation and delivery, and once or twice the other night he appeared wilfully to use the same mock-serious intonations. But I am convinced that these were merely expedients suggested by considerable nervousness and used to cover the extremity of not knowing where the next line was coming from; I am quite certain that in a fortnight's time Mr. Robey will be giving one of the best Falstaffs within living memory. It is in him to do so, but the audience must do its part. He has the authentic geniality of the old fribble, the genuine twinkle which kindles as easily as a taper that has been lighted many times. He has still to amend one or two impermissible and calculated occasions. These are when the actor slyly evokes his former self, the mask of Falstaff is dropped, the audience leaps at the gleeful discrepancy, and the ruin of the play impends. These stolen seconds — for they are no more than seconds — are a threat to the illusion the actor has laboured to create, and they must be resisted. It would be ungracious to omit to say how deftly, solicitously, and Shakespeareanly Lady Tree, in the very small part of Mistress Quickly, stood about ready to render Falstaff first aid.

More First Nights: March 3, 1935

KING HENRY IV, PART 2
(O.U.D.S.)

WHAT a piece of work is a theatrical producer! How noble in reason! In apprehension how like a god! But we must also remember the proverb which says that 'there's nowt so queer as folk'. Unless, of course, it be a theatrical producer. Mr. Bridges Adams, in a finely creative piece of work which got the best out of play and players, made two of those mistakes which, like revoking at bridge, happen only to the very simple or the very clever. What trembling newcomer to the great game of staging Shakespeare would have dared to deny the great speech beginning: 'I do see the bottom of Justice Shallow'? Falstaff's hand is all trumps, but this soliloquy is the ace; and to leave out the 'very genius of famine', and all that belongs to it, is to starve the part. Nothing in the theatre is more fantastic than the excuses your Shakespearean producer will make for omitting the best things. One has given up hope of ever hearing Hamlet's greatest soliloquy; I never thought not to hear about the cheese-paring and the forked radish. One understands that the time-factor was the trouble, and that Mr. Adams was anxious to have us out of the theatre by eleven o'clock. I submit respectfully that two minutes more would not have irked even the earliest Briton.

Then, again, the wilful misrepresentation of Feeble as a well set-up, lusty youth was one of those misplaced subtleties from which the stupid are immune. Just as in Beatrice Shakespeare anticipated Meredith's entire gallery of disdainful womanhood, so, in Feeble, he drew Mr. Polly three hundred years before Mr. Wells's hero was born. The stout soul in the shrinking frame, the little dyspeptic who goes to meet the bully armed only with his theory of 'sufficient beauty' — what is this but Feeble's 'We owe God a death; I'll ne'er bear a base mind,' all over again? Subtlety will have it that Shakespeare, in giving the woman's tailor manly bearing, meant to get away from that simplicity of humour which called Wart ragged and made Bullcalf roar. But subtlety is wrong. For Falstaff, who has not heard Feeble's confession of faith, says straightforwardly: 'And for a retreat; how swiftly will this Feeble, the woman's tailor, run off!' Mr. Bridges Adams may say that this is a small matter, and ask with Pistol whether etceteras are nothing. My point is that these were the only two blemishes in a production which was otherwise extraordinarily satisfying. Only a producer of genius aided by a company of Master Bettys could have made so much of the stage-direction: 'Enter Beadles, dragging in Hostess Quickly and Doll Tearsheet,' or have differentiated between the ribaldry of that jeering crowd and the loyal transports of that which welcomes the new-made king. No playgoer has ever fathomed what those battles were about to which Feeble went so valiantly; but the restoring of the war-scenes did have the effect of throwing the whole piece into the past. In the tavern scene it really did seem as though some Time-machine had carried us back to middle England and the dying Middle Ages.

It is curious how much of death there is in this fullest-blooded and most generous of English comedies. We owe God a death indeed, and here Shakespeare pays it for us royally. The King, the Justice, the woman's tailor, the great gormandizer who helped himself to Life as to some inexhaustible joint — the grave gapes for all of them. Yet not with menace; it is still afternoon, though the shadows encroach upon the gold. Death is certain; in the meantime there are bullocks at Stamford Fair. Stevenson could think of no work in which the end of life is represented with so nice a tact as in Dumas's *Le Vicomte de Bragelonne*, but we must suppose that he had forgotten Old Double and Falstaff's 'Do not bid me remember mine end'. It was in this scene that Time, having transported us to the year of grace fourteen hundred and thirteen, seemed to stand still. There must have been good producing and good acting here for us to feel, as we undoubtedly did feel, that we were in the same room with Falstaff and that the old man had yet to die. Yet to die, not in some following batch of history, but in a year or two. He was alive before us, and we could not bear to think on his end. Neither could Shakespeare. 'I have killed Porthos!' said Dumas, rushing from his study with streaming eyes. But I submit that in sparing us Falstaff's dying the English poet showed the finer taste. Warwick says simply of Henry:

He's walked the way of nature;
And to our purposes he lives no more.

That Falstaff must pass through nature to eternity we know, but his passing is not to our purpose. Hazlitt, discussing the essential meanness of the Prince's treatment of his old friend, said, 'We speak only as dramatic critics'. Of the unbearableness of the fat knight's end we speak as playgoers, not as philosophers.

The skill of Mr. Bridges Adams was again brilliantly shown in the management of his actors. Well may he have asked himself, in considering Mr. R. W. Speaight's claims upon the big part, how much a producer should care for the limb, the thews, the stature, bulk and big assemblance of a man. In *Peer Gynt* this young actor had shown us an apprehensive, quick and nimble spirit; but there was nothing in his slight habit and petulant temper to suggest that he could play the slow-moving mountain even tolerably well. However, as all Oxford knows and one hopes London may some day see, Mr. Speaight confounded even his

best friends. There was nothing of amateurishness in his performance, which was a piece of impersonation in the vein in which
Coquelin understood that art. It was a triumph to stir one so
deeply alike at the words 'I am old, I am old', and in the unutter-
able dumb dismay of the end to give us not only the large stomach
but the brain in which it 'snows of meat and drink'. There was a
spirit went out of this great creature to lard the Warwickshire
earth — all good Falstaffs must do this — and Oxford should
be proud of their young player. Easier to do, but still difficult
enough, is the dying King, and here Mr. H. Grisewood acquitted
himself very finely, again without trace of amateurishness, and
having sufficient instinct for beauty left over from the big speeches
to seize upon such a gem as

> O Westmoreland, thou art a summer bird,
> Which ever in the haunch of winter sings
> The lifting up of day.

One thought that Mr. Franklin rather overplayed Shallow,
who should be lean and slippered yet not quite Pantaloon.
Nevertheless, it was on its lines an excellent performance which
showed feeling for the stage. Contrariwise, the royal progency of
Messrs. L. A. Nye, D. R. Tidy, D. B. Buckley, and P. Pryor
were all under-played, being so many walking advertisements for
modesty. Mr. D. B. Buckley's Bardolph was capital, and I think
I spy an actor in Mr. G. E. Williams, who gave the small part of
Morton very well indeed. Miss Clare Greet and Miss Olga Lindo
played the tavern ladies as they should be played, and not
otherwise; and I hope they will not take this scanty mention as a
slight. They could not have been bettered in London, but I
am writing about the O.U.D.S. One would say a word for the
extremely intelligent interplaying of the whole company. Brilliantly indeed did these young wits get themselves into the bodies
of these old men.

The Contemporary Theatre, 1926: February 14, 1926

KING HENRY IV, PART 2
(Westminster)

THERE are a couple of magnificent parts in Shakespeare's play —
Falstaff and Pistol. Pistol is more than a mindless braggart; he is
a braggart with a mind, and one who has anachronously fre-
quented the Elizabethan playhouse and knows all about Marlowe's
mighty line. Tamburlaine's

> Our conquering swords shall marshal us the way
> We use to march upon the slaughtered foe,
> Trampling their bowels with our horses' hoofs

is at the back of Pistol's mind when he says:

> Shall pack-horses,
> And hollow pamper'd jades of Asia,
> Which cannot go but thirty mile a day,
> Compare with Caesars, and with Cannibals
> And Trojan Greeks? nay, rather damn them with
> King Cerberus; and let the welkin roar.

The Emperor of the Turks has the following:

> You are my wife, my queen, and emperess
> Brought up and propp'd by the hand of fame,
> Queen of fifteen contributory queens,
> Now thrown to rooms of black abjection,
> Smear'd with blots of basest drudgery.

And Pistol echoes it with his:

> Thy Doll, and Helen of thy noble thoughts,
> Is in base durance and contagious prison;
> Haled thither
> By most mechanical and dirty hand.

Lastly, the Soldan's:

> While you, faint-hearted, base Egyptians,
> Lie slumbering on the flowery banks of Nile,
> As crocodiles that unaffrighted rest,
> While thundering cannon rattle on their skins

is Pistol everywhere. The whole point is that Pistol talks pure Marlowe, and does it better, being both louder and funnier.

In his essay entitled *A Gossip on a Novel of Dumas's* Stevenson says: 'The great eater, worker, earner and waster, the man of much and witty laughter, the man of the great heart and alas! of the doubtful honesty, is a figure not yet clearly set before the world.' Is it possible that for once in a way R.L.S. was a little lacking in percipience? Was not Dumas always drawing himself? Consider the words he puts into the mouth of Planchet: 'Monsieur, j'étais une de ces bonnes pâtes d'hommes que Dieu a fait pour s'animer pendant un certain temps et pour trouver bonnes toutes choses qui accompagnent leur séjour sur la terre.' And again does not Dumas, still in the same novel — the essay quotes the passage — draw himself in the character of Fouquet? — 'L'homme de bruit, l'homme de plaisir, l'homme qui n'est que parceque les autres sont.' And in case Dumas hasn't done it well enough, here is Stevenson making sure: 'In a man who finds all things good, you will scarce expect much zeal for negative virtues: the active alone will have a charm for him; abstinence, however wise, however kind, will always seem to such a judge entirely mean and partly impious. So with Dumas. Chastity is not near his heart . . .'

Where, in the Shakespearean connection, is all this getting us, the reader may ask. Simply that in Falstaff Shakespeare drew not only D'Artagnan's old servant and the French court's great spendthrift, but Dumas himself. There is nothing which Stevenson would have us think about Dumas that Shakespeare has not already made us know about his great comic creation. 'Ventripotent' is Stevenson's word for Dumas. It might be said of this play that it is the last word in fatness. One thing troubles me about Mr. Atkins's fat knight: Is he fat enough? Physically, I think not: the grave does not gape for him wider than for many men. In all other respects it is a superb performance. This is a Falstaff of breeding, and enjoying to the full the relish of his own wit. Although the dates are against me, I shall always regard Sir Toby as a study for the bigger canvas, and reflect that whereas Olivia's kinsman had only Sir Andrew for butt, Sir John plays upon the entire world. He is so much the intellectual superior of his entourage that he has nobody to commune with. May that be the reason that Shakespeare gives him so many soliloquies? Mr. Atkins conveys all this beautifully, and when his double must brim over he does so in a persistent low rumble like a basso ostinato. He has pathos too, the sense of lengthening shadows and the sense of melancholy. I think, perhaps, that what I most admire in this acting is the extraordinarily skilful way in which the old fribble and sorner sets the play in its proper period. When he is on the stage this is not only England but England at a particular date, pre-Elizabeth and pre-Crookback. Altogether an exquisitely moving performance, and the crowning achievement among many by this actor that have been remarkable for their Shakespearean temper and fidelity to the player's art.

The Prince of Wales, though doing nicely at his father's death-bed, has not enough presence, mien, majesty, and force of character to justify the magnificence at the end. Pistol is a great disappointment; the actor who has to say 'There roar'd the sea, and trumpet-clangor sounds' must have a voice like Benson, or at any rate Mr. George Jackley. And why does Bardolph eschew all those bubukles, and whelks and knobs to which his countenance is heir? Justice Shallow, too, is rather the pantaloon of Christmas pantomime than the living embodiment of Shakespeare's Sixth Age. And I think it is a mistake to present Feeble as a complete nitwit. The point about the Woman's Tailor is that he has a mind and will not have it base. Falstaff instinctively senses the virtue in Feeble, and it is a beautiful perception on the part of Mr. Atkins which makes the gross materialist give his hand to this waif of true valour. And why, pray, should Sir John's Page be

played by a little girl? In the mind's ear one hears Falstaff antici-
pating Pooh-Bah and saying, 'Go away, little girl. Can't talk to
a little girl like you. Go away, there's a dear.'

Lest the foregoing be thought grudging, let me say that Mr.
Tristan Rawson's rendering of the King's apostrophe to that
'summer bird', Westmoreland, took me back to a performance of
The Seagull by the Pitoëffs, in Paris. Turning up my notebook I
find that I wrote: 'An older player, called Pierre Risch, giving
Dorn an almost Shakespearean melancholy, said, "Ou je n'y
comprends rien, ou je suis fou, mais cette pièce m'a beaucoup plu"
as movingly as ever I heard words spoken on the stage.' Mr.
Rawson's delivery of the dying King's exquisite lines merits the
same praise.

December 6, 1942

KING HENRY V
(The Old Vic)

MR. SWINLEY

FOR the first time at this theatre I did not greatly enjoy the play.
But then, apart from its purple passages, perhaps *Henry V* is not
very enjoyable. Hazlitt has said the last word upon the chief
character: 'In private Henry had no idea of the common decen-
cies of life, which he subjected to a kind of regal licence; in public
affairs he seemed to have no idea of any rule of right or wrong,
but brute force, glossed over with a little religious hypocrisy and
archiepiscopal advice'. Despite the 'intertissued robe of gold and
pearl' which Shakespeare wove for Henry's kingly speech, I,
personally, can never forgive this royal Jackanapes for the trick
he played on his old friend. Henry apart, the rest are rather a
poor crew. Pistol, Bardolph, Nym, without Falstaff are, as somebody said, satellites without a sun. The Archbishop is a fearsome

bore, Charles the Sixth and Chorus wag a good tongue, whilst Fluellen runs all three pretty close.

Still, there is no getting away from Henry's marvellous speeches, every one of which could always be inserted in those old-fashioned compilations called 'The Beauties of Shakespeare' in one solid chunk. Henry is 'a very amiable monster, a very splendid pageant. As we like to gaze at a panther or a young lion in their cages at the Tower, and catch a pleasing horror from their glistening eyes, their velvet paws, and dreadless roar, so we take a very romantic, heroic, patriotic, and poetical delight in the boasts and feats of our younger Harry.' Mr. Ion Swinley played the King well, up to a point. That is, he made a richly decorative figure of him, and gave his underlying emotion in the scene with Scroop and his fellow-conspirators better than I have ever known. But I should like to suggest to this actor that he cultivate a little more lightness of voice. That organ-note of his is too cumulatively sombre. After three acts it becomes a little like Hugo's flood which

> profonde,
> Tourne et gronde
> Comme une onde
> Sur la mer.

Possibly Mr. Swinley had been a trifle overworked. Probably by the end of the week the performance was a very fine one.

It is amusing to note how modern this play is. The pow-wow between the two kings is like our own peace conferences. The boy's 'Would I were in an alehouse in London!' is that Tommy, 'fed to the teeth', who would so willingly have exchanged Bagdad for Bolton. Even the appeals to glory are our recruiting-posters in better English. The Dauphin's chatter about his horse is dismissed by Hazlitt as showing 'the vanity of that class of persons'. But I could have told the essayist of a second-lieutenant who, sent out soon after Mons, had nothing to say of the desperate battles of those early days, and wrote his chums in England long accounts of the ailments and unsoundnesses of his horse. By the way, the Dauphin's talk of his nag is much better than that uninspired 'Points of the Horse' passage in *Venus and Adonis*. The Williams of Mr. Ernest Meads was extremely good. I liked the way in which Chorus, in the person of Miss Ray Litvin, came bounding on to the stage as though she were a very Muse of fire. Mr. Hay Petrie's Fluellen was not quite so happy as some of his performances. Mr. Walter's Pistol was a broth of a boy.

October 22, 1923

KING HENRY V
(The Old Vic)

MR. RICHARDSON

HARRY of England demands every physical grace that an actor can beg, borrow, or steal. Yet exterior bravery alone will not do, since the man had a considerable mind. Mind is a loose word, and by it we may mean either character or mere intellectual dexterity. The colour of Harry's mind largely depends upon what we think of the change from the madcap Prince to the ideal warrior King. Without enormous strength of character, Prince Hal must have grown up into an earlier version of Charles II, for men of weak character do not desist from wild oats until they have lost the power to sow. But the fact remains that there is a casuistry in the later hero, though it be casuistry magnificently carried off. One knows which side any soldier would have taken in the Westmorland-Harry debate as to whether the English force could do with more men. This, however, is a play, and we are spectators in a theatre and not students at Sandhurst, and the speech is certainly the butt and seamark of Shakespeare's utmost rhetoric, and should, I think, be delivered with this consciousness.

Mr. Richardson disappointed here. He talked like one rendering assistance to the Army Service Corps of the day arranging their supplies, and having delivered the line 'God's will! I pray thee wish not one man more!' lent a hand with an orange-box before tackling 'By Jove, I am not covetous for gold.' This is to be too natural, for the speech is a firework ascending to the heaven of invention and not to be tethered to joint-stools. But one saw the actor's intention, which was to present Harry as a human being and not as a mailed fist, eating, sleeping, and thinking in armour. It was doubtless this which rightly made him reject the usual notion of the 'O God of battles' speech as something to spout, and deliver it as an overheard prayer, which, in fact, it is. He was admirable, too, in the 'royal fellowship of death' speech, which is too often a mere catalogue, but on this occasion was made most moving. I think it may be said that Mr. Richardson was content to leave the contradictions alone and play the text for what it is worth, with sufficient *panache* and a sense of warm humanity.

Somebody really should take Mr. George Zucco on one side and explain to him that when Shakespeare puts a word at the end of a line of blank verse he means it to belong there, and not to the beginning of the next line. Pistol was a great mouther and obviously delighted in rounding off his periods. In the passage:

> The *solus* in thy teeth, and in thy throat,
> And in thy hateful lungs, yea, in thy maw, perdy —

the operative word is 'perdy', and we may be sure that Pistol gave it its full value. Mr. Zucco stopped at 'maw' and then began again, 'Perdy and what is worse'. Otherwise his Pistol was excellent. Mr. Harcourt Williams contributed a fine cameo as the King of France. Mr. Robert Speaight got into the skin of Fluellen without clowning that philosopher, and Mr. Richard Riddle had great fun with the Dauphin, though less with the Archbishop of Canterbury. The production was first-class and imaginative except that the Duke of York, asking to be allowed to lead the battle, was permitted to wear a night-shirt which would have tripped him up half-way across the first field.

November 30, 1931

KING RICHARD III
(The Old Vic)

MR. ATKINS

THE first thing to be remarked about the Shakespearean performances at the 'Old Vic' is the quality of the audience. This, you feel, is no assemblage idly 'doing' a theatre, but a crowd of busy men and women determined to lay out leisure to good purpose. Your right-hand neighbour has put up his master's shutters and hardly gulped his tea; the fellow on your left is a railway goods porter, on duty at midnight. Such fellows will drink in a performance lasting four hours as greedily as sweating haymakers their ale. The recent production of *Richard III* was a generous draught of best English brew — they poured out nearly the whole barrel — yet one wanted more. One felt that Shakespeare had tired of these Yorkists and Lancastrians, and skimped his ending.

What, we wanted to know, became of Catesby, who stuck to Richard to the end and would have helped him to a horse? 'There is no creature loves me,' wailed Gloster, lying to the last; for Catesby, of a surety, loved him. The point is a small one, yet it marks Shakespeare's extraordinary power of creating men and women. Richard is flesh and blood; he leaves innumerable corpses in his wake, and remains credible. Think what an unbelievable welter Ford or Webster would have made! Whereas Richard was as actual to this audience as any murderer of the penny press. Only a little more sophistication was necessary to make these simple playgoers realize that great tragic embodiments are more 'real' than reality, more lifelike than life. For myself, I am childishly illuded by Richard, who seems to me to be dotted all over history. I do not conceive him as essentially different from Napoleon, or — *pace* Mr. Drinkwater — Cromwell, or even our modern newspaper-lords. He physically, these morally, were given shoulders 'ordain'd so thick to heave'. When it was the fashion their owners cut the heads off living men; to-day they cut the head off living truth, and it suffices. To have told that Waterloo Road audience that Richard was a figure of pure melodrama would, if they had understood what was meant, have been accounted the purest treason. We all knew Richard intimately and took to him, as we have taken to many another scoundrel, for his pluck. This did not prevent us from cheering his conqueror for his manly sentiments, uttered without priggishness by Mr. Wilfrid Walter. By a happy imaginative touch, the lord who, at the end, offered Richmond the crown, bent his head as he did so towards the dead body of Richard. 'You lost,' that gesture seemed to say, 'but you were the bigger man!' It was an inspired coda.

Twice the orchestra let us down badly — once, when it accompanied the din of battle with trivialities destructive of tension, and earlier by hardly preluding at all. Relying upon those interminable 'Henry VIII Dances', which, in the English theatre, usher in no matter what reign, I arrived some five minutes late, to find the curtain up and Lady Anne bidding the undertakers set down their honourable load. I gathered, from the fact that 'virtuous Lancaster' figured in the programme among the live actors, that the play had begun where it ought always to begin, with the murder of Henry VI, which has rounded off the previous 'episode' in this drama of strong 'domestic interest'. 'Begin to-day!' is all very well in a newspaper, or on the screen; without a synopsis of previous happenings this play is almost impossible to follow in the theatre. Even the connecting link will not always make matters clear to simple minds. For a time I stood at the back of the pit and was rewarded by an illuminating colloquy. 'Who's the bloke in the coffin?' one said. 'Dunno,' replied another. Let me confess that I, too, had but a vague recollection who the bloke was, and who the women. They take a deal of sorting out. Anne is a fool, and Queen Margaret and Queen Elizabeth are the most triumphant bores in Shakespeare. Add the Duchess of York, and we get a quartet of she-ravens which would have croaked any but the most magnificent play into its grave. Was it,

I wonder, necessary for all these royalties and semi-royalties to look so unutterably dowdy and dilapidated? Queen Margaret might have been doubling the part of First Witch at a theatre over the way, while the Duchess of York wore the air of a widow who has spent her life brooding in the bay-window of a villa overlooking the cemetery at Kensal Green. These were relicts, but not distinguished relicts.

But the play stands or falls by Richard. It was the first time I had seen Mr. Robert Atkins, and he disconcerted me for a while with a mask for Gloster reminiscent of so many others that it seemed hardly Gloster's own. There was something of Napoleon, of every actor's Cromwell, something too of that tragic eye which Lauder can cock at you so surprisingly. Mr. Atkins endowed Richard with a smooth champaign countenance in no way horrific and on the whole pleasing, as became the man who took in Hastings and won Anne. But such a presentation has this disadvantage, that, unlike Kean's, it is emphatically not one for Titian to paint. It is bourgeois. The actor did not make Anne's winning plausible, but then it is unthinkable that any actor except Irving ever did. Mr. Atkins realized from the start that he had a long way to go and did not force the pace. Indeed, his first act was unimpressive, save for a walk which had in it the lilt of the moral buccaneer. Later his cunning and quiet ferocity took on cumulative effect, and I cannot imagine that the scenes with Hastings and Buckingham could be better played. But Richard's distinguishing traits are not these, nor yet cruelty nor temporal ambition, but mental arrogance. He knew himself the biggest man in the kingdom, and deposed the others by right of brain. I must think Mr. Atkins wrong in playing him throughout like an upstart, a 'little corporal' instead of a princely usurper born in an aery 'in the cedar's top'. Richard is fulfilled, not diminished, by his crimes; and this hardly appeared. Here the actor's mentality was scarcely to blame; no player can go beyond his personality. Mr. Atkins, in short, made a Napoleon of Richard and did not allow us to forget the Corsican; he had all the nudgings and pawings, the ill-bred *bonhomie* of that adventurer. It is something to get through such a part with even a semblance of conviction; but from that to the sublime is more than a step. We are told that Kean was best in the last scene of all. 'He fought like one drunk with wounds; and the attitude in which he stands with his hands stretched out, after his sword is taken from him, had a preternatural and terrific grandeur, as if his will could not be disarmed, and the very phantoms of his despair had a withering power.' Well, that is all a long time ago, and perhaps it was Hazlitt and not Kean who was as great as all that.

The scenery was admirable throughout, by which I mean that it was almost non-existent. A few bits of cardboard covered with brown paper made up a battlement; some bigger bits, aided by good lighting, did for Richard's tent; the whole so imaginatively composed that it never got in the actor's way or stood between us and the play. I doubt whether this mounting cost a five pound note; I am certain that no production has ever given me greater pleasure, though perhaps their Graces of York and Ely need not have had quite such dirty hands.

The Contemporary Theatre, 1923: March 10, 1923

KING RICHARD III
(The Old Vic)

MR. HOLLOWAY

Richard III is really a boy's play — a play for one boy to write and another to see. It belongs to the poet's first period, and we behold in it the germ of things to be amplified later on. Thus Richard's

> But I am in
> So far in blood that sin will pluck on sin.

is to become Macbeth's

> I am in blood
> Stepp'd in so far that, should I wade no more,
> Returning were as tedious as go o'er.

117

Sin plucking on sin is a philosophical commonplace, whereas real heart-ache is in 'tedious'. Compare

> There is no creature loves me;
> And if I die, no soul will pity me.

with the greater pathos of all that passage about the sear, the yellow leaf. This early play is full of indications of the greatness to come. Is there not something of complicated Angelo in Richard's two wooings? There is a kind of ghoulish gusto about the scene with Anne which half suggests that the poet held at one time the more sadistic view of Richard as a man delighting in villainy for its own sake. But the idea seems to have been quickly dropped, and after this one scene Richard comes back to the simple rôle of opportunist-murderer, sorting one 'pitchy day' after another for such as stand in his light. Richard wanted the sun, the whole sun, and nothing but the sun, and that is why the tale becomes so simple. You feel as you watch the play that Marryat or Ballantyne, or any other dependable writer for boys, could have put the bones of it together. But it would be wrong to mistake the Crookback for an early Captain Hook. There is a kind of actor who sees in Richard, not a Gilles de Rais but an ogre out of the story-books murdering little children in their beds for the fun of the thing. Such a Richard, says Lamb, is very close and shrewd, and devilish cunning, for you can see that by his eye. But there is more in the character than this. There is the poet, betrayed by the romantic splendour of thought expressing itself in such phrases as those about the aspiring blood of Lancaster, and the aery building in the cedar's top. Everything about Richard is magnificent. His mental quality matches his physical courage, so that he may be said not to act, but to magnoperate. We demand for him at the end, not the gallows, but the Judgment Seat.

How much of all this does Mr. Baliol Holloway give? Well, first his Richard is a man, and not a mental abstraction. Next, he is a man of genius set apart from his fellows by superiority of mind and will. Then, again, he is alive, and alive in his own

century and not in ours. But I do not, alas! find the poet in this
Richard, owing probably to the actor's indifferent mastery of
verse. Mr. Holloway still persists in cutting up every speech into
granulated nodules, though this habit is less persistent than it
was. Yet it obtains sufficiently to stand in the way of that full
swoop and rush of delighted words which mark the poet. If one
must continue for a little in the matter of shortcomings, one would
say that Mr. Holloway failed to excite either pity or terror. He
did not melt us in the tent scene, but then we are to remember
that many Richards, including Edwin Booth, have failed here.
Nor did the actor quite succeed in making the 'seated heart knock
at the ribs'. He lacked the cold malignancy of Irving, and also
something of the stunning power of sheer noise. When Booth
played the scene with Hastings we are told that he turned
furiously on the latter's 'if' and hammered the courtier's death-
knell upon the table with blows of the sceptre which struck terror
into every heart. In short, our friend's performance wanted a
touch of the fiend.

But there is a great deal in it that is immensely good. Mr.
Holloway makes that incredible wooing credible; he listens to
Margaret's curses in a silence of admirable mockery; he toys with
Buckingham like a very large cat with a particularly small mouse,
and plays the 'I am not in the giving vein to-day' scene as well as
it need be played. Throughout one is conscious of Richard's
master mind, buoyant spirit, and all that knowledge of man and
character which the part contains. Mr. Holloway's closing scenes,
like Kean's, are the most brilliant. Like the older actor, he has
given to all the busy traffic of the play the greatest animation and
effect. He has filled every part of the stage, and pleased the eye
with a succession of splendid robes and striking attitudes. His
costumes have been blood-red, and red blood has run in this
capital tyrant. Now comes the fight, which is done with immense
vigour. Mr. Holloway has a marvellous facial expression when he
turns and sees his sixth and last Richmond. At that moment all
the venom of the bottled spider rushes to his face, which takes on
a superhuman ugliness. His onslaught and overthrow are a

great piece of work, almost lifting one out of one's seat. As the actor lies panting on the ground one plays with the thought that there is in that body still sufficient of the dregs of life to taste the bitterness of defeat. If the rest of the part were acted up to this level one would salute a performance of genius. But though genius is not the word one would use, Mr. Holloway's acting is undoubtedly fine.

Miss Edith Evans gave Queen Margaret's two scenes with a great sweep of passion and magnificence of diction. Here is an actress who can walk like a queen and rant like one also. We owe the Old Vic a debt for teaching Miss Thorndike to be a first-class actress; in descending upon this theatre in the full plenitude of her powers Miss Evans repays that debt. But the team at the Old Vic had rather too much tail. Mr. Duncan Yarrow made a conscientious Clarence, though one associates the playing of this part with something more liquid in grace and beauty. It is perhaps not disparaging to say that Mr. Neil Porter endowed Buckingham with a nose of more than Roman loftiness, and he certainly spoke his lines as though he intended the back of the pit to hear them. The two murderers were played uncommonly well by Messrs. Charles Marford and John Garside. Some of the other young gentlemen in the cast were amateurish, which fault time, perhaps, will remove.

The piece was done in admirably devised settings. Perhaps Richard's tent was not very well suggested, the ghostly victims wearing something of the air of a collection from Madame Tussaud's. Either Mr. Holloway omitted the words 'the lights burn blue', or I did not hear them. One remembers how Mr. Atkins said them, and how the mind was suddenly filled with the colour of the night sky. There was a touch of imagination here which the play's present production does not quite give.

The Contemporary Theatre, 1925: October 7, 1925

KING RICHARD III
(Strand)

MR. WOLFIT

O FOR a Clement Scott to persuade an inattentive public to realize that at the Strand Theatre, daily at two o'clock, and on Wednesdays, Thursdays, and Saturdays at six, in Shakespeare's play of *Richard III* there is on view a fine, and in some respects a great, actor. No excuses need be made for Mr. Wolfit. What he can't play, that cannot he play at all. Was it not Hazlitt who said this was one of the properties of genius? , Nature has denied this actor the tragic mask. There is a chubbiness, about him which points to comedy; indeed his Falstaff, rosy and unrepentant as Miss Mitford's spendthrift father, is the best now to be seen. But he has little subtlety, and no skill in poetry except of the outspoken order which permits him to make the same kind of play with the vocables of Ben Jonson that Volpone's hands make with the Fox's jewels. This is the voice for Tamburlaine, to 'make whole cities caper in the air'.

What Mr. Wolfit can play he does magnificently. His Richard is conceived in the back-of-the-pit, Saturday-night vein demanded by this roaring melodrama. Richard is a part to tear a cat in, and to handle it like a lady of quality nibbling a wing of chicken is nonsense: this actor gets his teeth into it like the king of beasts with some still quivering prey. Mr. Wolfit does more than frighten the other actors; he terrifies the playgoer. Here is no introspective figure of evil but a constructive villain, no 'interpretation' of Richard but Richard himself, the 'bottled spider', 'abortive rooting hog', and all the rest of it. And here, alas, I am constrained to note the two last of this good player's deficiencies — the eerie and the macabre elude him, while of pathos he has as much as the champion bull at the Royal Agricultural Show. I ask nothing better than that Mr. Wolfit shall now produce a

Macbeth which is poetic and autumnal as well as 'bloody, bold and resolute', and so confute me. To conclude, let it be said that this Richard is in all but the tear-compelling vein superb. The whole pageant of fifteenth-century England is in the red of his robes and the stern superbity of his armour, which this actor has the *voice* to carry. Cibber added a dying speech of ten lines, six from other Shakespeare and four of his own. Mr. Wolfit stands in no such need. His final 'A horse! a horse! my kingdom for a horse!' is agony made vocal. The spectator, no longer concerned whether Richard is a good King or a bad, is appalled at this cry of a man about to die on his feet. Baffled enjoyment of his well-laid schemes, vengeance on Richmond, the fury of the trapped animal — all these are merged in the hoarse scream which still rings in my ears.

January 18, 1942

KING HENRY VIII
(Empire)

MISS THORNDIKE'S QUEEN KATHARINE

WHOEVER wrote this play managed to get an extraordinary number of fine things into it, though unity of impression is not one of them. Why should it be? The play is not called the 'bloodie tragedie' of somebody or other, but declares itself simply as *The Famous History of the Life of King Henry the Eighth.* There are lots of things in this chronicle which can never be tidied up into any formal play — the passing of the Middle Ages and last kick of Rome, the rise of Protestantism and the growth of this country to the status of a first-rate power. One does not mean that the characters babble, or are even conscious of, these swelling themes. They do not, like the soldier in the melodrama, strike their breasts and declare that they are off to the Thirty Years War. It will be argued that it is through our own minds, and not through the actual words of this play, that the Middle Ages blow; 'there is not a breath of mediaeval atmosphere in Shakespeare's histories' has trumpeted Mr. Shaw. And he goes on to tell us that Shakespeare's kings are not statesmen, that his cardinals have no religion, and that his plays contain no hint that the world is finally governed by forces expressing themselves in laws rather than by vulgar individuals expressing themselves in rows. This is as it may be; and possibly we who, seeing this play, put into it something that is not there, are entitled to reflect how fortunate it is that Shakespeare, who would never have pretended to half Mr. Shaw's understanding of history, had some skill as a depicter of vulgar rows to fall back upon.

Can there be any doubt that Katharine's three scenes are as moving as anything in Shakespeare? Maiden virtue rudely strumpeted has always been a sure card with the tear-compellers, but is there not even greater poignancy when the virtue is wifely? The most pitiful pages in that great novel *La Cousine Bette* are those which concern the woes of the pious Adeline. Yet we find Hulot writing to his enchantress, Madame Marneffe: 'My wife has never, throughout twenty-five years, interfered with my pleasures. Yet to you I would sacrifice a hundred Adelines!' There, surely, speaks the very voice of Henry! How comes it, then, that this infamous gormandizer is not the villain of the piece? Is it not that we regard him as something which is as little moral or immoral as a volcano? Puritan morality, Stevenson points out, was not dear to the heart of that 'ventripotent mulatto', the elder Dumas. Nor to Henry, from whose loins were to spring Elizabeth and England's greatest age. We look upon him solely in his quality as begetter, and feel that to try his potency at the bar of private virtue is to bring the matter to the wrong court. But the drama needs a villain whose discomfiture shall compensate us for the Queen's martyrdom, and Wolsey fills the breach. How any play can be considered long or boring which contains this trio — one of whom is a magnificent essay in *goguenarderie* — passes my comprehension. Add the moving incident of Buckingham and the bugles of greatness-to-come blowing faintly but surely, and it seems to me that dullness can only be in the mind of the beholder. It lacks poetry? One would retort that a horse need not be good-looking to win a race.

How was the piece played? Queen Katharine is not generally considered a great part, but Miss Thorndike showed that greatness may be brought to it. This artist proved once more that there is only one answer to the question as to whether she is a great actress. The answer is: 'Yes, in a great play.' Her features may not launch ships for light-hearted capture; let them show moral anguish, and whole navies will flock to her succour. Her voice is not for balconies and conquests, yet in suffering moves you to shattering depths of spiritual pity. In sporting parlance this actress cannot 'come without the horse', and in second-rate plays her talents are not of the first order. But let a great dramatist cry 'Ho!' and this fine artist will give him successful battle. Her manner then changes, infelicity drops from her, and she puts on the whole armour of artistry. Anything more noble, more dignified, more womanly, or more truly heroical than this Katharine it would be impossible to conceive; and in the ringing challenge of the trial scene Miss Thorndike may be said to have touched the sublime.

The first five minutes of Mr. Norman V. Norman's Henry were a little disappointing; there was even the hint of barn-door crowing in this old rooster's turn of the head and cock of the eye. But the uncertain moment soon passed, and from Henry's second appearance everything went magnificently. Here were the authentic traits — sensuality, cruelty, arrogance, humour. And the fellow had temperament to boot. The playing of two of the other big parts finds me in some difficulty. One respected the Wolsey of Mr. E. Lyall Swete, whose fine performance as Warwick obviously paved the way for the Cardinal. But was this quite the Wolsey who ruled England? This figure lacked something of grandeur and awe; he suggested the prelate hardly at all; and one would always have backed Mrs. Proudie to rout him. The trouble was one largely of voice, too richly comic and at times recalling Mr. Bransby Williams. Mr. Arthur Wontner's Buckingham seemed to me at once 'actorish' and ineffectual; one was too busy noting the airs and graces to feel any tug at the heartstrings. Let it be said that this absence of reaction was purely personal and was not general in the house, which gave both performers a magnificent ovation. I am afraid I thought the Anne Bullen of that clever player, Miss Angela Baddeley, too childish and too slight. She looked about fifteen, while Anne's age at her coronation is given at the earliest as twenty-six, and is placed by some authorities at thirty-one. And the actress's physique could only give the lie to the Third Gentleman's description. All the smaller parts were well filled, Miss Ada King in particular contributing a little cameo which defies any kind of appraisement. There is no question here of better or best; the ribald dame simply walked out of the sixteenth century as out of a frame.

The whole production was put on with all the care, enthusiasm, and insight which spell Casson. The setting by Mr. Charles Ricketts came in for general commendation, though, personally, I cannot shout my loudest here. I find something in this artist's view of the times which will not let me believe that the oak was growing which was to defeat the Armada. Stained glass windows and a colour-scheme inclining to claret are admittedly pleasant, and I expect to be told that the date is pre-Elizabeth, and that this French atmosphere is correct. But I have the feeling that it is the early sixteenth century seen through the eyes of the late nineteenth.

The Contemporary Theatre, 1925: December 23, 1925

KING HENRY VIII
(Sadler's Wells)

MR. LAUGHTON

It is odd that nobody has yet written a play about Henry VIII. Odd, but not unexpected, because that is the English way. It is true that Henry figures in certain dramas, but only in the sense in which, in the popular imagination, King Alfred is the centre of a story about burnt cakes, and King Canute the hero of a beach incident at Broadstairs. Harold dies because he did not keep his eye down, and William Rufus because of the unfriendly glancing of an arrow, while a lion-heart and a hump are the salient features of the Richards. Fuss is made about Elizabeth's virginity, Charles II sports his oak, the early Georges cannot speak English, and so on. The evil, preposterous and silly things that monarchs do privately live in the popular mind, provided they come within the scope of What Can be Publicly Discussed. Conversely, there is an agreed silence about any abnormality or disease which altered the entire course of English history, attention being by-passed on to some Charter to Wool-Gatherers or Tax upon Inventors. Henry's share in the Reformation had infinitely less influence on English history than his failure to reform himself, or one might put it that while the Church took its medicine, the doctors had not yet discovered the medicine for Henry's syphilis. English history, in so far as it insists on being polite, is a gallery of distorting mirrors.

Mr. Laughton came to Sadler's Wells with all his blushing film-vulgarities thick upon him. I hasten to say that the vulgarities to which I allude were thrust upon him by his scenario. This also seems the place to say that I cannot without qualification subscribe to the twofold view that *The Private Life of Henry VIII* is a good film and that Shakespeare's *Henry VIII* is a bad play. Though we rank *Henry VIII* low among Shakespeare's plays and not too high among Fletcher's, any ten minutes of it taken anywhere as much exceed in quality the whole significance of the Leicester Square film as any twenty bars of Beethoven, culled even from *The Battle of Vittoria*, exceed the entire cake, rag and jazz output. Mr. Laughton has sensed this, and his performance in the play has a distinction unattempted in the film. But has it distinction enough? This Henry no longer throws chicken-legs on to the carpet. But is it argued that to desist from rank bad manners is the same thing as to put on manners of rank fit for a Cloth of Gold? Has our actor been a little misled by this King's sobriquet? There is treachery in nicknames, and the pitfall in Henry's is to accentuate the bluffness at the expense of the kingliness. It all comes back to the question which must be asked of any 'natural' performance. Conceding the naturalness, we are still entitled to demand: 'According to whose nature?' Henry was addicted to wenching as Falstaff was to sack, but kingliness must be no more left out in the one case than knightliness in the other. This Henry is hardly ever royal; his bonhomie and his bad temper are alike low-born. Also, he is not ripe enough in years; his shoulders, the nape of the neck and the hair over it are too boyish, just as the gestures are too quick; the man is not heavy enough on his feet for the weight he is supposed to be carrying. Henry was thirty at the time of Buckingham's death and forty-two when Elizabeth was born, figures to which ten years must be added in modern reckoning. It is these ten years that this Henry lacks. The play gives little opportunity to show the tortured, neurasthenic aspect of this many-sided monarch. However, I am not going to pose as an authority on Henry VIII, and will merely record my impression that he was never at any time really happy about his divorce, and that underneath his bluffness he knew as much about the necessity of drowning remorse as any man of the Renaissance. Given Mr. Laughton's interpretation, his performance must be hailed as virile and lusty and full of animal spirits. A man, you might say, who would butt and batter his way through opposition like a ram alike of Nature and artifice. There are times when he lets subtlety creep in, and the passage beginning, 'Go thy ways, Kate', is beautifully spoken.

Miss Flora Robson's Katharine began disappointingly, principally because this accomplished actress had not quite got the pitch of the house. Incidentally this was true of most of the company, which, accustomed to the perfect acoustics of the Old Vic, had not in the first act made the necessary allowances for a theatre less easy to speak in. The ensuing upbraiding of the Court was a trifle shrewish, Miss Robson being inclined to scold. But the scene with the two Cardinals was done most sensitively, and the death scene was exquisitely affecting.

About Mr. Robert Farquharson's Wolsey I speak with some

diffidence, because none of it seemed to me to be right. This Cardinal did not fill the eye. There was nothing about him of the proud and haughty prelate, as Ouida would have loved to call him, nothing of the founder of colleges, of the great getter and spender whose state vied with that of the King, of the vainglory which aimed through graft at the Papal See. This seemed to me to be a Uriah Heep who had taken orders, and perhaps Wolsey cannot be played with the mind alone. There was superbity about the man, and it is just this quality which is lacking from Mr. Farquharson's repertoire. Mr. Nicholas Hannen spoke Buckingham's speech with good accent and good discretion, but without being very moving. There is a comely jollity about this actor which stands in the way of the predestined gloom marking your Buckingham. Mercutios do not go to the block, and when they die it is with a word and a jest, and we feel that this kind of dying would suit Mr. Hannen better. He was much handicapped, too, by Mr. Tyrone Guthrie's staging, which deprived him of the crowd the author prescribed. No birds were flying overhead; there were no birds to fly. There were no Tudorbethans for Buckingham to address, and so he addressed the audience directly. This is one of those mistakes in which a production, through being too clever by half, halves effectiveness. In my humble opinion very nearly the best performance in the play was Mr. Marius Goring's Cardinal Campeius.

First Nights: November 7, 1933

KING HENRY VIII
(Regent's Park)

MR. HOLLOWAY'S WOLSEY

DR. JOHNSON said of this play that 'the meek sorrows and virtuous distress of Katharine have furnished some scenes which may be justly numbered among the greatest efforts of tragedy. But the genius of Shakespeare comes in and goes out with Katharine. Every other part may be easily conceived and easily written'. May it? The thing being so easy, it is a pity that the author of *Irene* did not himself oblige. I suppose Johnson must have had as much sense of fun as any human being who ever lived. He quotes Warburton's preposterous note to Norfolk's, 'Compelled by hunger and lack of other means,' and adds 'I have inserted this note rather because it seems to have been the writer's favourite, than because it is of much value. It explains what no reader has found difficult, and, I think, explains it wrong.' And how the old man could praise! With reference to the stage-direction: 'Enter Katharine Dowager, sick, led between Griffith, her gentleman usher, and Patience, her woman', Johnson says 'This scene is above any other part of Shakespeare's tragedies, and perhaps above any scene of any other poet, tender and pathetick, without gods, or furies, or poisons, or precipices, without the help of romantick circumstances, without improbable sallies of poetical lamentation, and without any throes of tumultuous misery.' Yet there are not wanting modern critics to say that this is a poor play. I suspect them to be *young* modern critics. Let 'em mewl and puke!

Of course the play contains a good deal that is pedestrian. I will not, for example, insist upon the poetical quality of the Surveyor:

> Not long before your highness sped to France,
> The duke being at the Rose, within the parish
> Saint Lawrence Poultney, did of me demand
> What was the speech among the Londoners
> Concerning the French journey: I replied . . .

etc., etc. I agree that this is hardly the pink of poetry. On the other hand, this play has certain passages which, though devoid of poetical flourish, happen to move some playgoers strangely. There is no verbal beauty that I can see in Buckingham's:

> My noble father, Henry of Buckingham,
> Who first raised head against usurping Richard,
> Flying for succour to his servant Banister,

Being distress'd, was by that wretch betray'd,
And without trial fell; God's peace be with him!
Henry the Seventh succeeding, truly pitying
My father's loss, like a most royal prince,
Restored me to my honours, and out of ruins
Made my name once more noble. Now his son,
Henry the Eighth, life, honour, name and all
That made me happy, at one stroke has taken
For ever from the world.

The reason that some playgoers are so moved is that whenever
they hear this the entire pageant of Plantagenet and Tudor
history not only unrolls itself, but unrolls itself in terms of remembered theatrical experience. They say that a drowning man sees
all his life in a flash; at the words 'Henry the Eighth' I feel all
of Shakespeare's impact heaped up from boyhood. How, then,
can I hold this play to be a poor one? Really, I sometimes
wonder what playgoers demand. Do they want anything grander
or more unexpected than the last speech of Buckingham — good
enough to end one of anybody else's tragedies, but royally thrown
away by Shakespeare in what in any practicable version becomes
the first act? Do playgoers want anything better than the taut,
vibrant passion of Katharine at her trial, and her gentleness and
resignation afterwards? Do they want more moving pictures?
If they do, they had better go to them! And last, the fall of Wolsey.
This play may not overtop the world like the big tragedies. I
do not claim for it that it is a Snowdon. But it has four great
bosses of exalted emotion, and a range which contains Carnedd
Llewelyn, Carnedd Dafydd, Glyder Fawr, and Glyder Fach is
not to be despised.

Mr. Carroll has done the play the honour of noble casting, and
Mr. Robert Atkins, besides skilfully paring and pruning, has
found a way of treating the piece so that we do not miss the indoor
theatre. Of course, there are one or two little difficulties, though
he is a poor playgoer who lacks the spirit of accommodation.
There is the difficulty of making-up for a performance which

begins in natural and ends in artificial light. The face of Wolsey
— cheese-green with ambition at the end — is at the beginning a
horrible cocoa-brown. On the other hand, Buckingham's face,
which starts as apricot, presently turns to peach, possibly owing
to the dew of imminent execution. But, as I say, given the right
playgoing spirit, these things don't matter. After all, the acting
is the thing, and the players, realizing their responsibility, take it
in both hands. Wolsey must always be the trouble. There has
been an old tendency to present this character as an ascetic,
largely because Irving's nose was built that way. But are we to
believe that Wolsey piled up his riches solely to bribe his way to
the Popedom? We are told otherwise by Griffith, who describes
him as in bestowing most princely. Is it absurd to fancy that
there was something in Wolsey of Nicolas Fouquet, who out-
possessed and outspent his master, Louis XIV? Admirably
though Mr. Baliol Holloway plays one side of Wolsey he never
suggests the gormandizer, the man of an unbounded stomach in
more sense than the Queen means, the glutton for palaces and
pictures. We perfectly believe that Mr. Holloway's Cardinal
endowed Ipswich and Oxford. But he also suggests that he never
had a square meal in his life. And we just don't believe this of
Wolsey. Mr. Gyles Isham delivers Buckingham's farewell in the
bland manner, rather as though a person about to be executed
should cover himself with cold cream; all the same, it is a moving
performance. Mr. Lyn Harding's Henry is exactly right, since
he makes that monarch a quivering compound, not only of tissue,
but of neuroses. The ultra-modern way of playing the part with
the neuroses on top fails for the reason that such a Henry would
not have deceived his time. Better to play the part straightforwardly and leave a modern audience to guess how many thin
anxieties that bluff envelope was used to cover. Miss Vivien
Leigh plays Anne Boleyn with the right admixture of meekness
and the neck-or-nothing spirit, while as the chaperon Miss Hilda
Trevelyan has great fun telling us what every old Shakespearean
woman knows. But the great achievement of the evening is Miss
Phyllis Neilson-Terry's Katharine. Kean's voice was said to

sound like the soughing of the wind through cedars; Miss Neilson-Terry could act beside one and not be overtopped. To the tones of a voice rich, yet full of pathos, she adds presence, gesture, and gait. She moves with the sweep proper to a tragedy queen, and if an actress is playing a queen in tragedy this, I submit, is the proper thing to do. There is nothing false about such coinage. It is the doubloon and moidore of acting, a welcome change from the threepenny-bit à la mode.

June 22, 1936

ELIZABETHAN TRAGEDIES

THE TRAGICAL HISTORY OF
DOCTOR FAUSTUS

BY CHRISTOPHER MARLOWE

(The Phoenix Society)

THERE are other reasons besides the likeness to Mr. Walkley —
'And live and die in Aristotle's works' — which incline us to
regard Faustus as a Great Man. His tragedy is that of all the
Shakespearean protagonists — the overthrow of a soul essentially
noble. The lust of Faustus is the lust for something of vaster
scope than material pleasure. He would rule a world of honour
and omnipotence, command all things that move between the
quiet poles, enjoy dominion stretching as far as the mind of man.
It will certainly occur to those whose conception of this great
legend has been vitiated by Gounod's operatic trash — and it may
occur to others as well — that Faustus did not get very much out
of his bargain with the Devil, which was to live 'in all voluptuous-
ness' for four-and-twenty years. Faustus plans to bridge the moving air, which is an engineer's project, and to make Spain and
Africa contributory to his crown, which is the dream of a Napoleon or a Rhodes. But in the subsequent action these things are
not realized; while to indulge in a Pageant of Sinfulness and play
tricks on the Pope and a horse-coper seem to be less part of a
philosophic scheme than a desire to entertain the groundlings.
One feels that even a confirmed money-grubber would be able to
find pleasure more exciting than a personally-conducted tour
through Italy. The play, in short, waits for Helen and for all
that Helen means to your *homme moyen sensuel*.

But now the great poet in Marlowe takes hold of the playwright
and turns the bodily presence of the world's paramour into air

and cloud. It is interesting to compare the description of Helen given in the prose *History*. The author of this translation from the German *Volksbuch* tells us that she wore a most rich gown of purple velvet, costly embroidered. Her hair, fair as beaten gold, was 'of such length that it reached down to her hams'; her eyes were 'amorous and cole-black'. Our prose historian goes on to say that his heroine 'looked about her with a rolling hawke's eye and smiling wanton countenance, which near-hand inflamed the hearts of all the students, but that they persuaded themselves she was a spirit, which made them lightly pass away such fancies'. So Marlowe purifies his spectator's spirit by dissolving Helen into pure poetry. One would make bold and say that

> Sweet Helen, make me immortal with a kiss,
> Her lips suck forth my soul; see where it flies! --
> Come, Helen, come, give me my soul again.
> Here will I dwell, for Heaven is in these lips,
> And all is dross that is not Helena,

has a glory of pure passion not exceeded even in *Antony and Cleopatra*, and that the ethereal quality of

> Oh, thou art fairer than the evening air
> Clad in the beauty of a thousand stars;
> Brighter art thou than flaming Jupiter
> When he appeared to hapless Semele:
> More lovely than the monarch of the sky
> In wanton Arethusa's azured arms,

is not excelled even by the Flower Speech of Perdita. And if one must be quoting and comparing one would suggest that the last speech of Faustus, containing the famous

> See, see where Christ's blood streams in the firmament!
> One drop would save my soul — half a drop: ah, my Christ!

is not to be beaten anywhere in Shakespeare. I have always had the fancy — though this is probably highly uncritical — that the image of the streaming firmament was suggested by the sunset shining in the actor's face. We know that the piece was originally performed in a playhouse half-open to the sky, and that the performances took place in the late afternoon. I do not stress the point, for the objection is obvious that the hour is between eleven and midnight. But that mattered little at a time when night and darkness had to be suggested in full sunshine by the presence on the stage of a flaming torch. Yet obviously the line has the suggestion of the last sunset upon which the doomed man is to gaze.

The Phoenix Society did the play very well, probably as effectively as it ever can be done with a purely formalized stage. Is it all, until we draw near to the two great passages at the end, a trifle bare in interest? We have ceased to believe in the devils which were real to the Elizabethan audience, and in the magic which still held something of truth for Marlowe. Leave the Ghost out of *Hamlet* and you impair the play very little, whereas the whole of *Faustus* is bound up with the belief in the actual existence of hideous things with tails. An Elizabethan audience had terror painted on half its face and amusement on the other half, whereas we to-day are neither amused nor affrighted. Perhaps we may be justified in thinking that if Marlowe had known of the resources of the modern theatre he would have turned his Procession of the Seven Deadly Sins into a ballet after the manner of Flecker or Sir Herbert Tree. But severity is the Phoenix note, and in that idiom the performance could not, one thinks, have been materially improved. The Faustus of Mr. Ion Swinley showed once more how wrong it is for this fine romantic actor to make petty descent from Olympus. Mr. Swinley has almost everything that a great actor should have — poise, gesture, manner, looks, voice, and diction. He lacks two things only, pathos and the perfect recollection of his lines. But even so the actor shows intellectual mastery and the power of scaling heights with his author. Mr. Swinley does not entirely succeed in shaking our souls in the great speech at the end; but he obviously shakes his own, which in these days is no small matter.

The Mephistophilis of Mr. Ernest Thesiger was flawless. Here the conception is of a spirit fallen from nobleness, and of a hell whose fiends are filled not with delight but with weariness. This actor gave every line of his part its uttermost meaning, so that the words 'for where we are is Hell' had the directness of a shaft sunk into the infernal regions. We are always told that the comic passages in this piece are interpolations by another hand, but Mr. Hay Petrie made us think otherwise. This actor is either a genius or he is nothing, and his Robin comes easily into the former category. The enormous cast was thickly dotted with good names, and one would not willingly conclude without mention of the admirable performances of Messrs. Bruce Winston, Alexander Field, John Gielgud, Charles Bond, H. R. Hignett, and Mesdames Leah Bateman, Beatrice Wilson, Florence Saunders and Elsa Lanchester. The stage pictures and grouping throughout were very fine, and from the moment when the curtain revealed Mr. Swinley seated at his books on a dais like some Dante troubled of flesh and spirit the eye was mightily delighted.

The Contemporary Theatre, 1925: October 25, 1925

EDWARD THE SECOND

BY CHRISTOPHER MARLOWE

(The Phoenix Society)

Edward II moves us as with some story of our own day. The amount of sympathy which Marlowe arouses for the least becoming of English kings is extraordinary. There is no maudlin repentance here, no hollow cry out of the depths; this man sees his fate and embraces it. Kingliness increases as the grasp upon kingship weakens. Marlowe's Edward is a better man than Shakespeare's Richard, puling his life away in aesthetic conceits. From disaster Edward comes, as Stevenson said of a friend of his youth, 'like a spent swimmer desperately ashore. . . . He had gone to ruin with a kind of kingly *abandon*, like one who condescended; but once ruined, with the lights all out, he fought as for a kingdom'. Richard does nothing but rail, and gives in too soon. Edward makes sure the game is up. Even when he resigns the crown he has his moment of temper.

Comparison of these two plays has always been a favourite theme with the critics. Lamb went all out when he said that Marlowe's death-scene moves us to pity and terror 'beyond any scene ancient or modern with which I am acquainted'. Swinburne declared the deposition-scene to be 'almost as much finer in tragic effect and poetic quality as it is shorter and less elaborate than the corresponding scene in *Richard II*'. But let us be fair to Shakespeare. Having to do all over again that which had already been perfectly achieved, he was content to poetize and elaborate. Probably the play of Richard would have been stronger in dramatic power if the earlier play about Edward had not stood in the way. Swinburne found horror rather than terror in the death-scene, a view which not everybody will share. Perhaps the point to make about any stage performance of this play is its exceeding interest. I do not think that anybody could have gone home until he had seen the King delivered from that dungeon. When the door swung open on Monday afternoon and the murderer recoiled at the stench, it was as though fetor filled the theatre, offending the senses of to-day, not of three hundred years ago. The last scene had a magnificently barbaric ring.

Marlowe's line in this drama is not mighty; it is what Hazlitt, alluding to some undistinguished parts of Shakespeare, calls 'good, sound poetry'. In this play he does not scale the mountain-tops of the greater genius, but neither does he descend into the other's valleys and depressions. He comes up to his friend's shoulder, and stays there. Or you might describe this drama as a majestic table-land. Like Great Gable, it can stand to be looked at, whatever higher peaks may abound. Twice the dramatic poignancy of a single line caught me in the throat — the King's reply to Leicester:

A litter hast thou? Lay me in a hearse;

and, when he is about to give the crown to the Bishop of Winchester:

Take it. What, are you moved? pity you me?

Both lines were, in the situation, 'as good as Shakespeare'.

If there was a fault in the almost perfect acting it was that sufficient attention was not paid to the verse. The word 'minion' ·was persistently pronounced 'minyun', thus robbing the line of a syllable. I except Miss Gwen Ffrangcon-Davies, who spoke throughout with perfect feeling for the poetry, and gave its full four-syllable value to the last word in the line:

You know the king is so suspicious.

This lady's Queen Isabella was a very beautiful performance. But the play stands or falls by Edward, and Mr. Duncan Yarrow set that monarch, and also the tragedy, magnificently on their legs. It is, perhaps, not sufficiently recognized how rich we are in good young actors. Mr. Yarrow was suffering from a bad attack of laryngitis, and it was immensely plucky of him to play at all. Still, with such a character and such a performance up his sleeve, one understands that doctors had to be defied. In the circumstances, beauty of voice was not to be looked for, but there was compensation in great wealth and grace of gesture. Not a shade escaped this actor, and the death-scene was a piece of authentic tragedy nobly and broadly sustained.

But, then, all the actors were good. They could not choose but be, if we like so to interpret Greene's description of Marlowe as a 'famous gracer of tragedians'. Mr. Edmund Willard's Young Mortimer was the most vigorous piece of acting this most robustious of players has yet given. Mr. Thesiger made a good guess at Gaveston, and indeed conveyed something of that impertinent flaunt which marks this page of English history. Very rightly he eschewed charm, and made Piers an intellectual. The Warwick of Mr. Victor Lewisohn was particularly good; you felt that this grave baron had a life of his own, away from the Court. Mr. Lawrence Anderson's Young Spencer bore himself bravely. And I have no room for a great deal more that was excellent.

The Contemporary Theatre, 1923: November 25, 1923

THE MAID'S TRAGEDY
BY BEAUMONT AND FLETCHER
(Renaissance)

THE better is the enemy of the good. But for another dramatist
it is possible that Beaumont and Fletcher might have kept the
English stage in the way in which Racine and Corneille still hold
the French. Only last Sunday week French actors at the Odéon
could have been heard in full blast upon *Mithridate*. Racine still
lives in France; not only is he the best that country possesses,
there is in him something which is still very much alive in the
French mind. And we ask: Is there, all pretence apart, anything
in the common heart of Beaumont and Fletcher as exposed in
The Maid's Tragedy which beats with ours to-day? I doubt it very
much. The play is as dead as mutton, and its interest is purely
the collector's. Having bagged two revivals my appetite is
appeased.

Let me not be deemed to deny a certain readableness in the
thing. There are good lines here and there, and the imagery is
tolerable. But that's for the study, and we may be sure that
Swinburne was not sitting at the play when he concocted all
that rhapsodic stuff about the Dioscuri of English poetry, and
how Beaumont was the heavenlier twin only as Pollux was on one
side a demigod of diviner blood than Castor. The truth is that
in the theatre only a poet of Shakespeare's genius could have got
away with such silly stuff as the plot of this tragedy is seen to be on
even a cursory examination. Beaumont and Fletcher never sweep
you off your feet; the play sweeps them off theirs, which is a very
different matter.

Must I substantiate the silliness referred to above? Very well
then. Why should the King marry off his mistress to a courtier
whom he is supposed to cherish? Why should he hit upon the
noblest youth about the court, and so break off the young man's
match with the sister of one of his best supporters? Why should

the lady accept a husband at all, since she is resolved to deny his love and thus reveal the King's dishonour? Why does the King acquiesce in Evadne's continued faithfulness, knowing that this must give him away to Amintor? Why wantonly show a monarch hedged in by his divinity and making use of that security to plague his world? But the King is not more despicable than Evadne, who says plainly that she intends to love the King until he is deposed, when she will be quite ready to love his successor. There's a baggage for you, upon whom tragedy is wasted. Her repentance is pure fudge, forced upon her at the sword's point, and throughout she wins neither esteem nor liking. Amintor is a male ninny given to repeating the 'O, what a rogue and peasant slave am I!' soliloquy at inordinate length and using an inferior text. Beaumont and Fletcher could create an unnatural situation, but they did not, in this piece at any rate, create either a natural man or a natural woman. And, *in the theatre*, neither their poetry nor their bombast is good enough.

The Renaissance Theatre does well to trot out these old things, and give us the opportunity of judging them for ourselves. England is a free country, and there's no divinity round bygone dramatic critics. I may be quite wrong about this play. It just didn't happen to impress me. Neither did Miss Edith Evans, and here I venture to think that I am not wrong. Nobody will accuse me of a prejudice against this actress, but she must not play tragedy. I respectfully suggest that Miss Evans is the most brilliant comic actress of our day, with a good turn of domestic pathos. .But the tragic mask, voice, and manner are not hers, and she will never acquire them. Miss Thorndike showed us how much can be done in the part, Miss Evans how little. And now if the former artist will produce her Millamant I shall be delighted to apply sufficient balm to any wounds which the above may have occasioned to the foremost *comédienne* of the day. Mr. Ion Swinley, always at his best in these out-of-the-way things, showed how nearly great an actor he can be, and Mr. Baliol Holloway approached the admirable. He has shortened his pauses, but they are still there. Mr. Stanley Lathbury got into the skin of an old

man in tetchy second childhood. The allotting of Aspatia to the
Chinese actress, Miss Rose Quong, was a daring and vocally
successful experiment.

May 17, 1925

'T I S   P I T Y   S H E ' S   A   W H O R E

BY JOHN FORD

(The Phoenix Society)

ANTIQUARIAN interest, on the stage, is all fudge; a play which is
dead is dead. No amount of artificial respiration will restore that
peculiar protégé of the Phoenix, John Dryden, dead as a door-nail,
Tutankh-Amen, or whatever symbol we may elect for one who,
whatever he may be in the study, on the stage is no longer alive;
no change in dramatic fashion can kill John Ford, the last of the
tragic Elizabethans. I do not think that there was a single member
of the audience who did not follow this story of a brother's and
sister's love with at least as lively a degree of interest as if it had
been unrolled before them on the drawing-room stage, the screen,
or among the *faits divers* of the sensation-mongering press. Add
to the exciting and grievous tale the last wash and surge of the
greatest tide in English poetry, half a dozen pieces of fine acting
and one that touched greatness, and there was reason why the
spectator of to-day should have been swept off his feet.

The play has long been a thorn in the critical side. Even so
determined a judge as Hazlitt could never quite make up his
mind about it. He suspects in one place that the 'exceptionable-
ness' of the subject constitutes the play's chief merit; in another
that it will 'no more bear acting than Lord Byron and Goethe
together could have written it'. In this matter of exceptionable-
ness Hazlitt is wrong; perhaps he was only making obeisance to
the squeamishness of the time. It is become a commonplace of
criticism that defilement is not in the pitch but in him who
touches it; and we may find significance in the fact that it is to

God, through His representative, the Friar, that Giovanni first unburdens his soul. We see nothing of the storm and stress which have preceded confession; the unlawful passion is declared, absolute and inevitable, beyond human resistance. Everything here depends upon the actor who plays Giovanni: he must strike the note of one who is now *on the other side* of passion, stepp'd in so far that not only 'returning were as tedious as go o'er', but inconceivable. Mr. Ion Swinley was exactly right here. This bosom, one felt, was surcharged with self-blame, and therefore unassailable by alien prejudice. 'What is, is,' says Giovanni in the words of the unexceptionable Mr. Locke, caring no fig whether our Tupperish masters of the want of human understanding should declare the contents of that bosom to be for the best or the worst. Nor, we may suppose, did Ford very greatly care. He, like Tourneur, was permeated with the spirit and morals of the Italian Renaissance. They took their plots where they found them, and went ahead with dramas of incest, rape, parricide and matricide, as though these things could really happen — and perhaps the reader of the modern Sunday newspaper may concede that in mediaeval Italy they did. Ford was a poor moralist in the Puritan sense, and his sop to morality, in the form of Annabella's repentance, lacks conviction. The play remains, as an acted story, one of the greatest interest and power, over which the dramatist has thrown such a mantle of poetry that the mawkish may, if it please them, forget the matter and take cover in the manner. It may be said that the flame of the poet's genius burns so brightly as to consume, and purify, the candle.

Yet there is much in respect of which the play is intolerable to modern sense. One would instance the killing of Bergetto. It may be that the baiting of innocents was legitimate in Ford's day, and that the very humanity and sympathy of Mr. Harold Scott's playing were wrong. The actor was extraordinarily funny, showed the soul of the wander-wit to be most ludicrously loose about him, and yet he established so great a degree of likeableness that it was unbearable to see him dispatched. The putting out of the Nurse's eyes is not to modern taste. Then there is the, to modern notions, quite extraordinary lack of irony. Soranzo piles invective upon invective as a composer heaps up his tonal power, and develops his whole jealous symphony to a climax of vitriolic paranoia.

> Must your hot itch and plurisy of lust,
> The heyday of your luxury, be fed
> Up to a surfeit, and could none but I
> Be picked out, to be cloak to your close tricks,
> Your belly sports? Now I must be the dad
> To all that gallimaufry that is stuffed
> In thy corrupted bastard-bearing womb!
> Say, must I?

He does not see that as he is cuckolded so has he wronged Richardetto. But possibly the principle of not doing to others as you would not be done by had not made much headway in the seventeenth century. There was some admirable acting by Mr. Michael Sherbrooke, who endowed Vasques with a passion Jewish rather than Spanish, and by Miss Barbara Gott, who played the Nurse like a Rembrandt come to life. I find it difficult to say much of Miss Moyna Macgill's Annabella, which was pretty and insignificant where it should have been, oh, ever so much more. Mr. Ion Swinley's performance was quite perfect. Here is an actor in a fair way to become a tragedian; that is, if the managers will permit him. He has looks, figure, voice, admirable command of gesture, phrasing, and variety in nobility. When he withdrew the dagger from Annabella's womb he did not discard it as a piece of useless furniture, but rather identified himself with it. He became, as it were, *all dagger*. His attitudes throughout the last scene were very fine indeed, and recalled those pictures of old actors who, by taking thought, would seem to have added a cubit and more to their stature.

The Contemporary Theatre, 1923: February 3, 1923

THE WHITE DEVIL

BY JOHN WEBSTER

(Renaissance)

Polonius: 'Will you walk out of the air, my Lord?'
Hamlet: 'Into my grave?'

To descend from Shakespeare to Webster is to walk out of air into the grave, to leave the workaday world of good and evil for the charnel house of corruption. In the blackest of Shakespeare's tragedies you still feel that there is a heaven, and that God is in it. But in such a play as *The White Devil* there is no heaven for God to be in; evil by becoming normal has ceased to be extravagant, and goodness no longer is. It is difficult to see in Vittoria Corombona anything beyond the 'vamp' of the American film. It is true that she is married to a popinjay and is in love with the handsome Brachiano; but there is no kind of conflict in her soul, and she prepares the murder of her husband and her lover's lawful wife with the same cold-blooded gusto with which she would afterwards despatch her brother Flamineo. As we watch this play we cannot help thinking how differently Shakespeare would have treated the unhappy passion of Vittoria and her duke. He, we feel, would have made another *Macbeth* of this theme, and by working out tragedy to its remorseful end have revealed the essential goodness ordaining that such things shall not be.

But Webster's lovers do not work out their own damnation, and at no time in the play are they conscious of it. Their end comes upon them neither out of themselves nor from their sin; it is pure mischance. Or, if not mischance, one would say that punishment depends from a scheme of vengeance too loosely knit to be tragic. A strange, decayed Count, one Lodovico, wanders through the play. He has been banished by the Duke of Florence, and his grudge against Vittoria is that she did not induce Brachiano to plead for his pardon. What he has against Brachiano is not clear, but it is this neglected, desultory gentleman who is chosen by

Webster to slay the lovers with the help of Brachiano's wife's brother, who for no discoverable reason disguises himself as a Moor. The plot, you see, is complicated, and it is difficult for the spectator to be muddled and moved at the same time.

The Renaissance Theatre had clarified the text a good deal, and possibly a little too much. In the original the murders of Isabella and Camillo are revealed in dumb show to Brachiano by a conjuror, Isabella being made to kiss her husband's portrait which has been previously poisoned, and Camillo having his neck broken during a vaulting match. This dumb show is exactly in the vein of the dead hand, the Masque of Madmen, and Bosola's coffin, cords, and bell in *The Duchess of Malfi*. One suggests that the attempt to bring Webster by omission into touch with sweet and Shakespearean reason was to diminish him. Probably the best way to enjoy this gloomy dramatist is to put the greater man out of mind and concentrate on the things that are Webster's and Webster's alone. First, then, one would cite his mastery of the apparatus of horror, the vigour of his personages and his prose, and that tumult of being which reminds one of life lived in a moral stoke-hold or black engine-room. (I have the notion that if Webster were alive to-day he would be an admirer of Eugene O'Neill.) In this play only one or two escape. There is Marcello, brother to Flamineo, and there are the old woman Cornelia and the child Giovanni. These are, indeed, flowers of the purest and most human pathos. Certainly Giovanni's

> What do the dead do, uncle? do they eat,
> Hear music, go a hunting, and be merry,
> As we that live?

has nothing to fear by comparison with any child-passage in Shakespeare. Webster, master of a prose which ripples like the muscles in a statue of Rodin, and of a verse solidifying as we read into marble and bronze, is seldom the poet of gentleness and melancholy. Yet the dirge beginning —

> Call for the robin redbreast and the wren,

is a poem of absolute beauty. Lamb compares it to that other

dirge in the *Tempest* — 'as that is of the water, watery; so this is of
the earth, earthy'. The comparison is just; both poems do indeed
resolve themselves into the elements of which they treat. Webster
must have been conscious of having achieved a fine thing here,
for he at once empties his stage and gives to Flamineo, whose mind
up to this point has been as black as that of Shakespeare's Aaron,
these significant lines:

> I have a strange thing in me, to the which
> I cannot give a name, without it be
> Compassion.

These few human moments apart, one feels that in this play
Webster's relation to essential goodness never gets beyond the
line —

> The last good deed he did, he pardoned murder.

Mr. Esmé Percy played Brachiano with all that show of beauty
and display of temperament which the portrayal of a Florentine
noble of the period demands. He made of his penultimate death-
scene — for Webster is generous in this matter — a smiling, ineff-
able affair which showed how much of his art this actor learned
from Sarah Bernhardt. Miss Laura Cowie's Vittoria was all her
own, in so far as it was not a portrait by Holbein, and in this part
she showed the best of her intellectual mastery and perfect
technique. Mr. Cedric Hardwicke gave a careful study of
Flamineo. Mr. Terence O'Brien made a dignified figure of the
Cardinal, and Mr. Charles Carson did very well as the bereaved
Francisco until in the fourth act his disguise compelled him to
minstrelsy of the Moore and Burgess order. Miss Viola Tree made
a very weeping-willow of Isabella, and in a long cast one would
feel inclined to mention specially Mesdames Marie Ault, Rose
Quong, and Patricia Hayes. Mr. George Skillan hardly knew
what to make of the decayed yet peripatetic Lodovico, and I for
one did not blame him.

The stage-pictures were very fine, and the Cardinal's robe was
as a cascade of blood from the Websterian fount.

The Contemporary Theatre, 1925: October 12, 1925

THE DUCHESS OF MALFI
BY JOHN WEBSTER
(Embassy)

ARE we to rank Webster, as Mr. Shaw did exactly forty years ago, as among 'the whole crew of insufferable bunglers and dullards whose work stands out as vile even at the beginning of the seventeenth century, when every art was corrupted to the marrow by the orgy called the Renaissance?' Is he just one of the Elizabethan literary rabble who, formulating in rhetorical blank-verse cheap ideas about murder, lust, and obscenity, 'made the stage pestiferous with plays that have no ray of noble feeling, no touch of faith, beauty, or even common kindness in them from beginning to end?' Or is Webster a great dramatist whom the froth of criticism can no more destroy than the fleck and foam of two seas can wear away Gibraltar? How seriously are we to take Mr. Shaw, and how far was his attack the lusty crowing, kicking, and laying about him of a full-grown dramatic critic who was also an infant playwright getting himself born into a world at the opposite pole from Webster's? Sitting at this play the other evening, I could not help wondering what sort of man Webster must have been that, at one time the friend of Shakespeare — so it is surmised — and presumably having witnessed the great Shakespearean tragedies with their deepening message of moral responsibility, he could still stick to his Punch and Judy themes.

Those rascals, Ferdinand and his brother the Cardinal, between them do not possess an ounce of what Hamlet would call 'the motive and the cue' for the passion they work themselves into about their sister. Why should they be in such a frenzy to keep the Duchess from marrying again? Late in the play Ferdinand says something about inheriting vast sums if his sister dies husbandless. This passage was omitted at Swiss Cottage, and I think rightly, since it is a belated explanation stuck in doubtless to meet the objection of some snarling *Sunday Times* critic of the period!

Besides it isn't valid, since the Duchess has a perfectly good infant son by her first husband. Nor can snobbishness on the brothers' part be alleged, since not knowing upon whom their sister looks favourably, they cannot complain that he is only her steward.

The play starts, as it were, *in vacuo*. Webster asks us to suppose that if the Duchess marries again, her two brothers will for no reason tear her limb from limb. All right, let us suppose it! He next asks us to suppose that one Bosola, whom the brothers have 'forced' upon the Duchess, cannot discover who her new husband is, though she keeps having children all over the place; and that for two years the villainous pair are perfectly content to do nothing, which is out of all keeping with their filthy temper at the beginning. Well, we'll agree to this complicated nonsense also. Two questions at once emerge: What is there about this play which made it acceptable to the playgoer of 1614? Is there that about it which makes it acceptable to the playgoer of 1935?

To answer the first question one must go to the scholars; for an answer to the second one need only consult oneself. But even the scholars have perhaps not insisted strongly enough upon the consciousness of the first audience that it was watching carryings-on not in England but in 'furrin parts', and would therefore be no more flabbergasted into disbelief in these knaveries than we are by our modern plays of the underworld in Chicago. Mr. F. L. Lucas, in his admirable edition of Webster, recently reminded us that things were different in an age and land in which, for instance, the six sons of Lelio Massimo, on their father's second marriage, entered the bridal-chamber next morning and shot the bride in bed, because she was a cast-off mistress of Marcantonio Colonna. There is also the story of the professional cut-throat who, being offered a higher price by the victim to murder his employer instead, accepted but insisted on first fulfilling his original contract! In the light of such happenings there is nothing essentially improbable about the action of *The Duchess of Malfi*; the point is that to the Elizabethan mind such action was acceptable whether it exceeded probability or not. Here again, what Webster's audience wanted was something full-blooded; so long as it got that, it cared very little for the logic which set the full-blooded thing going. Further, the play is full of examples tending to show that the habit of the centuries is much nearer to kissing and commingling than to drawing apart. The incident of the dead hand and the wax figure is pure Grand Guignol. There is some confusion about the Masque of Madmen. A colleague has made the point that, as done at the Embassy, this is not terrifying: Mr. Lucas gives cogent reasons for thinking that Webster did not intend it to be. Masques of lunatics were a popular 'turn' at that time, and it is arguable that this particular masque, while intended to mortify the Duchess, was meant to amuse the spectator. Compare the knocking in Shakespeare's play, which has the double effect of striking terror into the heart of Macbeth and at the same time of bringing about the one comic scene in the play. Incidentally, and begging everybody's pardon, I think one should not ask a dozen of Hampstead's walking ladies and gentlemen to horrify an audience accustomed to the extravagances of modern Russian Ballet. And now, perhaps, that is enough about the playgoer of 1614.

Victor Hugo's 'Insensé, qui crois que tu n'es pas moi!' — any School of Languages will translate this for a shilling — must be my excuse for saying how this play affected me. I found that the tragedy's improbabilities did not worry me in the least, and that I had no need to justify them on the score that Webster was merely hashing up an old joint that half a dozen earlier story-tellers had cut and carved each after his own fashion. Never once did I have to murmur the word 'Renaissance', that magic cloth from behind which your sixteenth-century story-teller produces cardinals and noblemen splashing about in Machiavellian wickedness like goldfish in a conjurer's bowl. At Swiss Cottage Webster's gloomy gentry seemed good enough without any suggestion of magic, given that the black dog of sixteenth-century melancholy was gnawing at their vitals.

The same dog bites the heels of that very Shakespearean character, Bosola, who is Don John plus Iago, but also with a touch of Thersites plus Jacques. Bosola would be honest if he thought that there were any such thing as honesty. His acts, though they are those of a hypocrite, do not make him one; he is in the wretched case of a Hyde who cannot help every now and then turning into a Jekyll. Indeed, it occurred to me that an age which can accept Stevenson's balderdash, supposing you call it so, ought not to boggle at Webster's bunkum. Nor did I find the end too long-drawn-out, though perhaps this is due to the prevailing taste for the modern crime-novel which tends to expatiate on why a murder is committed rather than how. After all, the three villains must have something to say for themselves, and one wants to hear it. About Bosola we know; his melancholy has been fashionable in Denmark. The Cardinal is a more difficult problem, though I think straightforward guilt answers for him.

> How tedious is a guilty conscience!
> When I look into the fish-ponds in my garden,
> Methinks I see a thing arm'd with a rake,
> That seems to strike at me.

Surely this is only the visual form of Macbeth's 'How is't with me, when every noise appals me?'

Obviously a great deal depends upon how these two parts are played, and I thought they were done admirably on this occasion. Mr. Roy Graham made Bosola a fair-haired rogue, a slippery thing with diamonds in its ears, almost a waterfly, whose presence at Court might well seem to the Duchess to be innocuous. Yet, by an ingenious disposition of the ruff, the head seemed to the spectator to be sunk so low into the shoulders as to connote dishonesty; here, you said to yourself, was a moral hunchback. Mr. Neil Porter's Cardinal was also in excellent key; his Eminence walked about like a poker, and was much too straight in the back to have anything but a tortuous mind. This brings me to Ferdinand, who has to be taken as a figure of pure evil, the case for any other motive being too thin. Or you can think of this character as possessed; that he ends as a lycanthropist is not an accidental horror, since his remark about the strangled children:

>   The death
> Of young wolves is never to be pitied —

shows him to have wolfishness on the brain. Webster doesn't make
it too easy for the actor, because he cannot resist the line which has
since become so famous:

> Cover her face: mine eyes dazzle: she died young.

I do not believe that anybody in the theatre believed that Ferdinand would have said this, which is the kind of thing Stephen Phil-
lips, if he had been enough of a poet, would have given to Giovanni
to say over the dead body of Francesca. Indeed, I have always
thought that —

> I did not know the dead could have such hair.
> Hide them. They look like children fast asleep!

was a barefaced plagiarism. Having got on to this sentimental
tack, Webster followed it up with Ferdinand's remark about being
his sister's twin, which is unlikely but effective. It is the old
argument of whether Hamlet had a real existence apart from his
fashioner, or whether Shakespeare exercised the right to do what
he liked with his puppet even at the cost of consistency. Here
Webster certainly exercised this right. My difficulty with Ferdinand was that Mr. Laurie, despite his rantings, writhings, reelings,
never came near frightening me; one brushed him off the mind
like a fly. This actor's voice is too light, and what he falls into is
a pet rather than a rage; the harder he acts, the more peevish that
pet becomes. But one felt that Mr. Laurie knew what the part
was about, which is always something, whereas another actor, say
Mr. Ernest Milton, would have shown us, which is something else.
  Miss Joyce Bland's Duchess? The difficulty is that the part
starts off by being a good one, and then somehow isn't. She begins
by being like Shakespeare's Beatrice, then courts Antonio with
Portia-like largesse, fills in a Lady Macduff-like picture of domestic felicity, and is then struck more or less dumb while the morti-
fication takes place, though in the course of this she must give out

two terrific sentences: 'Am not I thy Duchess?' and 'I am Duchess of Malfi still.' These must boom like Big Ben or they are nothing, and the play here calls for a Siddons. Miss Bland does not pretend to be an actress of this force, and, while she did everything that charm and intelligence and a conscientious reading of her part could do, her performance remained too bland. Last, Mr. Torin Thatcher gave all possible graciousness of presence, voice, and manner to that poor fish Antonio. But the truth is that this is the very whale of a play. Burbage acted in it, and if I were to cast it within living memory I should choose Irving for the Cardinal, his son Laurence for Ferdinand, Ernest Milton for Bosola, Henry Ainley for Antonio, and Ellen Terry for the Duchess. I should rehearse these for three months to shake their schools together, engage Gielgud to produce, with music by Delius, and then see whether an instructed audience would endorse Mr. Shaw's 'Tussaud laureate' and Archer's 'ramshackle looseness of structure and barbarous violence of effect . . . hideous cacophonies, neither verse nor prose . . . Bedlam-broke-loose . . . poor Webster.'

More First Nights: January 20, 1935

DOUBTFUL PLAYS

THE TWO NOBLE KINSMEN
BY SHAKESPEARE AND FLETCHER
(The Old Vic)

A GOOD half of the entertainment in a performance of *The Two Noble Kinsmen* is bound to consist in apportioning the work between the two collaborators. Metrical tests, rhymes, the presence and quality of the prose scenes, all this has been elaborately done by the commentators to whom winnowing and sifting are the breath of life. But it is always an amusing game, and one in which the ordinary playgoer will want to take a hand. Consider, for example, the second verse of the Boy's Song with which the play opens:

> *Primrose*, first-born child of Ver,
> Merry spring-time's harbinger,
>   With hare-bells *dim*;
> *Oxlips* in their cradle growing,
> Marigolds on death-beds blowing,
>   And lark's-heels trim —

We murmur to ourselves:

> Violets *dim*
> But sweeter than the lids of Juno's eyes
> Or Cytherea's breath; pale *primroses*,
> That die unmarried, ere they can behold
> Bright Phœbus in his strength, a malady
> Most incident to maids; bold *oxlips* and
> The crown imperial —

Shakespeare, we say. And then remembering that no two lyrics or lyrical passages of Shakespeare are even remotely alike, and reflecting that one who possessed inexhaustible magic had no need to plagiarize himself we change our minds and say: Fletcher.

Definitely one would say that certain words, if there is any sensitiveness in words at all, give proof of Shakespeare's hand. For example:

> THIRD QUEEN: O, my petition was
> Set down in ice, which, by hot grief uncandied,
> Melts into drops.

Then take Arcite's:

> O great corrector of enormous times,

where the word 'enormous' is used in the strict sense of 'abnormal', as when Lear says that he 'shall find time from this enormous state'. And 'plurisy' in Arcite's 'and curest the world o' the plurisy of people' can only be Shakespeare.

In the matter of whole passages is there not a resemblance between Emilia's:

> But Palamon's sadness is a kind of mirth,
> So mingled as if mirth did make him sad,
> And sadness merry: those darker humours that
> Stick misbecomingly on others, on him
> Live in fair dwelling —

and Cleopatra's:

> He was not sad, for he would shine on those
> That make their looks by his; he was not merry,
> Which seem'd to tell them his remembrance lay
> In Egypt with his joy: but between both.
> O heavenly mingle! Be'st thou sad or merry
> The violence of either thee becomes,
> So does it no man else.

Certainly when Palamon says that by death:

> We prevent
> The loathsome misery of age, beguile
> The gout and rheum, that in lag hours attend
> The gray approachers —

he is echoing Vicentio's:

> Friend hast thou none;
> For thine own bowels, which do call thee sire,
> The mere effusion of thy proper loins,
> Do curse the gout, serpigo, and the rheum,
> For ending thee no sooner. Thou hast nor youth nor age,
> But, as it were, an after-dinner's sleep,
> Dreaming on both; for all thy blessed youth
> Becomes as aged, and doth beg the alms
> Of palsied eld; and when thou art old and rich,
> Thou hast neither heat, affection, limb, nor beauty,
> To make thy riches pleasant.

May one say that Pirithous's long description of Palamon's steed repeats that pre-occupation which we have already noted in *Venus and Adonis*, some thirty years lying between the passages? We note that the older poet now takes a more than poetic interest in the horse. It is the fancier grown pursy who insists upon the parenthesis:

> a black one, owing
> Not a hair-worth of white, which some will say
> Weakens his price —

This is the observation of a man who has dealt in the noble animal, and in the matter of horseflesh 'hath had losses'.

It is to be feared that the spectator who takes no interest in catching out each collaborator will not have much of a time with *The Two Noble Kinsmen*. After all, there must be a reason why a work of art should languish in oblivion, and three hundred years make a fairly conclusive test. Any play which is ever to come into its own should have done so in less than three hundred years; hence this play can have very little to come into. There is a pleasantly pathetic moment when the Jailer's daughter, who is no relation to Ophelia, but entertains a reasonable, Freudian ecstasy, goes mad with horn-pipe effects. But one cannot think that commentator overharsh who said of this scene: 'She fancies she sees a ship, and there is some affectation of nautical language — why,

Heaven only knows—and the rest is mere incoherent nonsense.'
Then there is that capital little scene between the Jailer and his
Daughter's wooer, which we take to be Shakespeare's from the
mere fact that it begins in the middle without any of the indifferent
writer's unnecessary preliminaries. The conclusion of this is a
gem. Palamon and Arcite appear at the window of a tower and
this colloquy takes place:

> JAILER: Look yonder they are. That's Arcite looking out.
>
> DAUGHTER: No, sir, no; that's Palamon: Arcite is the lower
> of the twain; you may perceive a part of him.
>
> JAILER: Go to! Leave your pointing: they would not make us
> their object: out of their sight!
>
> DAUGHTER: It is a holiday to look on them. Lord the difference
> of men!

'It is a holiday' must be Shakespeare. One returns, you see, to the
play's unique point of interest — which of them did it? Remove
this preoccupation and *The Two Noble Kinsmen* would seem to be
little more than a libretto for a Rimsky-Korsakov. Arcite did, in
point of fact, wear on his battle-tunic the image of a golden
cockerel! Further acquaintance, say some three hundred years
hence, might rate the play higher; and reading the two battle-
speeches one is conscious in their harsh, ugly splendour of a Shakespeare in the mood of the late, unsensuous Beethoven.

The piece was most charmingly dressed and mounted in good
Chaucerian vein, and one gathered that it was quite adequately
acted. As Palamon Mr. Ernest Milton moped more than intelligently, and as Arcite Mr. Eric Portman wore with gusto the same
romantic air and boots which he used for Juliet's lover. Miss Jean
Forbes-Robertson lent her grave beauty to the Jailer's Daughter,
and Miss Barbara Everest did her best with Emilia. But her best
could not be good enough, since the art of acting has yet to be
invented which shall cope successfully with a young woman allowing herself to be transferred from one lover to another like a sack of
corn.

March 19, 1928

ARDEN OF FEVERSHAM
ATTRIBUTED TO SHAKESPEARE
(Renaissance)

WE must ask antiquarians to look among their treasures and see whether they cannot find the manuscript of this play. Internal evidence counts for a good deal in matters of this sort, as, indeed, it should, since there is little other evidence worth having. But Swinburne, a critical whole-hogger if ever there was one, would have it that the play is Shakespeare's not only upon proof or suggestion offered by single passages, but because of the 'evidence of character'. It seems to him not pardonable merely, nor permissible, but simply logical and reasonable to set down this poem as Shakespeare's 'taking into account the really wonderful skill, the absoluteness of intuition and inspiration, with which every stroke is put in that touches off character or tones down effect, even to the sketching and grouping of such minor figures as the ruffianly hireling Black Will, the passionate artist without pity or conscience, and above all the "unimitated", "inimitable" study of Michael, in whom even physical fear becomes tragic, and cowardice itself no ludicrous absurdity, but rather a terrible passion'. This is just uncritical rodomontade. Black Will the 'passionate artist without pity or conscience', has been likened to Shakespeare's Pistol, whereas the braggart whom he more closely resembles is the more robustious of the two robbers in the pantomime of *The Babes in the Wood*. To talk of the 'terrible passion' in Michael is also nonsense. His fear is an infirmity which is ludicrous, so that there is no more to be said on that score. Towards the end, the play suddenly becomes serious. All that happens after the murder is first-class, and it is as though another hand had taken the piece here and pulled it together. But one refuses to believe that the hand was Shakespeare's. Mr. Poel produced the play in the only possible manner. That is to say he made it a roaring farce with one or two moments of wistfulness and beauty, and stuck a fine tragic lump on it at the end. He was not too well served by his actors, many of whom were insufficiently audible.   December 13, 1925

SHAKESPEARE'S TRAGEDIES

TROILUS AND CRESSIDA
(The Old Vic)

MR. PETRIE'S THERSITES

HAZLITT dealt finally with *Troilus and Cressida* when he said that it rambles on just as it happens, but overtakes, with some indifferent matter, a prodigious number of fine things in its way. It is sprinkled with tremendous passages, undream'd felicities, and those odds and . ends of speech which only Shakespeare could have uttered.

The lines which, on Wednesday, seemed to me to be most magnificently Shakespeare were the simple

> Farewell, revolted fair! and, Diomed,
> Stand fast, and wear a castle on thy head!

harking back, as they did, to Troilus's earlier boast:

> Were it a casque composed by Vulcan's skill,
> My sword should bite it: not the dreadful spout
> Which shipmen do the hurricano call,
> Constringed in mass by the almighty sun
> Shall dizzy with more clamour Neptune's ear
> In his descent, than shall my prompted sword
> Falling on Diomed.

This is Shakespeare talking through the very tallest and glossiest of his hats. 'The parrot will not do more for an almond than he for a commodious drab,' is the philosopher at his least gentle; whilst the poet is his immortal self in the reproach to Achilles:

> Sweet, rouse yourself, and the weak wanton Cupid
> Shall from your neck unloose his amorous fold,
> And, like a dewdrop from the lion's mane.
> Be shook to air.

158

Be sure the last four words came from no mind but Shakespeare's.

As a play there is not much to interest a modern audience. There are too many of those tedious captains, drinking delight of something less fierce than battle with their peers, 'far on the ringing plains of windy Troy'. You would have said the floor of some antique Senate House. One guesses that these old bores were made bearable by being cast after models well known to an Elizabethan audience and lost to us. As it was, their interminable councils were whiled away by comparing the make-up of Mr. Reyner Barton's Ulysses with Shakespeare himself, of Mr. Ernest Meads's Agamemnon with our old friend Athos, whose Dumasian respectability was admirably recaptured, of Mr. Wilfrid Walter's Achilles with John Philip Kemble posing for Sir Thomas Lawrence.

One wonders exactly what it was which so fascinated Shakespeare in this old story, to which he is always referring. Every schoolboy knows the kind of night it was when Troilus 'sighed his soul toward the Grecian tents where Cressid lay'. Either I dream, or the lady crops up in *Love's Labour's Lost*, and half a dozen other plays. Is it possible that Miss Florence Saunders was a shade less than magical? But then Cressida is an impossible part, and requires a personality to launch whole navies and burn the topless towers of a hundred cities. ('Why "topless"?' we can imagine Julia Mills entering in her diary.) Mr. Ion Swinley was in good vein as Troilus. He was giddy, according to text, and expectation whirled him round. Perhaps we have no other actor to-day who can enter and quit the scene so well. This Troilus, leaving the stage on that castellated admonition to Diomed, bids him stand fast with the entire line of his body — shoulder, hip, and heel. This is acting. Yet Troilus might conceivably have been better. This lover did not bring out of his instrument, passion, all the tones which Bernhardt drew when, at sixty years of age, she portrayed an amorous stripling. That was not to be expected; genius is not born every day. All the more reason why, when the miracle happens, we should be quick to note it.

Mr. Hay Petrie is a great comic genius — the finest Shakespearean 'low comedian' I have ever seen. The flame which is in him is kin to that which illuminated Bernhardt, Irving, and Dan Leno. Only, in tragedy, the flame demands an altar before it will descend, and insists that the chosen become celebrants. It plays in kindlier fashion round the heads of clowns, leaving them, as you might say, a trifle 'touched'. Mr. Petrie's acting has the quality of a message of which he is the inconscient mouthpiece. Thus the wisdom proceeding out of the mouths of guileless fools; so the malignancy of those evilly possessed as Thersites. That the actor has made his calculations to a hairbreadth is no affair of the audience. Let them listen to this misshapen dwarf echoing the extreme of Lear's distemper. Let them watch him hitch the world's evil to the crook of a twisted forefinger. Let them mark him lurking in the shade, hardly perceived, yet dominating the entire stage.

The Contemporary Theatre, 1923: November 11, 1923

TROILUS AND CRESSIDA
(Westminster)

MR. MACOWAN'S PRODUCTION

THE managements at the Drury Lane and Westminster Theatres seem to me to be faced with the same difficulty, though with an important difference. Drury Lane's difficulty is to persuade people to come to see a popular play; that of the Westminster is to induce them to see an unpopular play. Then why in Heaven's name does the Westminster make it more difficult by calling itself the London Mask Theatre? Call a theatre a theatre, a play a play, a management a management, and the average man will be, in the vulgar phrase, all for it. He will at least go with an open mind. But to tie round your venture's neck a label like 'Mask' or 'Cothurnus' or any other highbrow appellation is like presenting a nervous, untrained horse with the stuffed dummy of a police-man. The horse shies, I shy, and the public shies. And this may be very unfair to the venture. Now let's change the subject.

Is it fair or unfair to this difficult play to present it in modern dress? Mr. Macowan, the producer, tells us in a prefatory note on the programme that much of what Shakespeare wanted to say can only be seen clearly by relating it to contemporary experience. Very much, I suppose, as the boys of Dotheboys' Hall could only get a clear vision of spelling by relating it to practical experience, cleaning windows and the like! What Mr. Macowan is really trying to say, though he does not quite dare, is that he believes the only way of getting people to see a piece they are not inclined to is by giving them something else of the same name that they have more mind to. The matter of this new-fangled dressing is really very simple. The Elizabethan playgoer, attending an Elizabethan play, heard language that his ears were attuned to, while looking at costumes to which his eyes were accustomed. There was no discrepancy. I suggest that two minutes after the performance had begun the Elizabethan playgoer entirely forgot all about costume, and had his whole attention centred on what the actors were saying. Now dress up a Shakespeare play in to-day's costume, and what happens? First, there is a colossal discrepancy between dress and speech. Second, you never stop thinking about the costumes, with the result that you have less attention to spare for what is being talked about. At this point of the argument the reader will want to know why I should object to Mr. Macowan's discrepancy when I don't object to M. Giraudoux's. In the case of *Amphityron 38* we heard new speech wedded to old costume, which is the opposite of old speech and new costume. But the point in M. Giraudoux's case was that the mythological costumes were more or less what one expected mythological people to be wearing. Wherefore, having spent two minutes in appraising the costumes, one thought no more about them. Wherefore discrepancy vanished. But it doesn't vanish at the Westminster. I defy anybody not to go on being intrigued by the costumes.

Then wasn't the room placed by Pandarus at the disposal of the lovers exactly like your shop-window advertising a bedroom-suite for forty shillings down and the balance spread over forty years? Wasn't Pandarus exactly like the regretted Mr. Dulcimer? Wasn't his bringing of the morning tea exactly like a Shakespearean skit in a revue by Mr. Farjeon? Wouldn't the song he sang at the piano admirably suit Mr. Rex Evans? How did the soldiers of old tell the rank of their officers, since they didn't seem to be wearing badges? What were the wars, prior to the Trojan war, in which they won so many medals? How could any horse drag Hector's body through that field of barbed wire? Didn't Thersites' deplorable suit and fag never out of his mouth exactly suggest a Hyde Park orator in one of Mr. Sean O'Casey's essays in London sociology? Was not Ulysses' 'since things in motion sooner catch the eye than what not stirs' the forerunner of the winking sky-sign?

Yes, there were a lot of things in Mr. Macowan's production to attract and hold the attention. But so far as I was concerned — and I cannot speak for anybody else — they attracted and held the attention *away* from Shakespeare's tragedy. Of course, there are things in this play that no monkeying with the manner of its presentation can spoil. Every line spoken by Mr. Speaight's Ulysses was the purest gold; every word spoken by Mr. Stephen Murray's Thersites was the shrillest vinegar. Helen, as Mr. Bergel has beautifully pointed out, was any film star. About Miss Ruth Lodge's Cressida one feels inclined to repeat the late Grant Allen's remark about Hedda Gabler — that he took her in to dinner every night! That Cassandra was just a bore in black velvet was not Miss Rosanna Seaborn's fault; she is a bore anyhow. Troilus is inclined to take on wordiness unless there is a Swinley to speak the verse. Mr. Robert Harris tried nobly, but it wants more than noble effort to put up with Troilus's interminable maundering. Men were let down by witchery long before this young Trojan, and have not made so much fuss about it. Was Hector quite so lackadaisical a youth as Mr. Colin Keith-Johnston made him? And could anybody have played Pandarus better than Mr. Max Adrian?

This array of questions shows that the evening was not beggarly, though one didn't feel it had enough to do with Shakespeare to provoke one to a discussion of the play. At least I am not so provoked. I was too much entertained by the modern dressing to think about anything else. And despised myself for being so entertained.

September 21, 1938

TIMON OF ATHENS
(Westminster)

MR. MILTON

'Ah ça!' said Madame Perrichon, 'est-ce que vous allez continuer comme ça?' This was at least one playgoer's unspoken thought during Acts IV and V of this tragedy in which Shakespeare rises to a height unattained before or since in the art of saying the same thing over and over again. It is customary to compare this play with *Lear*, and to attribute the greater effect of the latter to the spectator's greater cause for sympathy. Lear — the argument runs — was a great baby, but then the fault was his second childhood's. He threw away his kingdom, but at least he parcelled it out among his nearest and presumably dearest. And we are told that because there is something to be said for Lear and nothing at all for Timon, the failure of the Athenian piece is due to our greater impatience with its hero. To which I reply: 'Garn!'

Let us consider the two plays apart from the question of sympathy with their leading characters. I imagine that what strikes us in any such comparison is the richness of invention in the one play and the poverty in the other. In *Lear* the mind is continually embarrassed with choice of riches — the devotion of the Fool, Kent's loyalty, Edgar's enveloping sympathy, all that business of Gloster, the intricate sub-plot of Edmund, the fact that the vipers stinging the old man's bosom are his proper issue, the reconciliation with Cordelia. So tumbled and pell-mell are the *matters for interest* that

163

merely in enumerating them you are forced to jumble the planes, since in the foregoing there are at least three — the plane of incident or what will happen next, the blood-thicker-than-water plane, and the plane of sheer sublimity which *Timon* nowhere reaches. On the last I place the fact that the hurt received by Lear is so great that he does not recover though cherished by at least three faithful souls. A man left to himself and going mad is not in the same case with the man losing his reason in the midst of friends; Timon solus in his cave can never rise to the height of Lear on his heath, alone and yet not alone. Grant, for argument's sake, that Timon's curses on humanity are the equivalent of Lear's. It may well be that his speech beginning: 'O blessed breeding sun' — or that other beginning: 'Common mother, thou — ' or any one of them, since they are all the same, is up to the level of Lear's 'Defy lechery' speech. Now let us do a little sum. Take the 'lechery' speech from *Lear* and what remains? Answer: The whole of the finest tragedy in the world less one speech. Take away Timon's tirades, which are all one tirade, and what remains? The answer is that nothing remains except the bright-armoured orations of that toy soldier, Alcibiades. No, I have not forgotten the churlish Apemantus. The point is that he spills himself and all he stands for at his first utterance and is of no further interest. And if the reader desires a simpler test still I will challenge him to lean back in his chair, close his eyes, think hard, and recall the name of any other character in this play.

To be brutal, the reason nobody admires *Timon* is that there is not enough in it to admire. Actually the play ends with Timon's: 'Uncover, dogs, and lap!' Why does it end here? Because the play, as a play, is played out. We have seen the man whose squandermania takes the form of giving to the rich. We have seen the well-to-do respond with their famous exhibition of ingratitude. And we have seen Timon get in his slap in the face. The rest, which should be silence, is interminable talk. Indeed, so little action and so much talk remains that Shakespeare seems to have foreseen the broadcast play! You would miss nothing whatever if you listened to Acts IV and V in a darkened room, and I submit that to stay at home is not what one goes to the theatre for. Even so, the first thing in the unseen actor is a noble and re- sounding voice enabling Timon's woes to come through like the thunderings of a Wotan rather than the whinneyings of a Beck- messer. On the stage the physical counterpart is necessary. This brings up my old unending war with the intellectuals, who will have it that subtlety of interpretation can blind the spectator to, or make up to him for, physical deficiency. I deny this. I deny that you can have a chubby Hamlet, a plain Romeo, an insigni- ficant Othello, a little Lear. I know all about Garrick and Kean, thank you, and patiently explain that their genius made the spectator believe that Lear was not only every inch a king but every inch of six foot as well! Irving could have conceivably looked Timon, though his asceticism would have been a stumbling- block in presenting this gormandizer — for nobody doubts that Timon ate and drank as much as any two of his guests. But Irving's voice would have let him down in the second half, and this was doubtless one of twenty good reasons for his never attempt- ing this play. 'Realms and islands were as plates dropped from his pocket,' says Cleopatra about Antony, and the point about Timon is that he must be big enough to suggest that plates dropped from his banquets as though they were islands and realms.

Now, Mr. Ernest Milton does not give this impression, his bodily aspect rather indicating that he would think a square meal grossly vulgar. This clever actor obviously knows what is in this part, though his offer to make the portion of Timon's servant equal to his fiancée's dowry has less of princely carelessness than of the meticulousness of the man who takes care to be in when the postman calls for the Christmas-box. He delivers the grace before hot water very well, after which and to the end of the scene he overmouths so much that no word can be distinguished. The second part of the play demands a great frame in ruins, and if that cannot be present then at least we must ask for a voice like the Albert Hall organ after the wrong boxer has been declared the winner. At the Westminster our ears, like our eyes, are unfilled. What signify the limbs, the thews, the stature, bulk, and big assemblance of an actor? I say that in the absence of overwhelming genius they amount to ninety per cent of one who attempts your heroic Shakespearean rôle, and that Timon must be drawn to heroic size. He has a world of grievances to support, and should be drawn to Atlas-like proportions. To be practical, the part requires the torso of a heavyweight boxer, the voice of an Ainley, the drive of a Benson at his physical fittest, and lashings of temperament. It is a part for a great actor, as great acting was understood before lesser actors began to drag brains into it. In the absence of a Phelps, this play should be an opera by Moussorgsky, with Chaliapine in the title-rôle. It is a play of hurly-burly, and hurly without burly is no good.

As Apemantus, Mr. Harcourt Williams is churlish with difficulty, and, in my view, the best performances come from Mr. Richard Fleury, who makes a distinct character out of the Painter; from Mr. Torin Thatcher, whose speech as Prisoner's Friend at the court-martial has a fine, warlike frenzy; and from that one of the Senators who stands up to Alcibiades. Mr. Nugent Monck's production is probably very satisfying to those who are up to this kind of thing. The dresses are like any haphazard section of any Three Arts Ball, Alcibiades being costumed like a Napoleonic general, and Timon's robes suggesting in the banquet scene this year's Paris model in bedgowns, and for the cave scene some négligé of yester-year. Personally, I think that a masque should be jolly and not a piece of stylized junk hight 'Baroque' or 'Early Perpendicular'. And last, let me confess that I am once again defeated by that music which insists on mirroring the spirit of a play. Timon bids the sun 'draw from the earth rotten humidity', and Mr. Benjamin Britten bids a concatenation of bassoon, oboe, clarinet, and something that sounds like the tongs and the bones echo this feat. A tiny orchestra of ladies accomplishes this *con morbidezza*, which presumably is what Mr. Britten desires.

More First Nights: November 19, 1935

CORIOLANUS

CORIOLANUS
(The Old Vic)

MR. OLIVIER

WHAT is all this about *Coriolanus* having no poetry? Well, there
was once a man who was prosecuted because his dog had bitten a
tramp. His defence was that the dog had not bitten the tramp.
Alternatively, that it wasn't his dog. If I were defending this play
for its alleged lack of poetry I should plead that it is full of poetry,
and, alternatively, that it doesn't need any; I think I should be
defeated on the first head; I know I should win on the second. But
why this absolute solicitude for poetry whatever the subject, this
Musset-like demand — 'Poète, prends ton luth' — to stand and
deliver blank verse? Ask some Trojan, tromboning it in Berlioz,
why he doesn't make his instrument sigh. This drama is a concerto
for the trombone; those who can hear nothing but the flute must
seek another play. The best defence is Hazlitt's: 'The cause of the
people is indeed but little calculated as a subject for poetry; it
admits of rhetoric, which goes into argument and explanation, but
it presents no immediate or distinct images to the mind, "no
jutting frieze, buttress, or coign of vantage" for poetry "to make
its pendent bed and procreant cradle in".' In other words, Shake-
peare's play of *Coriolanus* is full of such magnificent rhetoric that
you can almost plead that the tramp enjoyed being bitten! Anyhow, the title-rôle is something for an actor to get his teeth into.

Then how about the suggestion that the whole thing is a
perfunctory job done by Shakespeare to order? We are always
being told how Haydn was commanded to produce a quartet because the Elector of Umlaut was coming to dinner, and how Mozart
was ordered to prepare a serenade to please the Landgrave of
Dankeschön. To the musically uninstructed, quartet and serenade
now sound like pure genius, as against the superior view that
they are merely the common form of the time, with certain

167

idiosyncratic pribbles and prabbles which are the composers' finger-prints. Similarly, I will maintain that *Coriolanus* is full of Shakespeare's finger-prints, provided you have the ear to hear them. Vocally Mr. Olivier's performance is magnificent; his voice is gaining depth and resonance, and his range of tone is now extraordinary. Physically the performance is admirable, containing one startling leap and a superb fall at the end. If one has any reservations at all it is to suggest that this steadily improving actor should abandon that make-up like a Javanese mask and trust more to his own features. At present his face is not so much made-up as buried beneath loam and plaster. I think, too, that he must resolve to discard that clowning which he probably adjudges to be mordancy. There is not much of it in the present performance, but what there is is wholly bad. For where it is used it turns into a naughty boy a figure whose dignity should be pauseless. It is not right that Coriolanus, whose whole point is his refusal to tickle the mob, should play even to the Old Vic's gallery. These things being said, I regard this performance as Mr. Olivier's best to date, for it has a pathos we have not before observed. The playing in the great scene with mother, wife, and son has great tenderness. The famous speech, 'I banish you!' is delivered not in the Kean manner of 'ungovernable passion', but with Phelps's 'cold sublimity of disdain.' The end is the grand organ of acting, with all the stops out. It brings the house to its feet cheering, and yet those pajocks, the high-brow critics, must hurl at the playwright Horatio's 'You might have rhymed!'

Dame Sybil Thorndike discovers in Volumnia's early scenes a genial humour which would have made Geneviève Ward relegate this acting to something less than the top drawer. But mark this actress's face when her son comes back from the wars, and note how all the rest of her playing has the full authentic sweep. I doubt whether the Old Vic has ever had a more valuable secondary actor than Mr. Cecil Trouncer, whose Menenius is a beautiful piece of oddity, warm and shrewd, testy and true to life. His baiting of the Tribunes is wholly delicious. Mr. Casson's production strictly denies that Rome at any time looked like the pictures

of Alma-Tadema. The first act is even grubby. But there is fine
lighting throughout, and when necessary a fine darkness, as that
in which the red cloak of Coriolanus glows like sullen fire. Yes, this
is good Shakespearean producing, even if it does suggest that
Rome was built in a day!

The Amazing Theatre: April 18, 1938

JULIUS CAESAR
(The Old Vic)

MR. SWINLEY'S ANTONY

WHAT does the average man know about Shakespeare's Julius
Caesar? He imagines him crossing Rubicons and Alps, burning
boats, cutting Gordian knots, spouting that he came, saw, and
overcame. He knows that he went to war with Gaul and wrote
about it for the lower forms of schools. He knows that he was
murdered by Brutus and Cassius, because as Emperor and
Dictator he was getting too big for his boots. (Mr. Shaw would
have said that he was getting too big for their boots!) He knows
that Mark Antony said to Caesar's dead body:

> Thou art the ruins of the noblest man
> That ever lived in the tide of times.

But that is all he knows. Now compare his knowledge after he has
seen or read Mr. Shaw's *Caesar and Cleopatra* and has been sent by
him to Mommsen, the historian. Caesar makes an admirable hero
for our first writer of talkies because he is so thoroughly Shavian.
Caesar was, like Mr. Shaw, a thorough realist and man of sense,
his every action pervaded by the quality of cool, calculating
sobriety. Caesar had a marvellous serenity throughout good fortune and bad. He admitted of no control by favourite or wife,
mistress or friend. He had military genius of exactly the same kind
which Napoleon was later to possess, the power to achieve victory

not by the size of his army but by the quickness of its movement, not in long preparation but in rapid action even with inadequate means. Yet, though he was a great general, a great orator, and a great man of letters, he used each function only so far as it served its part in the character of a great statesman. Thus he exhibited more self-control than Napoleon. Napoleon turned back at Moscow because he had to; Caesar turned back on the Thames and on the Rhine because his mind was not affected by dreams of world-glory and because he saw that Rome would not be better off if he, Caesar, went further on.

Caesar was an Emperor, but he never played the tyrant. He neither hoped too much, nor, when things were going wrong, was he filled with inordinate despair. He was, says Mommsen, the entire and perfect man, and I would like to suggest that he was a Moderate of the most violent description. He knew all about wine, but was content with barley water. His head was full of the most glorious ideas, but he had a proper vanity and covered its baldness with a laurel wreath! If Caesar had a fault it was that he was not human but inhuman, because there is always something inhuman about perfection. He pardoned his enemies not out of mercy but out of contempt. When after a victory papers were seized which would have given him the names of all who conspired against him, he destroyed them without reading them, saying that it was unnecessary to know who had been his foes since in the hour of victory they would all become his friends. And Mommsen records that 'Although a gentleman, a man of genius, and a monarch, he still had a heart'.

We have, then, four Caesars — Shakespeare's, Mommsen's, Mr. Shaw's, and the actual Caesar. Reams have been written, and doubtless remain to write, as to why Shakespeare's great man is the least great of the four. Sir Arthur Quiller-Couch has said that it never does to neglect Johnson, and I shall say that it never does to neglect Mr. Granville-Barker. There is a canting kind of modern criticism which makes a virtue of necessity by pretending that a thing poorly done is really a kind of well-doing. With reference to the canting suggestion that Shakespeare's belittle-

ment of Caesar is intentional, indicating that towards the end
Caesar was not more than a façade, Mr. Granville-Barker simply
says, 'We need not credit Shakespeare with this theory'. The
point is that Shakespeare knew that the centre of his play was not
Caesar but Brutus, and that this being so the better he had done
by Caesar, the worse he would have done by his play: 'Certainly
to centre every effort upon presenting to us "the foremost man of
all this world" and then to remove him at the beginning of Act III
would leave a gap which no new interest could fill.' But does any
new interest fill it even with Caesar reduced to a shell? I venture
to think that in the theatre the answer is No, and that the second
half, though crammed full of philosophic interest in the study, is
one long anti-climax. It is all very well to say that Brutus, like
Romeo and the second Richard, is a stepping-stone to Hamlet;
any schoolboy will tell you that Brutus is an ass, and I agree
always on the condition that an ass can be magnanimous. He is
not 'the ass unpolicied' which Cleopatra called Octavius; he is a
donkey who thinks too much and too nobly for this world. Your
schoolboy will have greater respect for Cassius since he knows all
about bullies, and as a schoolboy I held that the quarrel between
Brutus and Cassius is pure waste of time since Antony with his
guile and Octavius with his cold determination are waiting for
them round the corner to give them the licking that will finish
them. Mr. Granville-Barker tells us that Shakespeare left the
character of Casca in two halves, which it is up to the actor to
join as best he may. I should like to go further and say that he left
his play in two halves which no company of actors, however skilful,
can succeed in putting together to our entire satisfaction.

The revival at the Old Vic is very well done, though with
certain qualifications. Mr. Cecil Trouncer's Caesar is the best I
have ever seen. Physically he has not enough nose, but he
makes up for this with a mouth as ruthless as the maw of a shark.
Mentally there is a cold splendour about the man which survives
his weakest lines and makes one believe that this is Caesar. Mr.
Ion Swinley's Antony is very fine indeed, and the presence of so
experienced a Shakespearean actor is to make all the conspirators

seem little more than boys. Cannot Miss Baylis have some auditions for the purpose of getting her young men to listen to Mr. Swinley's pronunciation of the five English vowels, *a, e, i, o, u*? Mr. Swinley's English might have been spoken at almost any time in the last three hundred years, whereas the vowel sounds of to-day's young actors were never heard before 1926, when they were begotten of Oxford and the Night Club. Mr. William Devlin's Cassius is 'werry fierce', and Mr. Leo Genn's Brutus, though noble and virile, is perhaps too much of a dear! Mr. Keneth Kent gets over the difficulty of Casca's two halves by looking, like Ethel Monticue, 'rather sneery'. But the remaining conspirators appear to be scared to death and badly in need of a couple of aspirins, while the unnamed senators are the perfect collection of fourth and fifth murderers.

October 24, 1935

JULIUS CAESAR
(Regent's Park)

MR. PORTER

WHEN I presented myself at *Julius Caesar* the other afternoon, everything was against an open-air performance of anything. Little dogs shivered, the gravel had a wintry crunch, and the amplifiers brought to the voices of the actors the melancholy of sea-lions calling across ice-floes. On the sward was the strangest assemblage of colour. Familiar, much-respected players had raddled their cheeks with burnt umber and gamboge. Antony, for some reason, was the yellowest of yellow ochre. A gentle claret, connoting moral indignation, suffused the rest of the conspiratorial countenances, with the exception of Casca, who remained an uncompromising white. Something of the same sort had happened to the ladies. While Portia was livid with anxiety, Calpurnia was puce with dismay. The mob, too, had undergone similar vagaries, the arms and legs of the soldiery running the gamut of primrose, daffodil, cowslip, jonquil, and marigold — a hint to Mr. Nichols for his next ballet of flowers! One understands the reason for this. It is the subconscious notion that anything so wildly untheatrical as acting in the open air must be the film, whereby film make-up is subconsciously adopted.

But these be toys. Underneath the make-up the performance was superb, and proved once more that great emotion operates greatly whatever the setting. Mr. Eric Portman gave Brutus just that shade of vocal fretfulness which consorts with those 'tahsome' magnanimities. As Cassius Mr. Laidman Browne interested principally because one hadn't seen him before; one felt that anything might happen, whereas generally when you know an actor by heart you realize that nothing will. It is unnecessary to say how resonantly Mr. Swinley vocalized the part of Antony; the point is how intelligently he played this august *farceur*, giving 'the choice and master spirits of this age' the precise shade of polite contempt, and so delicately that none of the dolts and gulls surrounding him could take offence. Though it is a commonplace that the good actor makes the part, one did not expect even Mr. Morland Graham to make as much of the part of Ligarius as did this admirable player. Mr. David King Wood, too, made a considerable something out of Decius Brutus, and I think it was hardly fair to Mr. Jack Carlton's rightly vaulting ambition that the programme should call the character he played Metellus *Climber*.

Who started the fashion of saying that Caesar is a bad part? I have always suspected Mr. Shaw. And I have the further and even stronger suspicion that if Mr. Shaw had written about Caesar at this particular juncture he would have made him talk for five acts without ever getting near his assassination. It is all a matter of title, which in the case I am supposing would, of course, have been *Pompey's Statua*. Which, equally of course, would for five acts have run pure Shaw! Shakespeare's real title was *Brutus and Cassius*, and with this in mind he gives us a magnificent Caesar, crowding a thumb-nail sketch with as much as a thumb-nail may reasonably be expected to hold. Mr. Neil Porter, patrician as a ramrod, used his magnificent nose to bridge the distance between modern and Roman times. A colleague has said that this actor discovers in Caesar an Aristotelian magnanimity that is often missed; I agree, except that most often it is the critics who miss it. Anyhow this performance was a superb one. 'The deadest deaths are the best,' says Montaigne, and Mr. Porter at the end was deader than one had thought feasible. He could not be seen to breathe, and though one realizes the mechanics of this, due meed of praise should be given to the inventor.

Let not Mr. Carroll wonder whether Calpurnia and Portia are parts unworthy of Mesdames Fay Compton and Phyllis Neilson-Terry. It was exactly the use of two such distinguished actresses which kept the tragedy in Rome. Normally these two small parts are entrusted to too small-part ladies, whereby the tragedy immediately forsakes Tiber and helter-skelters back to Thames. Or Thames Ditton, which is worse.

July 6, 1937

ANTONY AND CLEOPATRA
(The Old Vic)

MR. HOLLOWAY AND MISS EVANS

So little was cut out of this piece that one almost fears the management of the Old Vic has succumbed to the fetish of performing these plays as they were written. One or two small scenes might certainly have gone, and so long an interval between the dying of the two protagonists is certain to make for anti-climax. One feels that just as the same grave was made to clip the pair, so their deaths should be close in time. Perhaps this is to have too much respect for Cleopatra: and there may be irony in the scene in which she has that vulgar row with her treasurer in the presence of Caesar. But the end of a tragedy is no place for irony which

delays the action, and a capital motto for all Shakespearean producers is Cleopatra's own, 'resolution and the briefest end'.

The best Cleopatra I ever saw was Janet Achurch, who was
equally overpowering whether what she did was immensely right
or immensely wrong. Mr. Shaw put it on record that everything
that Janet did as Cleopatra was mistaken, but the fact remains
that her performance was unforgettable. There was majesty and
there was physical passion; there were looks which might have
unpeopled a city, and tones which might have quelled provinces.
Miss Edith Evans administers none of these shocks. 'Which is the
Queen of Egypt?' asks Caesar, on entering the Monument, and,
indeed, the jade is never very easily distinguished from her
attendants. Miss Evans appears to have purposely stressed the
childish element in Cleopatra; at times even she seemed to be
imitating Miss Ffrangcon-Davies's spoilt child of the other play.
I take it that any actress who is to play Cleopatra should show us
the most primitive of emotions worked up to its last subtlety of
acquired finesse. 'Her genius', wrote a great critic of Réjane, 'was
sex bejewelled with every invention of cunning and charm that in
civilized history — perhaps long before — the instinct has forged
for its armoury; so that you felt she was the last, up-to-date, of
the line of Helen and Sappho and Queen Cleopatra and Mary
Stuart, and all the women famous in history for womanishness.
The craft which spoke in her voice and her eyes was the sum and
perfection of what, in all but the most noble ages, most men have
wished women to have instead of high intellect.' But that is very
exactly not Miss Evans's *forte*. She has not enough passion and
vulgarity for Cleopatra, or you may say that she has too much
fastidiousness. This was a Queen of Egypt who had read Paul
Bourget. Brilliant comédienne though Miss Evans is, she has not
a great deal of pathos, and it was Antony in his scene with Eros
and not Cleopatra in her last scene with her dying lover, who
drew the tears of the house. I need not say that what brains and
skill could do was achieved. But the actress was simply not suited.

Mr. Baliol Holloway played Antony as well, one thinks, as that
difficult part could be played. He looked very noble and like a

man who has worn well, and perhaps — though I am not quite sure — beneath his charm of manner he was sufficiently vacillating and dissolute. The actor gave the poetry of his lines its value, and was very moving in places, though he did not get the full pathos out of 'Bring to me all my sad captains', and had not sufficient power, pace, and excitement for the passage about the hill of Basan. Antony here out-roared the horned herd too much like a bull who is not sure of his next line. But the performance was very good on the whole, as is everything which this clever actor attempts. Mr. Neil Porter made a very effective Enobarbus, and succeeded in delivering the most threadbare tag in Shakespeare as though it were newly minted in his mind. Mr. Duncan Yarrow gave Caesar dignity; and it is well that he did for this character possesses no other sort of interest. Pompey struck me as being capable, when in mufti, of the indiscretion known as Oxford bags. All the other young men did fairly well, and indeed to give identity to these Shakespearean odds and ends is a difficult task.

I am afraid I thought that the piece was rather meagrely put on. If ever a Shakespearean play calls for music, processions, and Tadema-like excesses in bathroom marble, *Antony and Cleopatra* is that play. Whereas, so far as I could see, Alexandria and Rome only possessed two pieces of furniture between them, and the population of these cities was about three to the square mile. Owing to the peculiarly cold quality of the lighting the Egyptian temperature seemed to be a good ten degrees below freezing point. Also, I did definitely object to Cleopatra's refusal to die sitting bolt upright on a throne. This is obviously the proper thing to do. Any objection that the Monument did not contain a throne would be frivolous; neither, probably, did it contain Cleopatra's robe and crown. And I submit that she would certainly not have bothered to put these on if she was going to curl up and die on the sofa like a naughty consumptive in the reign of Dumas *fils*.

The Contemporary Theatre, 1925: November 30, 1925

ANTONY AND CLEOPATRA
(The Old Vic)

MR. WILFRED LAWSON AND MISS NEWCOMBE

To strike twelve at once is no mean feat for an actor; it is a still greater feat for a whole company. This is what any company must do which tackles this great play. Two things are essential for this kind of success. The first is that the actor shall at once throw the spectator back into the time of which Shakespeare was writing; this is largely a matter of appearance. The second is that he shall act Shakespeare like a Shakespearean actor, which is largely a matter of voice. In my view all but three of the company fail, for reasons to be particularized presently. The three successes are Mr. Abraham Sofaer's Messenger, who looks exactly right and with each and every one of his small scraps of verse fills the theatre with Shakespearean music. The second success is Mr. Maurice Evans's Octavius, though I think a chillier note should be struck by this master of chicane. The third is Mr. David Horne's Enobarbus, though he imperils the time-factor by looking a little too like the late Lord Salisbury. When these three actors are about we have the fleeting sensation that this is Shakespeare's tragedy of *Antony and Cleopatra*. No other play by this or any other dramatist plunges so directly into the middle of things. The opening sentence: 'Nay, but this dotage of our general's O'erflows the measure' shows the piece well on its way. The next eight lines promise everything that we are to see. Incidentally, I wish some better instructed Shakespearean commentator would tell me whether the coincidences in which this play is peculiarly rich really are coincidences or intentional echoes and recapitulations. In the first speech Philo talks of his captain's heart having in the scuffles of great fights burst the buckles on his breast, and in his last scuffle with fortune Antony bids his heart be stronger than its continent and crack its frail case. Was it conscious art or something in Shakespeare's physiology which made him subconsciously repeat the pattern? Perhaps we may say of the poet what Antony himself says of the Soothsayer: 'Be it art or hap, he has spoken true.' However this may be, Philo's first speech presents us with the whole of this tragedy of looking backward.

'Money lost, little lost; honour lost, much lost; pluck lost, all lost.' Mr. Granville-Barker says in his admirable Preface to this play: 'Losers ought not to whine. Antony stays a soldier and a sportsman — and a gentleman, by his lights — to the end.' But a gentleman in ruins, and with a partiality for harping on earlier pomp and circumstance. Over and over again Antony insists upon what a lad he has been, and there is such magic in the poetry of his regret that it is as though Autumn should call attention to the glory of its former Summer. Cleopatra makes tremendous catalogue of all that Antony was; and the freed slave's 'noble countenance Wherein the worship of the whole world lies' is neither compliment nor lip-service. These things are the mind's-eye portrait of all those vestiges and remnants which the actor must present to the spectator's physical eye and ear. Here, the spectator must say to himself, of his own accord and without prompting, are the ruins of the world's arch-romantic, the master of largesse and unparalleled spendthrift. Though when the play opens Antony may be at the end of his tether, the actor's concern is not with this, but with the royally ranging fellow he has been before his tether runs out. Now I have great respect, and have often expressed that respect, for Mr. Wilfrid Lawson as a character actor. But this must not debar me from saying that Antony is a rôle which, though Mr. Lawson may conceive it perfectly, he can neither look nor voice. His first appearance with a shock of hair kept tidy by a gold band suggests a leading member of Peter Quince's troupe, and his voice is quite staggeringly unfitted for heroic verse. 'Grates me: the sum!' says Antony to the messenger from Rome. Alas, it is not the news that grates Antony so much as Antony's voice which grates us! In addition, the articulation is so indistinct that in many places the meaning is quite incomprehensible. Thus Antony nowhere justifies all that the other characters say about him, or our own preconceived view.

ANTONY AND CLEOPATRA

Miss Mary Newcombe's Cleopatra is a very good performance —
of some other character. Of, say, a brilliantly clever, highly complex, neurotic lady of our own times. Perhaps not quite our own
times, for Miss Newcombe has thought back, though not far
enough back; not further than Portia or Beatrice. Her dresses,
of which the principal feature is a fringed tippet, could be worn
at any of to-day's dinner-parties without exciting comment. On
the other hand, her verse-speaking is so far on the right lines that
it has obviously to do with verse, though I think she should mouth
it more, and in the line: 'rather make My country's high pyramides my gibbet', give the word 'pyramides' its four syllables.
Let me say that within the actress's conception her playing is
always subtle and at the end moving. Mr. Shaw said, apropos of
the Manchester production of 1897, that if managers will only
take care of the minor actors the leading ones will take care of
themselves. Either insufficient care or something else has gone
wrong with the casting of Charmian and Iras. Charmian is acted
as though she were a replica of the parts played by Miss Helen
Spencer in modern comedy, and Iras is just a round-faced little
Miss from Kensington Gore. Now, if the atmosphere of the East
is to be brought into this play, these are the two characters to do
it, since it then gives Cleopatra time to get on with the business of
inveigling and betraying Antony. Iras is mute almost throughout,
but when she speaks it is immensely to the point, and she has two
extraordinarily lovely lines:

> Finish, good lady; the bright day is done,
> And we are for the dark.

In Manchester they made Iras into a low-browed, walnut-stained
Egyptian, who throughout lay on her stomach and gazed at
Cleopatra in a mood half-way between breathless adoration and
sphinx-like criticism. She knew all that was going on, and told
Cleopatra when it was time to throw in her hand. Whereas the
present Iras is dumbly inefficient, and Charmian gabbles to no
purpose.

Despite the foregoing, the fact remains that Shakespeare's play

179

has come between me and every other I have seen this week. The production by Mr. Henry Cass is for the most part excellent, though I dislike the Chorus recruited from the canvases of Marcus Stone. Mr. Menges' music is colourful and happily remote from that facile Egyptologist, Luigini, though near the end there is a horrid concession to what is left of Victorian taste in the form of a voluntary which might have been ladled out by the lamented Liddle. If there is need for a concession to the senses, why not incense?

More First Nights: September 17, 1934

ANTONY AND CLEOPATRA
(New)

MR. WOLFIT AND MADAME LEONTOVICH

THE tail-end of your theatre programme is invariably composed of what Cleopatra would call 'lady trifles' and 'immoment toys'. Thus you will read 'Shoes by Thingummy' and 'Stockings by Thingumbob'. One turned to the New Theatre programme the other evening to see whether among the informative rag, tag, and bobtail, one would find: 'Words by Shakespeare'. One did not. The time-honoured phrase was in its usual place under the title of the play. But alas! the information turned out to be, in part and in the most important part, false. Cleopatra's words may have been Shakespeare's; they were spoken in the accent of Count Smorltork. But of this more later. Beneath the words 'by William Shakespeare' one read in thicker and blacker type: 'The Production is devised and directed and the Scenery and Costumes designed by Komisarjevsky.' But not a word about the disgraceful messing-up of one of the grandest of Shakespeare's openings. It may be useful to recall how this goes. The curtain rises, and to the unimportant Philo is given one of the most tremendous sentences in the whole of Shakespeare:

Nay, but this dotage of our general's
O'erflows the measure: those his goodly eyes,
That o'er the files and musters of the war
Have glow'd like plated Mars, now bend, now turn
The office and devotion of their view
Upon a tawny front: his captain's heart,
Which in the scuffles of great fights hath burst
The buckles on his breast, reneges all temper,
And is become the bellows and the fan
To cool a gipsy's lust.

There in ten lines is the whole of Antony. Next Philo bids us mark the entrance of the lovers, but still harping on Antony, and with Cleopatra dismissed in the single word 'strumpet'. 'Behold and see,' he tells Demetrius. Then follow the lovers' exchanges, beginning with Cleopatra's: 'If it be love indeed . . .' An attendant enters whom Antony will not hear. Let Rome in Tiber melt and the wide arch of the ranged empire fall sooner than that he shall be bothered with Caesar's foolish politics. 'Speak not to us,' he says to the messenger, and leads his queen away.

All this is Shakespeare's 'wide arch', the opening through which he desired that we should enter his play. Mr. Komisarjevsky will have none of it. He does not cut the scene, which would be bad enough. He postpones it, which is worse, and in favour of a tweeting soothsayer and a pair of gossipy girls. I do not think that foreign producers, however distinguished, should permit themselves to take such liberties. For this is a liberty which matters. Shakespeare meant to open his play grandly; this opening niggles. Like all other producers of this play, Mr. Komisarjevsky has been faced with the old difficulty about the multiplicity of scenes. He gets over this by pretending that no difficulty occurs. He has two formalized settings, one before the interval and one after. It is all exceedingly simple. If a Roman appears, then the place is Rome; if an Egyptian, then Egypt. This is fairly easy for the producer. But just as it is always said that easy writing makes hard reading, so easy producing means hard playgoing. Simplification has other dangers, one of which is that the spectator, having been induced into the mood of simplicity, may decline to get out of it. Consider the famous scene whose stage-directions are 'Enter, below, Antony, borne by the Guard' and 'They heave Antony aloft to Cleopatra'. Even if these directions are not Shakespeare's, the text clearly indicates that Antony is to be drawn up into the monument, and, I suggest, even on the Elizabethan stage in view of the Elizabethan audience. Mr. Komisarjesvky has Antony carried round to the rear so that nothing is seen save the backs of the hauling women, while Antony's broken: 'I am dying, Egypt, dying!' has to be shouted at the top of his lungs by an actor in obviously excellent vocal condition. Here the playgoer's induced simplicity comes in. Why, he asks, go to all that trouble when from the spot where Antony has fallen to the top of the monument there is a perfectly good staircase of six steps only? I am afraid this production is one of those cases in which what is wanted is a little less imagination and a few more scene-shifters.

I cannot hope to emulate the phonetic daring of one of my colleagues. But I confess to rubbing my ears on hearing Cleopatra say to Antony:

> Wen you suet staying,
> Den was de time for Wurst.

What had English tallow and German sausage to do with this Egyptian passion? It needed genuine effort to recall that what Shakespeare had written was:

> When you sued staying,
> Then was the time for words.

And so Mme. Leontovich continued throughout the entire play. Let me not be misunderstood. If except for the matter of accent this were a great Cleopatra, then one would make every effort to forgive the Russian accent just as one forgave Modjeska's Juliet her Polish intonations. But Mme. Leontovich is never Shakespeare's Cleopatra, though she might make a very good shot at Mr. Shaw's. We know our Russian visitor to be an extremely accomplished comédienne; the difficulty about Shakespeare's baggage is that she is a part for a great tragic actress who has a comédienne up her sleeve. And, alas, I do not think that Mme. Leontovich, born comédienne though she is, has any of the physical dispositions necessary for a great tragic actress. She has an eager, inquisitive little face resembling that of Spinelly. She has hardly any voice, and what she has is pitched too high, with the result that what ought to be poignancy is merely a squeak. Since we could hardly bear to listen to this Cleopatra we were forced to fill up occupation with our eyes, and therefore could not help noticing how little of majesty or queenliness there was in the little figure skipping about the stage. Incredible though it sounds, Cleopatra attended the sea-fight in a costume consisting of a Roman helmet, a golden breastplate, and a slashed skirt of forget-me-not blue satin, the whole irresistibly reminiscent of Miss Renee Houston in some naval-cum-military skit. But then absurdity was never far away from this Cleopatra's frocks, whose trains covered the floor like a peacock's, but afforded no protection elsewhere.

Of the essential Antony, Mr. Donald Wolfit, alas, gave little! At the beginning of the play he glowed like plated Mars, and he went on glowing to the end. But the whole point of the man is that he has ceased to glow and is now only the ruins of what has once been great. Antony is a lean wolf, bloated, out of training, with a middle-aged spread; a lean Wolfit, who is chubbier than he was, is not the same thing. The actor did his best, though his tragic expression was rather like that of the desperate leader in a tug-of-war whose team had given ground at the word 'go'. I suspect him, unfortunately, of not having much natural pathos of the kind possessed by Mr. James Craven in the small rôle of Eros. On the other hand, Mr. Wolfit may very well take up the challenge and ask what pathos I expected from an Antony whose pathetic passages had been cut. If Mr. Komisarjevsky does not know, he must be told that 'Call to me all my sad captains' and 'To-night I'll force the wine peep through their scars' are to the English ear and mind sacrosanct. While one is on this point of arrangement and rearrangement, what a mess was made of the 'music of hautboys as under the stage'. I recall how well this was done in the last revival at the Old Vic. It was night, and the Guard was set one at each corner of the stage. Then came the unearthly music, the First Soldier's: 'What should this mean?' and the Second Soldier answering him across the empty stage: ''Tis the god Hercules, whom Antony loved, now leaves him.' Mr. Komisarjevsky had this said at high noon by a soothsayer!

Mr. Ellis Irving preferred a forthright rendering of that polished snake, Octavius; this honest manly fellow would never have conceived the impertinent: 'Which is the Queen of Egypt?' As Menas, Mr. Lawrence Anderson elected for a gum-chewing gangster of our own day, and as Lepidus, Mr. Vernon Kelso was less anachronistically amusing. In the matter of Enobarbus I can only say that Mr. Leon Quartermaine, by turning the bluff soldier into the silky diplomat, was utterly and entirely wrong from the first syllable of the part to the last. Yet inasmuch as all the other syllables were pure and dulcet English exquisitely manipulated I forgive him; but then, I would at any time pay half-a-guinea to hear Mr. Quartermaine recite a page of Bradshaw's Railway Guide. The cleverest thing about Miss Margaret Rawlings's Charmian was that she refrained from wiping Cleopatra off the stage till after she was dead. The Queen once dispatched, the tiring-maid let us know in six lines who should have been playing what.

More First Nights: October 4, 1936

CYMBELINE

(New)

MISS THORNDIKE'S IMOGEN

IF this play be by Shakespeare and nobody else, then one imagines either that he was fulfilling a contract, or that he was

temporarily written out. Or perhaps the poet had grown contemptuous of his public, and threw them something which he
did not even take the trouble to perfect. One makes these sur-
mises with diffidence. Consider that this play was probably preceded by *The Winter's Tale* and followed by *The Tempest*, two
masterpieces which show that the four great tragedies together
with the three other plays which belong to this period, *Troilus*,
Timon, and *Measure for Measure*, had not entirely exhausted their
author's powers. Yet *Cymbeline* is strangely inferior to all these.
Is it possible that Shakespeare was, for the last time, merely
tinkering up another man's play, sewing his brilliant trimmings
on to the garment of an inferior tailor who, like his master, had
dipped for material in the common rag-bag of dramatic motive,
but pulled less magically out?

And to put together the patchwork *Cymbeline* there was need
neither of Holinshed nor of Boccaccio. A competent hack could
have done it out of the odds and ends of Shakespeare's other plays.
It is quite consonant with the theory of an 'arranger' that he
should give his résumé at least the air of a new play. What better
than a device which has always been, and always will be, to the
hand of the dramatist, though Shakespeare does not seem to have
been fond of it? Thus we get the 'wager' motive which, centuries
later, Dumas *fils* and Sydney Grundy thought such a capital
idea. Complicate this with the 'jealousy' motive, with which,
only yesterday, Mr. Matheson Lang was making carnival. (I
hasten to agree that gambling and jealousy are elemental passions.)
Add all that mechanical business from *Romeo and Juliet*, concerning
poisons which are no poisons, the changeling-cum-foundling
motive from *The Winter's Tale*, the masquerading from *As You
Like It*. Enliven with alarums and excursions, and prick out with
patriotism. And just as the Queen's boast about the 'natural
bravery of this isle', about 'Neptune's park' and all the rest of it
is inferior to John of Gaunt's 'other Eden, demi-paradise', so
Posthumus is inferior to Othello, and Iachimo is less than Iago.
Imogen, too, is a poor pastiche. She has less wit than Rosalind,
less gumption than Desdemona, less resolution than Juliet.

Would that last determined lady have prepared to follow Lucius with no more than a tear and a sigh, a beggarly two hundred prayers, and a sentimental smoothing of the earth over her dead lover?

Even when Shakespeare obviously displays his hand he shows omething less than his usual skill.

> Damn'd Pisanio
> Hath with his forged letters — damn'd Pisanio —
> From this most bravest vessel of the world
> Struck the main-top!

reads like the poet who could make Othello talk of the butt and sea-mark of his utmost sail. But what are we to think of the succeeding:

> O Posthumus! Alas,
> Where is thy head? Where's that? Ay, me! where's that?

Did, when the master was in form, such ten low words e'er creep in one dull line? Even those two lyrics lose something of exquisiteness when you hear them in their context. 'Hark, hark! the lark' should not have been sung by order of a Cloten to a disdainful lady. Even that soul-shattering line, 'To thee the reed is as the oak' loses significance when it is rehearsed over the body of one who will presently awake.

Mr. Casson's version gives the play the best of chances. He divides it into two acts, and by the use of curtains and an inner stage secures a continuity of narration and an appearance of cohesion. This no-man's-land in time and space is admirable; the costumes are of an arbitrary period, and 'Britain' is anywhere you like. Once Posthumus delivered a speech in a blue and yellow cloak against a blue curtain with admirable effect. Mr. Charles Carson was not the only actor who was indistinct; otherwise his Posthumus was a performance of admirably blended vigour and restraint. Mr. Robert Farquharson lacked only a horse for his Iachimo to look like the statue of Caligula in the entrance hall of the British Museum. The bravery of his address and bearing was that of a Florentine noble from the pages of Benvenuto Cellini. I heard one lady call this Iachimo 'rather a dear', though whether lovableness is the function of this character I beg leave to doubt. Still, I thought Mr. Farquharson gave a performance of both brains and beauty, and one almost entirely free from tricks of distortion and grimace. The long scene in the bed-chamber was very imaginatively and decoratively done. After all, one must not expect a Florentine noble to cut as stolid and unromantic a figure as a policeman or a commissionaire at a cinema; and if the actor attitudinized a little, so perhaps did the exquisites of Florence in the sixteenth century. For Iachimo is pure Renaissance even if Shakespeare makes him hob-nob with rude Britons of the time of Boadicea.

About Miss Thorndike's Imogen I am frankly in a difficulty. I have never been able to 'see' this fine and magnoperative artist in parts where a fragility of intellect must be suggested. Sybil can make a voracious meal of a Medea, mauling her like a lioness, and the spectacle is magnificent. But you cannot worry the virtue out of Imogen. Of course, her interpreter knows all there is to be known about this faint lily, and would probably lecture about her most illuminatively. But to analyse and to be are two different things, and nervous modernity is not Imogen's 'note'. Miss Thorndike gives me the impression of having swallowed the character at one gulp, and of looking round the stage for something about which to be effective. Hence those little cheerfulnesses and playfulnesses, and those stupendous exits with the left arm extended in swan-like exploration. Miss Margaret Yarde licked the Queen's platter clean, and enjoyed herself enormously. Mr. Ian Fleming and Mr. Lewis Casson were good as the Barrie-ish Britons. Mr. Willie Clarkson had a great success. His shop would seem to contain all manner of beards, save those of moderate length.

The Contemporary Theatre, 1923: September 19, 1923

TITUS ANDRONICUS
(Old Vic)

IT is the fashion to sneer at this play, and, on the whole, it is a bad fashion. *Titus Andronicus* may be a bad play for Shakespeare; it is middling and even highly creditable for anybody else. The horrors may not have the calamitous effect ascribed by Byron to Kean's acting of Sir Giles Overreach in *A New Way to Pay Old Debts*, but at least they are horrors, and not the occasion and cause of laughter as the gory wallowings of *The Jew of Malta* recently proved to be. The slaying of the young Goth is a capital spring-board for the drama to take off from. Titus, by his lack of clemency, 'asked for' all that was to come to him, to use a modern vulgarism. Mr. Wilfrid Walter, made up like an El Greco, played him very well, but without, I think, obtaining much of our sympathy. One felt that he must have been something of a bungler to fall so easy a victim to the Gipsy Queen. Mr. Ion Swinley made an eloquent and a decorative Saturninus, and was magnificent throughout the first big scene. But the character peters out, and is not a grateful one. Mr. Swinley managed to look surprisingly like old Irving in the third act of *The Bells*, and perhaps Saturninus has something of the romantic fire of Matthias in his nightshirt.

Nobody with either ear or eye for Shakespeare needs Schlegel to tell him who wrote this play. It is full of anticipations of *Lear* and *Othello*, and even, in the half-human Aaron, foreshadows Caliban. There is a little of that monster in the black, but there is also a very great deal of Iago. I would much sooner believe that Shakespeare is entirely responsible for Aaron than that he had even a little to do with Iachimo. Mr. George Hayes gave a really fine performance in this part, which he rightly imbued with some of the dæmonism of the fourteenth century *messes noires*. His power in the scene with the child was quite remarkable. The incident of the fly-killing brought Lear instantly to mind, as also did the passage about digging down to Pluto's region. Yes, there is a great deal of Shakespeare in this play, and, I should judge, hardly anything of anybody else. Mr. Hay Petrie made a great deal out of the tiny part of the Clown. Miss Florence Saunders was a lively Tamora, and Miss Jane Bacon a sympathetic Lavinia. This young woman's final dispatch can never, one thinks, be very effective. It is too much the fag end of horror. The production was excellent, and there was immense virtue in a flight of steps and some scarlet cloaks.

October 8, 1923

KING LEAR
(Phoenix Society)

MR. CARTER

WHAT are the essential qualities for an actor who shall play Lear? First, one hazards, a voice which shall not be too small for the play, like a tiny sail on a big vessel. Next, a presence which shall suggest not decrepitude, but the sense of the completeness of old age — the fulness of years, in a word. After that we must have pathos, a quality defying study, given unaccountably to one actor and withheld from another. Lastly a quality of ecstasy must be conveyed in which the soul stands beside the body, and becomes answerable to laws which it were unreasonable to enjoin upon mere clay. Records of anything like an adequate Lear are scanty. Salvini, they say, had the pathos, but I beg leave to doubt whether any Latin could give my postulated ecstasy its moral texture and English colouring. (*Lear* is as definitely English as *Le Cid* is French.) Turn this tragedy into an opera, with Cordelia for heroine and Edgardo, alias Edgar, for hero, the old man providing the heavy business as *père radoteur*, with bass rumblings by Massenet

189

or Puccini — call the thing *La Fille du Tyran*, and where is the Frenchman or Italian who would see any wrong? Irving's Lear had pathos, but only a clever simulation of power; it was useless for him to spout cataracts and hurricanoes in a voice which broke to a piping treble. In 1881 at the old Princess's Theatre Edwin Booth obtained what a critic of the period described as 'an almost unqualified success', finding shortcomings in the matter of dignity alone. Phelps, twenty years earlier, went mad too soon. Charles Kean, according to Henry Morley, treated the King of the first half of the play as a comic character. The performances of Betterton, Quin, Barry and John Kemble, who, like all the actors from 1681 to Macready in 1838, used Nahum Tate's version, are dark in the mists of time. 'Tate', says Lamb, 'has put his hook in the nostrils of this Leviathan, for Garrick and his followers to draw it about more easily.' Of Garrick's Lear we know that it shook Dr. Johnson out of his wits, which is a considerable testimonial.

Hazlitt bestirred himself even more than usual on the occasion of Kean's performance in 1820. He begins by reminding the reader how, when Garrick knelt to repeat the curse, the first row in the pit stood up in order to see him better, and the second row, unwilling to lose precious moments in remonstrating, stood up too; and so, by a tacit movement, the whole pit. John Kemble, 'that old campaigner', was next noted as having been 'very great in the curse'. Kean, Hazlitt goes on to record, thought no end of his own Lear, and said coxcombically that 'he was very much obliged to London audiences for the good opinion they had hitherto expressed of him, but that when they came to see him over the dead body of Cordelia they would have a very different notion of the matter'. To which the essayist wittily rejoins that as Kean persisted in Tate's version, London had no chance to see him 'over the body'. The greatest of English tragic actors proved, on the whole, to be disappointing. He 'chipped a bit off the character here and there'. He was too violent at first and too near mere dotage at the end. He scolded like Timon where he should have recited a Hymn to the Penates. He expressed Lear's crosses one by one, in single images of ruin, in place of a growing desolation. His face did not 'encrust and stiffen into amazement'. In one thing only had the actor been great — the attitude in which he put himself to repeat the curse. 'He threw himself on his knees; lifted up his arms like withered stumps; threw his head quite back, and in that position, as if severed from all that held him to society, breathed a heart-struck prayer, like the figure of a man obtruncated.' Probably the greatest of all Lears was that of the great German actor, Ludwig Devrient. But I must leave the past and come to the Phoenix.

It cannot be said of Mr. Hubert Carter, as of an earlier actor who essayed Lear, that 'it was not thought that he could make anything of it, and it was not, therefore, said that he did'. Great things were expected, and some of them were achieved. This actor belongs to the school of Mr. Oscar Asche, the excellencies of whose art have been compared to long driving at golf. Now the secret of long driving, Mr. Blackwell once told us, was to grip like the devil and hit like hell, and Mr. Carter, when I saw him play the lead in *Kismet* on tour, seemed to me to give Mr. Asche a good thirty yards and to be quite as straight. In the mind's eye, then, he lacked nothing which should make for a powerful and effective Lear, except, possibly, what I have called the ecstatic quality. Which just shows how wrong one can be in previsions of acting, since this was the one aspect which was presented with entire success. To begin with, Mr. Carter had not the right quality of voice. It was too light in timbre and rose to hysterical whinings and whimperings where it should have boomed and rumbled. Wind in the rigging will not do for Lear; in the big speeches you should feel that not only the actor, but you, the spectator, are supported on a sea of sound. The part is largely a solo for the voice. Then again, this Lear was too lusty. Let me admit that there is a difficulty here. What is *not* wanted is a display of senility like that of the Veteran of Waterloo; you cannot palsy your way through this storm. But there should be some evidence of four-score's weakening of mind and body, and this Lear looked not more than a well-preserved seventy, thought like sixty, and waved his arms, gat on to his knees and ambled up and down the stage like a boy of fifty. I have seen Falstaffs less jovial. All this is not to say more than that the actor was not physically suited. How about the spiritualities?

Well, the whole performance reminded me of the neat piling up of points by a boxer who lacks a punch: this little piece of irony was capitally delivered; that litre of passion was neatly decanted; the kindliness of the old man was touchingly shown in his covering of Edgar's nakedness; the decline to madness — about which Shakespeare took such extraordinary care — was conscientiously done, though in the end one was left with the feeling of an old roysterer with the wine in rather than with the wit out; the famous colloquy between Gloucester and Lear was conducted with an extreme nicety; the recognition of Cordelia had all the appurtenances of pathos; the dying was a full-lung'd affair. But we waited in vain for the onslaught on sensibility which should overthrow us quite, and as the afternoon wore on I, personally, began to find my sympathies centring in Gloucester. Perhaps Mr. Frank Cochrane acted too well here? I avow that he made Gloucester's case so pitiful that I forgot all about Lear, whose entry to his blinded subject came as a surprise. Yet that this was Lear, or the ecstatic part of him, was demonstrated by the fact that at the words 'Ha! Goneril, with a white beard!' Gloucester's viewlessness sank again properly to nothing in comparison with Lear's wide-eyed despair, which surveys the universe and knows no alleviation. If Mr. Carter failed to give the whole of this tremendous figure — though he was always interesting and even respectable — he failed in the greatest company, and perhaps for the reason which Coleridge assigned for some inadequate performance of Macready. 'He is, I fear, too improving an actor to be a man of genius. That little ill-looking vagabond, Kean, never improved in anything. In some things he could not, and in others he would not.' This last reproach cannot be levelled at Mr. Carter. He tried his utmost. If we were not in Lear's presence we were in his ante-chamber.

Mr. Frank Cellier played Kent as he plays everything else, that is with a perfection which I begin to find monotonous. He even got humour into this Enobarbus of another mould, and his closing sentences touched profound beauty. When will this actor fly a kite in Romeo or Antony, and so give me·a chance to have at him? Perfect, too, were the later scenes of Mr. Henry Oscar's Edmund; while Mr. Duncan Yarrow was excellent when he was unclothed and in his wrong mind. It is pleasant to be able to say that the Fool was just bad — pleasant, because I am always prepared to maintain Mr. Leon Quartermaine to be our best exponent of the sensitive and exquisite. Critical integrity must be preserved. The people in this play are early Britons; they are dressed and talk like Elizabethans; Mr. Quartermaine strolled in from a day of 'bus-strikes. He *meant* all right; you could see that by the way he laid his head on Lear's bosom. Mr. Quartermaine's difficulty was that, at any cost, he must not be Persian, must be Beowulf rather than Ishak. He ended by being an emphatic Briton, but not an early one; and a billycock might with propriety have surmounted his lank and natural locks. But, then, even a 'bad' performance by this actor is not without a great measure of joy, and always he dips into a natural well of poetry as lesser artists dip into Mr. Clarkson's shop for wigs.

Cordelia is a 'gumph' or, as we say in Lancashire, 'gormless', and was played as such, very prettily and appealingly, by Miss Gwen Ffrangcon-Davies. If Cordelia hadn't been a noodle — *pace* the shade of Helen Faucit and those ecstatic ladies who write whole volumes upon the psychology of Queen Gertrude and Ophelia — if Cordelia had had her wits about her there would have been no play. (Decidedly she would go well into opera with the song, 'Mon coeur se ferme aux enchères.') It is difficult for the Duchesses of Albany and Cornwall not to conjure up the Ugly Sisters of the Brothers Griffiths, but the exponents at the Phoenix surmounted the danger successfully. Miss Constance Robertson as Goneril was content to be baleful and uncomplicatedly chief villainness. Miss Stella Arbenina played Regan with great *finesse*, spoke with excellent point, and, indeed, endowed the wretch with life outside the play. This Regan, you felt, had an anterior existence, and if she had survived the poison, would have provided Mr. St. John Ervine with a prose sequel of exquisite malice — *King Lear's Daughter*. That is if Mr. Gordon Bottomley had not previously snapped her up in blank verse.

The Contemporary Theatre, 1924: April 6, 1924

KING LEAR
(The Old Vic)

MR. GIELGUD

ONE could almost imagine a young actor declining to join a Shakespearean company on learning that the season's programme must top up with this high-climbing play. No young performer would willingly hazard a hard-won reputation by asking for critical judgment in a part so unplayable that it defeats the ripest player, any more than the most hard-bitten and hard-biting critic would, in the circumstances, proceed to execution of his own free will. Yet any Shakespearean management may quite rightly hold that the lack of a sufficient actor is no reason why a repertory audience which has faithfully borne with Prospero should be deprived of that major reward which is Lear.

A common objection to presenting Lear as a doddering Father Christmas older even than Maeterlinck's Le Plus Vieil Aveugle is that such an one will not have the voice to spout those cataracts and hurricanoes. The way to get over the disparity between Lear's physical decrepitude and the winds and tides beating about his head, between volcanic passion and the hoar and spent old man who must be its mouthpiece — the way for the actor to overcome this is to bethink him of old age as Blake depicted it. Nobody could be older than Blake's Ancient of Days, who is yet 'a monstrously muscular old man, with hair and beard like a snowstorm, but with limbs like young trees'. The actor who should present Lear to the eye as though he were one of Blake's ruined giants has reconciled Lear's feeble pulse and his creator's pulsing mind. It was so that Rossetti painted Lear, and we know that Ludwig Devrient acted the character as though he were Nestor with some remainder sparks of battle, as evinced in the 'wild gorgon-like hair twining about forehead and neck like the snakes of the Furies'.

Mr. Gielgud, lacking the physique upon which to build something patriarchal, presented a man prematurely old, a man wasting away like King John in the orchard at Swinstead Abbey. In the early scenes he touched many right notes, suggested the arrogance and the impatience, was wholly lovely in his half-listenings to the Fool, invented one superb gesture when, returning to Goneril, he veiled his face, and achieved a fine climax in the 'terrors of the earth' speech, which, in the present arrangement, concludes the first act. It is here that, essentially, the play begins, and it is here that the actor of normal powers comes to the end of them. Even Devrient sometimes got no further, not only figuratively, but actually, since we have von Holtei's description of how, at this exact point, Devrient upon one occasion fell into a fit, and some hours later was carried out, still in the old king's costume, 'into the bright summer daylight like a dead man from the battlefield'. In the middle part, where Lear must be as old as the elements and attain to that preternatural grandeur which finds its only image in the heavens, Mr. Gielgud failed through lack of physical means. Again, before the hovel where Lear should be the broken column at whose foot the others bewail their lesser miseries, Mr. Gielgud was merely one of a quartet. On the other hand, he delivered the speech about 'loop'd and window'd raggedness' with extraordinary beauty and, in the last act, the 'Let copulation thrive' soliloquy with admirable point.

Meanwhile a curious thing was happening, which was that Lear seemed to be growing younger. For this two reasons are possible — one that the overburdened player preferred concentration on philosophical content to the lesser business of miming senility, the other that our capacity for going half-way in the antique pretence was exhausted. Alas that in all that is quintes-

sentially Lear we were still not wholly satisfied! Certain it is
that towards the end Lear had not sufficiently earned Gloucester's
description of him: 'O ruin'd piece of nature!' At this point we
should be conscious of an old man so borne down by cumulative
sorrows that he can now hardly feel the heaviest blows. But Mr.
Gielgud's hurts were no greater now than at the end of the first
act, and his hardly perceptible madness had not been as poignant
as his anticipation of it. What one saw now was a hard-pressed
and valiant actor from whom, somehow, the pretence of being
Lear had slipped away. One saw him putting forth final spurts
to cope with the pathos of Lear's end. 'As sobbing runners breast
the tape,' wrote the poet. But runners are young men, and the
pathos of this death-scene had less to do with Lear than with a
talented young actor's comments upon an old man's passing.
Mr. Gielgud must not take the foregoing as harsh criticism; and
it is perhaps not irrelevant to recall that Devrient was exactly Mr.
Gielgud's age when he first played the part, an age at which, says
Mantzius, 'it was impossible *in the nature of things* that Devrient
should be capable of a complete solution of this gigantic problem'.
At twenty-six what was to be the German actor's finest creation
was only 'a worthy first sketch'. I shall rate Mr. Gielgud's present
performance higher than that. In the manifest intelligence dis-
played throughout, and in the speaking of the verse, it is fine;
time only can do the rest.

Miss Dorothy Green's Goneril has always been magnificent.
Mr. Ralph Richardson's Kent was extremely moving. Mr. Leslie
French's Fool was agreeably so, and Mr. Eric Portman's Edgar
would have been adequate if he had not contrived to be both over-
strident and indistinct. Cordelia was colourless, and in the matter
of Regan, Edmund, Gloucester, France, Burgundy, and Cornwall, the company came by a whole crop of misfortunes.

April 13, 1931

KING LEAR
(Westminster)

MR. DEVLIN

Two of the prime cuts in the body of cant are the statements
that Shakespeare did not mean his play of *King Lear* to be acted,
and that it is in fact unactable. Both statements are nonsense,
and Lamb when he inaugurated the second of them was for once
in a way out of joint. That Shakespeare had the stage very much
in mind is proved by the dramatic business of the trumpets
sounding on behalf of Edmund, which is nothing to read, and
again when the doctor says at Lear's waking: 'Louder the music
there!' If ever there was a stage-direction in Shakespeare's
spoken word, this is it. I have a fancy, too, that there is a pointer
inserted in this play not for the benefit of any possible reader but
for the slower-witted playgoer. (I am aware that Shakespeare
did not contemplate the printing of the plays, and that when we
talk of *King Lear* not being meant for the stage we are really
thinking of the poet giving rein to his full mind without caring
whether the result could be fastened down to a stage performance.)
The passage I have in mind occurs when Kent is warned by 'a
Gentleman' that Lear:

> Strives in his little world of man to outscorn
> The to-and-fro conflicting wind and rain.

May we not take it that this is as much a pointer to the immediately ensuing: 'Blow, wind, and crack your cheeks' scene as the
steeple of St. Martin Ludgate is to St. Paul's? In the theatre a
bolt from the blue may be too sudden, and Lear's next appearance
is so terrific and so *outsize* that I can imagine Burbage saying to
the author: 'You must give 'em a lead here or they'll laugh!'
We know that Shakespeare prepared us for Lear's entrance
'fantastically dressed with wild flowers' in Cordelia's speech

beginning: 'Alack, 'tis he!' This speech is generally cut, perhaps because the talk of rank fumiter, burdocks, hemlock, nettles, cuckoo-flowers, and darnel reads too much like a brochure with the title, *Garden Weeds and How to Get Rid of Them*.

It is even more demonstrable that Lear can be acted, as anybody can be convinced who takes the trouble to see how the great players of the past have come off in the alleged unequal and unfair contest. According to Forster, Betterton's performances of Lear between the years 1663 and 1671 'are recorded to have been the greatest efforts of his genius'. But Forster does not mention who were the recorders, perhaps for the reason that Steele, the first accredited dramatic critic, was not born until the year after Betterton relinquished Lear. A century later Spranger Barry and Garrick divided the town in this part. Of Barry it was said that he was 'every inch a king'; of Garrick that he was 'every inch King Lear'. According to Hazlitt, the impression made by the latter on Dr. Johnson was so terrific that he could never again see him in the part. Johnson, however, in his preface to the play does not allude to this, saying merely: 'If my sensations could add anything to the general suffrage, I might relate that I was many years ago shocked by Cordelia's death, that I know not whether I ever endured to read again the last scenes of the play till I undertook to revise them as an editor'. I had hoped to prove that all the greatest actors have been greatest in Lear, and that the mark of second-raters like Edwin Forrest, Vandenhoff and Charles Kean was to fail in the part. But facts are stubborn things, particularly theatrical facts. According to Hazlitt, Kean, whom I have always regarded as the greatest of all English actors, merely 'chipped off a bit of the character here and there'. My father, who ran away from school to see Macready, implied in after life that if he had not played truant he should not have thought so much of him. I can never get it into my head that Macready was really first-class. Yet here is Lewes saying that Lear was his finest Shakespearean character, and Forster opining that Macready's was the only perfect picture of Lear since the age of Betterton. Then, of course, there was Irving's mishap. Of this

Mr. Graham Robertson has written: 'I saw the play again on the fifth night, and Irving's rendering was magnificent, its pathos terrible. I can still see him, weary and half dazed, sitting up on his couch and staring at the daughter he had banished, as she bent tenderly over him. "You are a spirit, I know. When did you die?" he whispered; and I can almost weep now when I recall his voice.' The trouble on the first night was Irving's nervousness, and I shall always believe that his Lear was a sublime failure in the sense that it was a failure on the first night and sublime for the rest of the run. In any case, I personally had always more pleasure in seeing Irving fail than any other six actors succeed. To sum up, the part of Lear can be played by a great actor — if he is the kind of great actor who can play Lear.

There is a sense in which a very young player Shakespeareanly bent is not ill-advised to tackle Lear; nobody is to be blamed for not climbing Everest, whereas he is a fool who falls off Skiddaw. About Mr. William Devlin, who is twenty-two, I shall say straight away that his acting in the part is good enough for me to disregard his age. As the performance of a youngster and a beginner it is incomparably finer than anything I have ever seen; in fact, I have never seen anything at all like it. Setting this against the performances of mature actors in the part, I find that, with the exception of Benson's Lear, it is again incomparably the best I have known. Whatever one may have politely said about individual performances, I know none in my time that began to be Shakespeare's character, whereas Mr. Devlin's starts by being Lear. This is a snuffy, rather dirty old king, made out of the earth of Britain, and not your intellectual actor's octogenarian, *soigné*, redolent of the pouncet box, and breathing Oxford's youngest accent. With that logic which so pains readers of this column, I shall now explain why the rest of it will probably be devoted to dispraise of Mr. Devlin, the point being that, whereas I have given marks to other actors for their little victories over nothing, I may have to take marks off Mr. Devlin for occasionally falling short of perfection. For example, he is not tall enough, and when this Lear talks about being every inch a king he has not enough

full height to draw himself up to! Over and over again throughout the play one feels that Lear must look as though he had steppec'
out of a canvas of Michael Angelo or a drawing by Blake — that is
to say, just a shade bigger than life-size. But. things without
remedy, of which height is one, should be without regard,
and Mr. Devlin has that with which Garrick and Kean made
up for their lack of inches, a magnificent voice full of oak-
cleaving thunderbolts and all the rest of it. He would do well,
by the way, to devote attention to the middle register, which is a
trifle weak. He has abundance of gesture, skilfully contrived in
the grand manner, and is obviously an actor who has no difficulty
in acting. Mr. Devlin presents Lear along the traditional lines
without any annoying intellectuality and with due attention to
each point as it comes along. I think that presently — in the
course of the next forty years — he will be able to elaborate the
physical characteristics a little more and show how as mind and
body crumble the spirit becomes more and more towering. Lear,
who at the beginning has still some vigour, comes at the end to
physical babyhood; contrariwise, the childish mentality with
which he sets out becomes the greatest mind, though disordered,
that Shakespeare ever drew. It was wise of Mr. Devlin not to
insist too much upon the presentation of senility, which is the
mark of your second-rate actor; there will be time to make more
of this when he is confident of taking it in his stride. His understanding of the text and his sense of beauty are everywhere
apparent, and the whole of his conception hangs well together.
His most moving passage is perhaps the 'Come, let's away to
prison' speech, and his pathos is as good as any young man can be
expected to achieve, though here one thinks the actor must have
years. 'Nature's above art in that respect,' as Lear remarks.
But the sovereign merit of the performance — aided by the superb
Goneril of Miss Dorothy Green, the unusually effective Oswald
of Mr. Julian Somers, and the goodish Kent and Edmund of Mr.
Neil Porter and Mr. Francis James — is that it enables the play
to be seen as a whole. Here Mr. Hugh Hunt helps through having
the extraordinary notion of presenting the play as a whole, or

very nearly. This is attained through the use of curtains and a simple, stylized setting having nothing to do with those geometrical arrangements whereby Goneril and Regan must stand on the apices of triangles while Lear sinks back into a parallelopiped. The result is that the philosophy of the play comes through as well as its poetry, and to a greater degree than I have ever known before.

The reader will note that I make no claim for Mr. Devlin as a great actor. I merely say that, apart from Sir Frank Benson, his is the best Lear I have ever seen. On the other hand, Mr. Devlin may be the worst possible Hamlet and an incomparably fatuous Macbeth. Or he may not; it is impossible to tell. One cannot estimate an actor's facial expression or mobility of features when they are obliterated by the papier-mâché and horsehair of the make-up for Lear. Mr. Devlin creates for himself in this part a magnificent head, which, however, remains the same throughout, except that he holds it at different angles like a figure in a carnival. The simile is apt because the head is too big for the body, a fault which would be less noticeable in parts not of the Father Christmas order.

More First Nights: October 8, 1934

KING LEAR
(The Old Vic)

MR. GIELGUD

LEAR is sometimes described as an oak-tree riven by the thunderbolts of fate. I think it better to say that he is an oak which has obeyed Antony's 'O, cleave, my sides! Heart, once be stronger than thy continent, Crack thy frail case!' But whether the assault be from without or within, the tree remains an oak and not an ash. I hope it is not mean to say that the present Lear is an ashtree storm-tossed with infinite grace, whereas the sturdier oak has no need of graces. Mr. Gielgud composes a noble head for the part, though a little less grand than Blake would have drawn. I do not feel that this Lear's rages go beyond extreme petulance — they do not frighten me! — and I am not made apprehensive by his 'I would not be mad!' because the actor does not make me feel that he is in danger of madness. A player may pad out his figure, paint age upon his face, and by high heels add inches to his stature. He can simulate the cracked voice of old age. But not, I think, the near-to-spent surge and boom of a voice like Isaiah's. Mr. Gielgud's:

> Do not laugh at me;
> For, as I am a man, I think this lady
> To be my child Cordelia.

is hung on the air, a very miracle of pathos. But it is a youthful miracle, indistinguishable vocally from the same actor's delivery of Romeo's 'Eyes, look your last!' All of which is merely a note on Mr. Gielgud's lack of physical correspondency.

Mantzius tells us that the weak point in perhaps the greatest of all Lears, Ludwig Devrient's, was lack of 'volume and sonority of voice — Lear's defects, in short, were physical rather than spiritual'. And again: 'It was beyond Devrient's power — especially, of course, in his younger years — to body forth the gigantic figure of a Colossus of heathen antiquity.' I would apply this, word for word, to Mr. Gielgud. With the necessary corrections, his performance is a thing of great beauty, imagination, sensitiveness, understanding, executive virtuosity, and control. You would be wrong to say — this is not King Lear! You would be right to say that this is Lear every inch but one.

I have two small suggestions for the producer. These are that Gloucester should not be allowed to mask Lear at the 'toasted cheese' speech, or Burgundy to get in front of Cordelia in her 'Nothing, my lord' declaration. Why Mr. Stephen Haggard's exquisitely conceived Fool is a tailing-off performance would take too much space to explain. It is an almost impossible part, though I once saw it played perfectly by a child at Oxford. Is

Mr. Haggard a little too consciously clever? But he is right in seeing the part as a silly bucket of folly, silly in the Coleridgean sense. Anybody who wants a comic fool should go not to this tragedy but to *The Yeomen of the Guard.*

April 21, 1940

KING LEAR
(St. James's)

MR. WOLFIT

THOSE who see a moral purpose behind the phenomenon of the artist must be discouraged when they are told — I doubt whether they ever realize — that the faults of the great actor are more impressive than the virtues of the player who has no more than talent. The voice of the greatest actor I ever saw, or ever shall see, was a staccato, raven croak, his walk a halting, ungainly limp, his speech a mass of slurred consonants and unintelligible vowels. And did not Mr. Shaw say of this great player that he 'had no voice, and when you looked closely at him, no face'. Yet I remember an educated man, a professor at Owens College, afterwards Manchester University, telling me that when the play had been *Louis XI*, he had to stay the night in town because he could not endure the mile-long walk along a lonely country road for fear of that dead face following him. What then, if Irving had no face, did he use to fright us withal? Your actor of talent may bid the charnel-house give up its horrors, and our hair is not raised; your actor of genius can make us gibber with a recitation of the multiplication table. Which, of course, is highly unmoral.

But to come to the revival at the St. James's. There is one over-riding reason why Mr. Wolfit must be relegated to the category of the immensely talented; *he does nothing which we cannot explain.* Obvious effects proceed from recognizable causes, and, to para-phrase Montague, while this acting never fails or flops it never lights on the floor of magic. No question here of 'amazed and

sudden surrender to some stroke of passionate genius'. What of
Mr. Wolfit considered on the next-best plane? Let it be admitted
that Nature has denied him almost everything that we look for
in a tragic actor's appearance. If Irving had no face Mr. Wolfit
has too much; that broad moony countenance — Lamb's word
for the comedian Dodd — is a handicap to a tragedian. Then,
again, his voice is all middle register, like a baritone with a compass of an octave and a half, and though a very fine noise can
be made, resonance is lacking. Mountaineers who attempt
Everest are assessed not by that which they achieve but by the
amount by which they fail. So with the actor attempting to scale
Mount Lear. One reads of your persevering climber that he
must have succeeded but for this mishap or that piece of bad
luck, in a word, that he morally reached the top. Morally, Mr.
Wolfit may be said to have attained this play's summit. The
make-up was good, the scenes with the Fool were beautifully
done, the episodes in the hovel were masterly, the crumbling of
the mind was beautifully graded, there was intellectual passion,
and there was even pathos. We left the theatre full of admiration,
but wondering why we had not been swept off our feet.

The reason, I think, is to be found in Lear's

I will do such things, —
What they are yet I know not, but they shall be
The terrors of the earth.

The great actor in this part does not know, nor do we who look
on know, what exactly his terrors have been made of, or how they
have been achieved. What we do know is that we experienced
them. Perhaps it would help if Mr. Wolfit did not so often put
his head on one side like Mr. Chillip in the first chapter of *David
Copperfield*. What is peculiarly unmoral about this business of the
artist is that talent, produced to infinity in the Euclidean sense,
never attains to genius any more than perpetual burnishing of
silver turns that metal into gold. However, there is one glory of
the sun and another glory of the moon, and it would be uncritical
not to recognize that, on its plane, Mr. Wolfit's performance is

very fine. One does not need reminding that if this country had had to wait for genius it would have seen six Lears and no more.

Miss Rosalind Iden struggled bravely with the wretched part of Cordelia; Goneril and Regan were played by two young ladies who gave utterance to the most fearful sentiments while preserving masks inexpressive and creamy; the part of Edmund was cut to ribbons, and Gloucester seemed out of voice. Some clever person explained to me recently why the Fool should be middle-aged. I have forgotten the explanation, but I concede that given this reading Mr. Richard Goolden's performance was admirable.

January 31, 1943

ROMEO AND JULIET
(Fellowship of Players)

MR. ANDERSON AND MISS FORBES-ROBERTSON

THIS immortal masterpiece roused Johnson to the most inept of his criticisms. 'Here', he writes, 'is one of the few attempts of Shakespeare to exhibit the conversation of gentlemen, to represent the airy sprightliness of juvenile elegance.' And again, 'Shakespeare's comic scenes are happily wrought, but his pathetic strains are always polluted, with some unexpected depravations. His persons, however distressed, *have a conceit left them in their misery, a miserable conceit*'. Worms as chambermaids, flesh wearied by the yoke of inauspicious stars, lips which seal bargains, poisons as pilots — it is odd to know that in Johnson's opinion these conceits are miserable.

One's sympathies go out to any actress who is playing Juliet for the first time. If she is an actress of experience she must know that she will not look the part, and if she is a young girl her modesty should tell her that she cannot play it. Always there looms ahead that fearful potion speech, which so many inexperienced Juliets play with an amount of apprehension to combat a beetle and an endeavour to restore balance by cramming their mouths full of blanket. The mere knowledge of this terribly difficult passage has caused many a Juliet to break down long before she got to it. With the foreknowledge of this middle danger and the irretrievable woe enwrapping her at the end, Juliet has yet to begin by being gay. She is not an uncomplaining lamb like Hero, sad in the pastry sense like Mariana, or an unpractised silly like Cordelia and Desdemona. She belongs to a wittier and a livelier order of Shakespeare's heroines, and you feel that in jollier circumstances she would have put on the trews with Rosalind, Imogen, and Viola. Juliet must steer between solemnity and the madcap spirits of Beatrice. She is a creature of banter and the sun, passing through pure love into the 'rotten jaws of death'. Her body is cloudy with innocence, yet her eyes are frank.

My only doubt about Miss Forbes-Robertson's Juliet concerns the extent of its relationship to Shakespeare's heroine. That the performance could only be one of greatest delicacy everybody who remembered her appearance in *Uncle Vanya* and later pieces must have been aware. This young actress possesses the extraordinary quality of knowing the last things about her art almost, you might think, before she has had time to learn the first. She has only to appear in any character and before she has crossed the stage you feel that you are in the presence of a spirit whose excess of fineness cannot escape the world's pain, of a soul importunate for things not of this earth and, in Herbert's phrase, 'divinely loose' about her. It was said of Duse that her countenance in repose showed the ravages of past storms, and it might equally be said of this young actress that in her face is the foreknowledge of storms to come. On the spiritual side this Juliet was perfect. She was Sonya all over again, Sonya in all her truth, purity, loyalty, Sonya in hopeful love. This was a Juliet steel-true and blade-straight — the rustless steel of the untarnishable soul. Of such a Juliet as this Malherbe might have written:

Et, rose, elle a vécu ce que vivent les roses,
L'espace d'un matin.

For her death was not untimely. She had told all that we need ever know of innocence, and when at the end she bent over Romeo and took his head in her hands the gesture showed the tenderness and depth of feeling of the innocent who had passed through inviolacy into motherhood.

But Juliet has earthly values as well as spiritual; the containing vessel is the lovely clay in whose perishable beauty is all the ache of the sonnets. Miss Forbes-Robertson showed us the white wonder of Juliet's soul, but we are to remember that Romeo bothered a good deal less about this than about the white wonder of his lady's hand. Is it possible that this Juliet breathed an air too rare, and that she would in the end have thoroughly disappointed a Romeo desiring less a goddess than a mistress who 'when she walks, treads on the ground'. Is it possible that Juliet was, in Gilbert's phrase, too 'Francesca da Rimini, niminy-piminy' for a Romeo of the 'pushing young particle, what's-the-next-article' sort? Mr. Lawrence Anderson's Romeo did not belong to Shakespeare's world; one felt that, like Archibald Grosvenor, he would have fittingly enlivened Verona's Saturday afternoons with a stick and a pipe and a half-bred black and tan. This was largely owing to a distressing make-up and a black wig which was the lawful adjunct of Second Murderers. Mr. Anderson can get beauty and to spare into his voice, but seems to banish it wilfully from his presence. Of this I am certain, that if Miss Forbes-Robertson is going to make an entire success of Juliet she must insist upon a Romeo of fire and air inhabiting the same ethereal world. But as such Romeos are hard to come by, the young actress might be advised to read the text again with an eye to Juliet's purely human quality. Instead of twitting Paris before the Friar, she gave him mournful responses. Why, when the nurse says 'See where she comes from shrift with merry look' should Juliet enter with a face longer than any fiddle?

Mr. Robert Loraine was a manly Mercutio, Mr. D. A. Clarke-Smith proved his versatility by turning his and Mr. Shaw's entertaining Bloomfield Bonington into the least boring of Friars, and Mr. Ivan Berlyn contrived in the three minutes allotted to the

Apothecary to play all but Juliet off the stage, most improperly diverting our sympathy from hero to druggist. In the even smaller part of Balthazar Mr. Carol Reed was exactly and Shakespeareanly right. Mr. Reginald Tate, who, as an amateur, gave a brilliant rendering of the principal part in Mr. Monkhouse's *The Conquering Hero*, made a first professional appearance as Paris. And a very nice little appearance too. The play was hacked and cut to fit into something like two and a half hours, to the happy annihilation of many of Johnson's 'miserable conceits'.

The Contemporary Theatre, 1926: December 19, 1926

ROMEO AND JULIET
(New)

MR. OLIVIER AND MISS ASHCROFT

THURSDAY evening was all that an evening in the theatre should be — exciting, moving, provocative. Here in conjunction were the flower of Shakespeare's young genius and the best of young English acting talent. The producer was our leading Shakespearean actor, and the scenery and costumes were by the artists who had attained fame through the productions of *Richard of Bordeaux* and *Hamlet*. In other words, Mr. Gielgud had once more invested him in his Motley and given these young ladies leave to speak his mind. Let me begin with a word or two about the production, normally tucked away at the end. The difficulty of producing plays written for the Elizabethan and transferred to the picture stage must always be resolved by compromise, which means that good and bad must go hand in hand. The good point about this production is that it enables that fiery-footed steed which is this tragedy to gallop sufficiently apace. Now, though the acquisition of speed has been a triumph, it has entailed certain sacrifices. For Mr. Gielgud's, and consequently Motley's, method is a combination of the Elizabethan and modern stages, with Juliet's bedroom and balcony a permanent part of the setting; that people may walk beneath it the thing is supported on posts, so that it looks rather like a hotel-lift which has got stuck half-way up to the mezzanine floor. The device also precludes the full use of the stage, so that the action seems to take place not so much in Verona as in a corner of it. I fault the lighting, too, in that gone are the sun and warmth of Italy and the whole thing appears to happen at night, the tomb scene being the cheerfullest of all! The costumes are charming, even if the football jerseys of the rival factions remind us less of Montague and Capulet than of Wanderers and Wolves. Elsewhere Motley have rightly differed from Dickens's Flora, who could not conceive any connection between Mantua and mantua-making. In the theatre there is every connection, and Motley have caught the spirit of the place and time, brilliantly for example in Romeo's case, though in Juliet's oddly reminiscent of the pre-Raphaelite way of looking at Ellen Terry.

Mr. Olivier's Romeo suffered enormously from the fact that the spoken poetry of the part eluded him. In his delivery he brought off a twofold inexpertness which approached virtuosity — that of gabbling all the words in a line and uttering each line as a staccato whole cut off from its fellows. In his early scenes this Romeo appeared to have no apprehension of, let alone joy in, the words he was speaking, though this may have been due to first-night nervousness, since he improved greatly later on. But throughout one wanted over and over again to stop the performance and tell the actor that he couldn't, just couldn't, rush this or that passage. If ecstasy is present in this play it must be at the meeting in the Friar's cell, where Romeo's words hang on the air like grace-notes:

> Ah, Juliet, if the measure of thy joy
> Be heap'd like mine, and that thy skill be more
> To blazon it, then sweeten with thy breath

This neighbour air, and let rich music's tongue
Unfold the imagined happiness that both
Receive in either by this dear encounter.

This is music and must be spoken as music. Again, what is the
use of Shakespeare writing such an image as: 'The white wonder
of dear Juliet's hand' if Romeo is not himself blasted with the
beauty of it? Never mind Shakespeare's precepts; his verse must
be recited line upon line, here a little hurry and there a little
dwell. Apart from the speaking there was poetry and to spare.
This Romeo looked every inch a lover, and a lover fey and fore-
doomed. The actor's facial expression was varied and mobile,
his bearing noble, his play of arm imaginative, while his smaller
gestures were infinitely touching. Note, for example, how lovingly
he fingered first the props of Juliet's balcony and at the last her
bier. For once in a way the tide of this young man's passion was
presented at the flood, and his grief was agonizingly done. 'Is it
e'en so? Then I defy you, stars!' is a line which has defied many
actors. Mr. Olivier's way with this was to say it tonelessly, and
it is a very moving way. Taking the performance by and large,
I have no hesitation in saying that this is the most moving Romeo
I have seen. It also explains that something displeasing which I
have hitherto found in Mr. Olivier's acting — the discrepancy
between the romantic manner and such ridiculous things as cuff-
links and moustaches. Now that these trivia have been shorn
away and the natural player stands forth, lo and behold he is
very good!

Mercutio is always a problem, for the reason that the Queen
Mab speech, obviously inserted to satisfy an actor's demand, is
not in keeping with that arch-materialist. In my opinion the way
to play the part is to go all out for the sensualist, treat the speech
as a cadenza, — in the way a fiddler will plonk one of his own
into the middle of somebody else's concerto — bow, decline an
encore, and then get back into the character! Mr. Gielgud
reverses the process and builds his Mercutio out of the Queen Mab
speech which, of course, he delivers exquisitely. This means a

new death scene and saying 'A plague o' both your houses!' with a smile which is all a benison. Not good Shakespeare, perhaps, but very beautiful Gielgud. In these circumstances Mercutio is not our old friend but a Frenchified version, say Théodore de Banville's:

> Jeune homme sans mélancolie,
> Blond comme un soleil d'Italie.

Miss Peggy Ashcroft's Juliet has been greatly praised. Certainly the eager and touching childishness of the early part could not be bettered, so that we prepared to be greatly moved. Personally, I found the performance heartrending until it came to the part where the heart should be rent. And then nothing happened, though all the appurtenances of grief, the burying of the head in the Nurse's bosom and so forth were present. When Juliet lifted her head, her face was seen to be duly ravaged, but she continued to the end with the same quality of ravagement, which as a piece of acting spells monotony. In my view Miss Ashcroft implied Juliet without playing her. That is to say, she did not move me nearly so much as any of the children who have played in *Mädchen in Uniform*. But then it is very difficult indeed, perhaps impossible, for any Mädchen to put on Shakespeare's uniform. Mr. Granville-Barker dismisses as 'parroted nonsense' the saying that no actress can play Juliet till she is too old to look her. Let this acute observer produce an actress past or present to support him! According to a great critic of the 'eighties, Ellen Terry herself failed not only to conjure up the horrors of the charnel house but to make the scene impressive. In my judgment Miss Ashcroft succeeded in the first half, only to fade away later. On the other hand, the success so far as it went was complete.

I have not space to enumerate the admirable supporting cast, and can only congratulate Mr. Gielgud upon a production triumphant everywhere despite the fact that Romeo cannot speak his part, Juliet cannot act more than half of hers, and Mercutio is topsy-turvy. To crown all, remains Miss Evans's Nurse, knocking the balance of the play into a cocked hat, just as would happen if the Portia were the centre of *Macbeth*. She ruled the entire roost. Obviously of the German-Flemish school, this was Hugh Walpole's Agatha Payne metamorphosed into good instead of bad angel. It was a grand performance, and the pathos of it should have taught young playgoers what pathos was in younger days. One felt that whenever such grief is heard in the theatre, Mrs. Stirling's heart will hear it and beat, though it should have lain for a century dead.

More First Nights: October 17, 1935

ROMEO AND JULIET
(New)

MR. GIELGUD AND MISS ASHCROFT

'ROMEO's himself again!' seemed to be the note of the applause when Mr. Gielgud came on the other evening, while the roar greeting Mr. Olivier suggested that Mercutio had regained his kingdom. Rivalry is always a good thing for the theatre, and it is pleasant to reflect that we do it better now and in England than it was done in the past and in France. I refer to the famous row between Mlle. George and Rachel, which always amuses me, and with which every reader may not be familiar. The older actress went to call on Victor Hugo, and with tears in her eyes told him how Rachel had snubbed her. She would not receive George, and if George wanted Rachel to play at her benefit, she must write to Rachel. George's indignation need not be imagined, because Hugo has left an account of it which I here translate and abridge: 'I am as much a Queen of the Theatre as Rachel. Like her, I have been a courtesan, and the day will come when like me she will be a beggar. Does the freak think I am going to wait upon her? Ah, but no! I suppose she has forgotten how she used to go round the cafés singing for coppers? Now my fine lady gambles for stakes of ten thousand francs, but I say that the day may come when her shoes will be in holes and she will have less right to the name of Rachel than I have to George!' There is a lot more, and George leaves Hugo vowing that rather than write to Rachel she will throw herself into the Seine. However, George did not throw herself into the river, but asked the great Samson to approach Rachel, who thereupon promised her patronage and assistance.

It was upon Sunday, May 27th, 1849, that the battle royal took place. The piece chosen for the benefit was *Iphigénie en Aulide*, with George as Clytemnestre and Rachel as Eriphyle. The first two acts were, as George had probably foreseen and Rachel certainly hadn't, a triumph for Clytemnestre, the rôle permitting the setting star to outshine the rising one. It was a tragic duel, the older actress slowly but surely putting it across her young rival. 'I have never seen anything more terrible', wrote Jules Janin, 'than those two serpents straining for an opening. One would have said that the younger actress was shaken to the depths at sight of this unquenchable verve, fire, pride, and majesty, and that the older actress meant once more, and for the last time, to regain the throne and sceptre which this chit had usurped.' Not only Rachel but her partisans lost their tempers, and George at her entry in the third act was hooted. The hint was not lost upon her supporters, who, when Rachel next came on, returned the compliment with interest. And here are two sentences which I refuse to translate. Fleischmann writes: 'Le vent des grandes batailles romantiques balaya cette houle de têtes furieuses, vociférantes.' And Auguste Vacquerie has this: 'Tandis que Mlle. George, escortée de la sympathie générale, s'épanouissait de plus en plus dans l'ampleur de sa beauté et de son talent, Mlle. Rachel, abandonnée, irritée, seule, se rétrécissait et disparaissait.' In other words, a good old 'un proved better than a good young 'un. When the curtain went up at the end, there was only one actress present, Rachel having turned tail and fled. She did not appear in the after-piece, and Malibran's sister, Pauline Viardot, finished off the evening.

If a thing may be described by its opposite, the foregoing is a fair account of the state of affairs at the New Theatre, where the clash of magnanimities is almost embarrassing, Mr. Gielgud going to the length of not letting us see what he thinks of Mr. Olivier's diction in the Queen Mab speech, and Mr. Olivier tempering Mercutio's death agony to permit us a glimpse of Romeo's contrition. It is the merest cant to pretend that comparisons, on such an occasion, are odious. They are inevitable, since two actors agreeing to fly at the same part put themselves in the position of two golfers engaging, not in a match by holes, but in a medal round, the par of the course being the ideal performance of the character. Now the par of Mercutio is pretty well known: he is to Romeo what Grosvenor is to Bunthorne, a jolly, sensual sort of fellow, who 'takes life as it comes and death when it comes'. Incidentally Mercutio has to let off the most elaborate set-piece in all Shakespeare's poetical fireworks, and for myself I have never known any actor except Frank Rodney who could both be the man and let off the speech. Mr. Gielgud when he played this part gave us the cascade, but failed at the bluff; there is plenty of honest rock about Mr. Olivier's Mercutio, though he turns on the poetry in the way that athletic young fellows turn on the morning bath.

But the par of Romeo is something upon which the best analysers of golf-courses have never agreed. Thus Hazlitt says roundly: 'Romeo is Hamlet in love', and Mr. Granville-Barker says no less roundly: 'Romeo is not a younger Hamlet in love'. All are agreed, however, that Romeo is a mighty poetical fellow, which he could hardly help being since he is the first tragic hero of a mighty poet. Here, in the matter of comparison, there is cut-and-come-again. Mr. Olivier's Romeo showed himself very much in love but rather butchered the poetry, whereas Mr. Gielgud carves the verse so exquisitely that you would say the shop he kept was a *bonne-boucherie*. Yet is this Romeo ever really in love with anybody except himself? If not, we must presume Mr. Gielgud to take the Hazlitt side of the argument, and his Romeo to be, like Hamlet, in love with love, its metaphysics

MACBETH

and vocabulary, the passion rather than the object of it. It is
impossible to pin so delicate an opinion to any word or look or
gesture, though I have the feeling that this Romeo never warms up
to Juliet till she is cold. But the whole thing is a lovely exercise.
Or you might put it that the performance is better as absolute
than as programme music. Miss Ashcroft's Juliet is gaining in
depth and power while losing nothing of childish fragrance, and I
fancy that Miss Evans does not run off with the play quite so
boisterously as she did. Alas; I still dislike the cramped setting in
which everything is sacrificed to that suspended conjurer's box!
Alternatively, it makes you think that the tragedy happens in
Verona's Birdcage Walk at midnight.

More First Nights: November 28, 1935

MACBETH

(Prince's)

MR. AINLEY

SURTOUT, pas trop de zèle! Or, as we say, moderation in all
things. Does unabridged Shakespeare really suit the picture
stage? And if you give the dramatist his head, should you not
leave him his full complement of acts with the climaxes where he
put them? The pause at the end of this play's real Act One is
useful as marking the passage of time. Duncan has supped late
and gone to bed. At the beginning of Act Two, Fleance thinks
the hour is after twelve, Macduff makes his call; and later we are
told definitely by Lady Macbeth that the murder took place
round about two o'clock. Run these acts together and Duncan
is apparently murdered within twenty minutes of his arrival at
the Castle. We lose the sense of the most awful pause known to
tragedy. Mr. Casson places the dagger scene and the 'staircase'
colloquy in the Courtyard, in which he is, of course, strictly

215

accurate. But Elizabethan *locale* was merely the matter of a placard, and I suggest that these events take on greater dread when they happen indoors, as our modern stage permits. The essence of all this business is that it is a closet horror. The constantly shifting scenes at the end were too much cry for too little wool, a tableau of young gentlemen flicking lethargically at each other with battle-axes being frankly absurd. The final duel was lamentably ineffective; Duncan's arrival was attended by a rally of enthusiastic Scots suddenly struck dumb; Macbeth collogued with Banquo's murderer within two feet of half the court; the bagpipes reminded one too insistently of tossing the caber at a Highland gathering at Braemar; dummy apparitions rising belatedly from the cauldron irresistibly recalled an inexpert showman sending up Punch, Mr. Ketch, and others; there was an entirely ludicrous procession of scullions *à la* 'Scheherazade' bearing sirloins, and suggesting that Macbeth's immediately ensuing 'If it were done when 'tis done' had reference to the *pièce de résistance*. Lady Macbeth's 'Was the hope drunk?' etc., should not be accompanied by the skirl of pipes from the supper-room, punctuated by ejaculated 'Heughs!'. Nor is there any earthly reason why the King's Evil speech should be retained. King James is dead. These things apart, the production is handsome if a trifle Christmassy.

With the greatest possible reluctance I must confess to not caring very greatly for Mr. Ainley's Macbeth. An auburn wig gave him the air of a Wagnerian tenor *un peu bête*, and his fullness of countenance and short beard a distinct likeness to a Van Dyck Charles the First well in flesh. Mr. Ainley was never dæmonic nor did he quite touch pathos. And then, possibly through nervousness, he gabbled. 'My thought, whose murder yet is but fantastical,' was reeled off as though the crime did not here first definitely present itself. By the way, shouldn't Gould's reading of 'matter' for 'murder' be adopted? In the dagger speech the actor discounted his effect by playing with a palpable weapon before being startled by the impalpable one. A number of misplaced words and a sad bungle of the 'Sleep no more!' speech

were obvious accidents. But this will not account for a perfunctoriness which can pass from 'My way of life is fallen into the
sere, the yellow leaf', to 'I'll fight, till from my bones my flesh be
hacked', without change of intonation. Mr. Ainley can play
better than this, and I do not need persuading that he will be a
different Macbeth in a week's time. But he must wake up, live
the part instead of reciting it, and forget about Fluther Good and
'not being derogatory'. His best scenes were with the murderers
and when confronted by his fit and the ghost of Banquo. Here
Mr. Ainley really began to act. Miss Thorndike, in robes which
would have served equally for Portia or Cardinal Wolsey, grasped
her nettle firmly, and achieved all expected things. She showed
mind and common sense in the intrigue, majesty at the banquet,
and pathos at the end, though her night-gown was too elaborate.
I never heard 'The Thane of Fife had a wife' better said. But alas!
that neither the lady nor her husband exhibited any sense of awe,
superstition, poetry. They were not in touch with any world
larger than themselves, and the tragedy which began at Dunsinane
ended in the police-court of the Seddons. Mr. Lewis Casson
made an unimpressive, priggish Banquo, until after his death,
when suddenly he did terrifically as his ghost, being fearsomely
uncoffined. Mr. Basil Gill was an extremely fine Macduff, and
the Weird Sisters of Mr. Ivan Berlyn, Mr. Ronald Kerr, and Miss
Zillah Carter bettered anything in my recollection. The performance began at a quarter to eight and lasted till much after eleven.
Could not Malcolm's long speech of self-inculpation, a very
Récit de Théramène if ever there was one, be considerably shortened?
And do we really need the old cobbler out of *Chu Chin Chow*?
At the end Mr. Ainley blessed the audience, and Miss Thorndike
thanked everybody who has taken any part in the production
except, of course, Shakespeare.

December 26, 1926

Mr. Casson has speeded-up the production so that the tragedy
is now concluded well within the three hours. But the curtain
still descends some two and twenty times, which gravely disperses

the interest instead of concentrating it. Mr. Casson's difficulty is that of all Shakespearean producers finding themselves in the quandary imposed upon the good lady whose business in life was to manage Mr. Micawber. If the members of her family did *not* choose to place their money in Mr. Micawber's hands — which they didn't — what was the use of that? If the public will not flock to see Shakespeare produced austerely and imaginatively — which they won't — what is the use of Elizabethan staging? Compromise is indicated. I suggest that the best compromise means one more act and fewer set scenes. Mr. Casson has chosen to present the play in three slices, running the first right up to the discovery of the murder and the second to include the sleepwalking scene. To my way of thinking no division could be unhappier. Consider how much the play gains by the use of four acts. The first act should be Shakespeare's, and end with Macbeth's decision to bend up each corporal agent, the rhymed tag about the false face hiding the false heart bringing the curtain down perfectly. The interval marks the passing of time, and the curtain rises again on Banquo's 'How goes the night, boy?' This act should in my opinion end with the flight of the sons, the small scene which follows being pure anti-climax. The third act has the magnificent opening: 'Thou hast it now: King, Cawdor, Glamis, all.' And after cutting most of that very dull patch about Malcolm's pretended misdeeds, the act ends with Macduff's newfound resolution. And I submit that whatever division be adopted the sleep-walking scene *must* be the beginning of the last act. Only so is the pattern preserved. Macbeth begins the play, and to him in immediate support comes the stronger mind. Lady Macbeth's defeat by conscience withdraws the murderer's last support, and its withdrawal should *immediately* precede his fall. The rest of the play should be all Macbeth, towering in his rage, impotence, and folly. He has forgotten his wife. Nor do we want a full parade of Malcolm's army, since all that it exists for is to allow of Macbeth's several magnificent entrances: 'Hang out our banners,' 'They have tied me to a stake,' and 'Why should I play the Roman fool?' In the matter of scenery I suggest that the best compromise would be, say, three or four scenes of maximum splendour, the rest to be done as barely and suggestively as possible.

My principal reason for visiting the play again was the conviction that Mr. Ainley was not at his best on the first night. On Thursday evening he gave us a great first act, or as great as his physical attributes permit. For this actor suffers in this part from his many perfections, including nobility of voice and serenity of countenance. Duncan calls the thane 'noble Macbeth' and his lady believes him too kind. But that these are skin-deep qualities is hinted in Duncan's 'There's no art to find the mind's construction in the face,' uttered when that monarch is transferring absolute trust from one traitor to another. Macbeth is essentially bloody-minded, and he is a murderer from the beginning, though lacking the nerve to take the first step. He has resolved to murder Banquo and Fleance long before his wife's 'In them nature's copy's not eterne,' and she has no knowledge of the decision to annihilate Macduff and his family. Mr. Ainley nowhere suggested a soul as black as this, largely owing to that quality of voice which fits him so admirably for Brutus. After all, you would not cast a light baritone as Mephistopheles. I repeat that Mr. Ainley on Thursday gave us a very fine first act, his nervous collapse after the murder being admirably done. But he did not keep it up. His second act fell away into the entirely unremarkable, and in the third he merely walked through his part, divesting the lines of power, beauty, and any kind of significance. It was as though he had taken 'Out, out brief candle!' literally, and voluntarily extinguished himself. I suggest that Mr. Ainley should hesitate before offering his admirers, among whom I count myself, a performance unworthy of his great reputation. There was more terror in the little finger of his Gauguin than in the whole of his Macbeth. Frankly, I am at a loss to understand this. Mr. Ainley has studied the part carefully. He uses the later folio reading of 'our place' for 'our peace' in the line 'Whom we, to gain our peace, have sent to peace'; and adopts Keightley's 'on earth below' to fill in the dropped half-line after 'Makes wing to the rooky wood' and before 'Good things of day begin to droop and drowse'. One may not like these emendations, but they are evidence of careful reading. It is surely the reverse of careful acting which omits 'his hour' from the line about the poor player that struts and frets upon the stage.

Miss Thorndike's lady Macbeth seemed to me to be pretty good, and within the actress's physical means entirely perfect. Mrs. Siddons may have been more terrible, but I always suspect the good Sarah of a likeness to Mrs. Vincent Crummles. Not 'standing on her head on the butt-end of a spear, surrounded by blazing fireworks', in which attitude Mr. Crummles first saw her, but sedate and even sepulchral as in *The Stranger*. Miss Thorndike is never sepulchral, and makes you sorry for the poor Queen — about whom there is nothing of Mrs. Haller. May I discreetly inquire why the sergeant who is faint with wounds is allowed to bawl his speech louder than any toastmaster? Mr. Hubert Carter is much too good an actor to yield so readily to the temptation of over-playing.

The Contemporary Theatre, 1926: January 2, 1927

MACBETH
(Court)

MR. MATURIN

Too much ink and not enough logic has been spilled over this controversy, which can be reduced, surely, to a simple question of accountancy. What is the balance of profit or loss in the change from costume to modern dress? What is it that we can *hope* to gain? And who is to hope? The players or the audience? And, if the latter, what sort of audience? To take the players first. It is alleged that costume has the same exuberant effect upon the actor that the sight of writing materials had upon Mr. Micawber, and that it tempts him to prefer sound to sense. 'Good morrow, lord. Go you to Milford Haven?' uttered with a sweep of the cloak, swells to a tour which comprises not only the Welsh seaport, but the sun, moon, and stars. Personally, I do not mind this; the converse fault would seem to me to be the graver. Better too much rotundity in Shakespeare than none at all. The modern young actor who has no Shakespearean training may be able to say such a line as:

> There's husbandry in heaven
> Their candles are all out.

But he will not convince us that the words are the coinage of Banquo's mind, since the manner will necessarily be that not of the vault above but of the vaults below in which the characters normally played by him must sip their cocktails. The effect of clothes upon the actor is, I submit, a matter for the actor. If the innovation is bad for the audience, the fact that it is good for the actor should not weigh with us. What should we think of a concert-giver who announced that the Emperor Concerto would be performed on the ukelele because his soloist could manage the passage-work on that instrument but not on the piano? Should we not advise him to hang up the concerto until he had caught and taught a competent pianist? So it is with actors and Shakespeare.

Now in the matter of the audience, which we will divide into people accustomed to Shakespeare and people unaccustomed to Shakespeare. Let me deal first with the unaccustomed lot. It is said that Shakespeare in a top-hat may entice the uneducated who believe archaic costume and boredom to be the same thing. But has not this been said of archaic language? Has it not been argued that the plays are popular in Germany because the German version is modern German, and that a good way to make the plays popular in English would be to get hold of the German versions and turn them into colloquial English? The logic here is sadly to seek. The reason Shakespeare's plays are popular in Germany is that in that country educated people have not given up going to the theatre, and that the people who go to the theatre are educated. But I do not see why people of taste in this country should have that taste affronted to seduce the cinema-going public which, when the novelty of the 'stunt' has worn off, will obviously not continue to 'fall for' works of imagination contradicting in every conceivable way the poverty-stricken realism in which it is their use and delight to wallow.

This brings me to the normal playgoer, the person of average education and average taste. What is he expected to gain? Sir Barry Jackson suggests two things. First, that clothing to which our minds and eyes are most accustomed frees us to concentrate on the story. Second, that it helps us to realize that 'with but slight differences the characters are thinking and talking as we should do to-day'. He argues that the plays will then put on 'the vividness and actuality of present-day happenings'. We will take the second half of the argument first. 'The characters are thinking and talking as we should do to-day.' At once we ask whether the habit engendered at Sandhurst and matured in Whitehall incline the modern soldier to chatter of temple-haunting martlets, pendent beds, and procreant cradles? But neither, presumably, did the army training of Shakespeare's day. Did the murderers of Rasputin and the Tsar — cited against the possible view that the savagery of *Macbeth* has gone out of the world — feel subsequent twinges about incarnadining the multitudinous seas? Probably not. Yet who can doubt that they would if a poet with Shakespeare's command over language were to make them characters in a modern play? Therefore we will pass the talk. Does the modern murderer think like Macbeth, that is to say, not like a particular murderer but like the entire brotherhood of Cain? Again, no. But again one suggests that he would have those thoughts if another Shakespeare had the handling of him. So we must pass the thinking, in so far as Macbeth and murder are concerned. But how about *The Taming of the Shrew* which is to be the next venture? We have thought differently about women since 1878 and Ibsen's *A Doll's H̄*

The gist of the whole thing, it seems to me, is in a word used in the first clause of Sir Barry Jackson's argument — the word *concentrate*. Does the modern costume liberate the mind from inessentials, or preoccupy it with them? Sir Barry contends that five minutes after the curtain had gone up on his production of

Hamlet one was no longer concerned with what Hamlet wore or
how he looked. Accepting Sir Barry's statement, let me ask him
if that is not exactly what happens in the case of normal costume
production of Shakespeare. Surely five minutes exhaust in any
normal production our preoccupation with Macbeth's costume
and with the costumes of everybody else? On the profit side of the
account then, I can see no entry and no possibility of entry. Even
if Sir Barry Jackson can make good his five-minutes claim he
is only marshalling us the way we are going already. But his
production of *Macbeth* was extravagant proof of the failure to make
good that claim. Speaking for myself — and one's self is the only
criterion — I cannot remember any period longer than five minutes
in which the costumes did not obtrude themselves to the occlusion
of the drama. The shadow not of tragedy, but of the furniture-
dealer's plain van hung over that lounge-hall with its tasteful
little table, standard lamp and pot of primulas accurately recalling windows in Kensington High Street and Tottenham Court
Road. The banqueting scene had all the excitement and colour of
a Ruritanian coronation, the third act appeared to be set in some
musical comedy of the Balkans or the film version of Mr. Noel
Coward's *The Queen Was In The Parlour*. There were undoubtedly
several consecutive moments when the costumes did succeed in
partially effacing themselves. One was during the Porter's Scene,
which came off better than I have ever known it, partly because in
the matter of drunkards Nineveh is Glasgow, and partly because
Mr. Frank Pettingell played the scene better than I have ever
known. Another was the murder of Lady Macduff and her son,
when the sofa and the tea-things simply didn't exist. A third was
the breaking of the news to Macduff. To me — and again I must
postulate the personal criterion — the only absolutely moving moment in the play occurred at the four-line speech of the Second
Murderer. Here I am sure that it was the acting, for Mr. Douglas
Payne made his declaration about the vile blows and buffets of the
world with so much authenticity of passion that one ignored his
seedy frock-coat and willy-nilly was translated into Shakespeare's
world. Had the rest of the playing been on the level of this tiny

but perfect performance, there might have been an entirely different story to tell about the method of production, since it is quite possible that one concentrated upon the clothes for lack of something to concentrate upon in their wearers. Sir Barry said at the end of the performance that he was making an experiment. Before deciding whether the experiment is a success or a failure, I submit that he should make it with a cast capable of giving a first-class performance in the familiar, ordinary Shakespearean costume. Say that Chaliapin in a morning-coat and a bowler hat should fail to impress us with the death of Boris. We should argue, and argue rightly, that the get-up was wrong; whereas the failure of a singer possessed of inadequate voice and little or no gift for tragedy would prove just nothing at all.

I have the greatest respect for Mr. Eric Maturin, who when cast in his right line of parts is a most excellent actor. I cannot know what Mr. Maturin feels about Macbeth. All I know and am entitled to say is that his playing of the character has nothing of the tragic momentum, pathos, and intellectuality which are proper to it. This Macbeth does not grow either in perception, terror, or sadness of heart. He does not age, and when he talks about the sere and yellow leaf we do not believe him. He is violent without attaining to power, and there is no suggestion that Macbeth is talking the loveliest verse that has ever fallen to the lot of actor to utter. There is not even the implication of thought behind the words, which are merely recited. In fact, it is not a performance of Macbeth at all, but an essay in self-sacrifice which the actor ought not to have been called upon to make. The spiritual home of Miss Mary Merrall's Lady Macbeth is obviously the more exclusive portions of Finsbury Park, but at least the actress knows what she is at, and she gives the sleep-walking scene very well indeed. I confess that I never thought to see the speech beginning:

> What beast was't then
> That made you break this enterprise to me?

with the speaker reclining in abandonment and luxury and the arms of her Sheik on an art-coloured divan with a distant gramophone playing the opening to the fourth act of *Carmen*.

Let me sum up the whole thing by saying that at the conclusion of the proceedings I had no feeling of having attended *Macbeth*, or even any tragedy by anybody. One enjoyed the words, of course. But then one would enjoy them if they were read audibly and distinctly by the strictly formal players in the strictly formal costumes of the Happy Valley at Llandudno.

February 6, 1928

MACBETH
(The Old Vic)

MR. GIELGUD

IN many respects this is the best production that I can remember of this, on the stage, always slightly disappointing tragedy — disappointing, or perhaps baffling, in several ways. First, comprehensively, in the sense that no actor has ever made a success of the first magnitude in the title-rôle, while many great actors have failed in it. Second, with any but a terrific Macbeth the play is broken-backed; or you might put it that up to the end of the banqueting scene the play goes up like a rocket and then comes down like the stick. Third reason is that definitely barren patch, the long pow-wow between Malcolm and Macduff concerning the qualifications for kingship. Shakespeare was obviously in a difficulty here, for he had nothing else with which to fill in the gap between the murder of Lady Macduff and the narration of that event to her lord. Obviously there must be a gap to suggest delay, and indeed the passage is so long-drawn-out that one feels that the messenger might almost do the journey in the time.

But there is yet a fourth reason, and this concerns the spectator rather than the poet. Indeed, it accounts in large measure for reason number one, or the play's universal failure to come up to stage expectation. This reason is to be found in the different kinds

of satisfaction which this play presents to ear and eye. Coleridge
has told us of the molten and brassy quality of the verse imposed
upon *Antony and Cleopatra* by the necessity of matching the
torridity of soil and passion. Hamlet being the most civilized of
Shakespeare's heroes, the verse of *Hamlet* has a quality of urbanity
to be found nowhere else in Shakespeare. And so we can go
through all the plays, including *Macbeth*, where a strange thing
happens. Shakespeare here strikes his richest vein of poetry. If
tapestry can be splendid and sombre at one and the same time,
then nowhere is the spectator's mind so gloriously and darkly
hung as in such a passage as:

> Come, seeling night,
> Scarf up the tender eye of pitiful day,
> And with thy bloody and invisible hand
> Cancel and tear to pieces that great bond
> Which keeps me pale! Light thickens, and the crow
> Makes wing to the rooky wood:
> Good things of day begin to droop and drowse,
> Whiles night's black agents to their preys do rouse.
> Thou marvell'st at my words. . . .

If this passage were newly discovered to-day its colour would
instantly assign it to *Macbeth*. It paints the bare gaunt time and
the bare gaunt scene. Now probably in Elizabethan days, when
a Palace in Alexandria and a Castle in Scotland were to the
spectator the same thing, *Macbeth* pleased as well as any tragedy.
But the modern eye has been too lusciously titillated by representational scenery and thus spoiled, spoiled in the sense that the
modern playgoer will only consent to dreadful happenings provided they take place in luxurious surroundings. The Macbeths
and the Macduffs, the Banquos and the Malcolms are, and must
always be, a forbidding lot, with their tartan manners, berserk
headgear, and uncouth whiskerage. If Macbeth had been a
Roman General, and the 'sure and firm-set earth' the marble
floor of a palace in Alma-Tadema's best manner, if Siward's
army had been composed of plumed and polished legionaries

MACBETH

instead of a mere English rabble, if, in short, the eye in this play had been feasted instead of starved — why, then one may think that *Macbeth* would have received that fullness of stage-success which performance nearly always denies it. Be sure that if Colley Cibber had be-Romanized the play the audience would have been content to ignore the vandalism and applaud the deed.

It is, of course, futile to compare infinities, and certainly, in the presence of such acting as Mr. John Gielgud gave to the principal part, the mind could afford to stop teasing itself as to this play's exact place among the tragedies. The piece became sufficient to itself and to us, so that for the time being there was nothing else to be thought about; in the old phrase, the actor carried us away. I have to admit that for the first time in my experience Macbeth retained his hold upon this play till the end. There is a technical reason for the difficulty, the fact that Macbeth is given hardly anything to grip the play with. With the banqueting scene, which is only half-way, the part is almost over. After that we have the apparition scene, in which Macbeth is virtually a spectator. Then comes the murder of Lady Macduff, the long business about Malcolm, the revelation to Macduff, and the sleep-walking scene. Macbeth's next appearance is with Seyton, and whether the play is to stand or fall depends upon the power of the actor to suggest the ravages of mind, soul, and even body endured since we saw him last. Mr. Gielgud did not begin again as so many Macbeths do, but came on the stage as though he had lived the interval. Macbeth has to say: 'I have supped full with horrors,' and the actor must make the audience realize that this supper-time has been the time of the interval. Mr. Gielgud did this perfectly, and in addition filled out all this part of the play with the noise which is its due. Vocally he was superb, and quite rightly let the fine shades go and the sound have it, dropping into quietude for the 'to-morrow' speech, which must always be lovely speaking, however fustian — it is, I think, Mr. Shaw's adjective — the philosophy. Poetical delivery is for the earlier part of this play, and Mr. Gielgud is not a Terry for nothing.

Every good performance of any Shakespeare play is recognizable by the fact that it arouses fresh shock at something which one knows so well that one takes it for granted — to each spectator his own shock, of course. We know Macbeth to be a murderer and so cannot think ourselves into the state of mind of the audience first realizing that he is, in fact, going to obey the promptings, in that order, of his own heart, his wife, and the witches. But other shocks are possible, and my own occurred when Macbeth came away from the murder carrying with incredible clumsiness both daggers as witnesses. To experience this shock is to believe in the murder, and this again is to believe in the actor. But I am afraid that I succeeded in believing less in Lady Macbeth than in the intelligence, subtlety, and artistry with which Miss Martita Hunt tried to overcome certain physical disabilities. But Lady Macbeth must not be winning, and the fault with Miss Hunt's Lady was that she was always too likeable. This was curious, because the same actress's Regan was very fine. I suggest that Lady Macbeth is of a still deeper dye — say, Goneril plus one of Strindberg's hyenas. Some day Miss Miriam Lewes must give us the part, and then I think we shall get the play as Shakespeare wrote it. However, Miss Hunt, who is an admirable comédienne, nowhere let us down.

Macduff was magnificently given by Mr. Donald Wolfit. But, oddly enough, throughout the whole evening I did not notice Banquo, a part in which, doubtless quite wrongly, Mr. Lewis Casson made a significant and even terrifying impression. The piece was excellently, if simply, staged by Mr. Harcourt Williams, who carefully kept the stage bare of all colour until the dull scene between Macbeth and the murderers, which he cleverly enlivened with a scarlet throne. The music to the play took the form of a bleak and appropriate assemblage of threnodies and coronachs, dirges and unco'-Scottish laments. March 19, 1930

MACBETH
(The Old Vic)

MR. LAUGHTON

It was a trick of Racine to begin a tragedy with the word 'Oui'. This, says a commentator, was a dodge to put the audience into a mood of acquiescence towards the highly improbable story to follow. 'Ah, mais non!' presumably went up from every bosom in the Old Vic audience when it was seen that the curtain rose not on a Desert Place but on a Camp at Forres. I hasten to say that actually the curtain did not rise even where I have just said it did, for the production was in the coy Elizabethan mode, meaning a formalized, unchanging display of a child's box of bricks. It was the ear which was shocked, since it expected the First Witch's 'When shall we three meet again?' and got instead Duncan's 'What bloody man is that?' prompting at least one playgoer to whisper his neighbour: 'What bloody nonsense is this?' The fitful gleam of a match revealed a programme-note denying the authenticity of the first Witch Scene and arguing that 'by making the three Weird Sisters open the play, one cannot avoid the implication that they are a governing influence of the tragedy.' Having treasured the programme for further perusal at home, I find that the note goes on to contend: 'Surely the grandeur of the tragedy lies in the fact that Macbeth and Lady Macbeth are ruined by precisely those qualities which make them great . . . All this is undermined by any suggestion that the Weird Sisters are in control of events.' At this point I permit myself to remind Mr. Tyrone Guthrie, the producer, that the play is not a tract by Samuel Smiles but a tragedy by William Shakespeare. I have no doubt that Mr. Guthrie can produce authorities to say that the first scene is quite too definitely bogus. It may be; and in any case I am too old a bird and Spring is too much in the air for any dusty quarrel. I shall merely remark first that the bogus collaborator

229

did pretty well to cotton on to Macbeth's 'So foul and fair a day' for his Witches' motif, and second that I sympathize with Sir Arthur Quiller-Couch when he writes: 'The commentators, ready as usual, surmise that Middleton, or somebody like Middleton, interpolated Hecate. I hesitate to accept this. It does *not* appear likely to me that a whole set of foolish men were kept permanently employed to come in and write something whenever Shakespeare wanted it foolish.' But is that doubtful first scene foolish? I think not. Like Macbeth's dagger it marshals the play the way that it is going. And, anyhow, to open the drama not in murk and storm but the cheerful lighting of a sunny day at Eastbourne belongs to the silly-symphony order of too-clever-by-half producing. Perhaps Mr. Guthrie would like a copy of my treatise proving that Beethoven began his Fifth Symphony at the sixth bar, the Fate Motive having been dug out of the main body and wittily prefixed by Breitkopf and Härtel or somebody. Indian papers and Mr. Newman please copy!

No play suffers more from the formalized setting than does *Macbeth*. I am not referring to the indoor scenes; our fears in that banquet have always stuck deep, despite platters of capons, boars' heads, dolphins, Loch Ness monsters in miniature, and other fry. Where the Elizabethan trick served the play worst was in the Murder Scene, one of the great points of which is that it happens in the courtyard with the hospitable murderers without and Duncan under their watch and ward within. On the general head, why does nobody ever make the point that to the theatre-goer with three hundred years of representational scenery in his blood the Elizabethan stage is much blanker than it can have been to the Elizabethans? It may be presumed that his ear would tell an Elizabethan that 'How goes the night, boy?' is the opening of an outdoor colloquy. But modern scenic development has robbed your modern playgoer of Elizabethan word-consciousness, and when somebody calls a spade a spade he expects to see one. This going back to Elizabethan conditions because they were the only ones Shakespeare knew seems to me like saying that Rameau, Couperin and all that push would have

refused to avail themselves of the pianoforte if they had known of
it. Or would they? Indian papers and Mr. Newman please reply!

The house was packed, and the giddy audience, containing
not one sailor in the gallery but four in the pit, were all of
Troilus's mind: expectation whirled them round. What like
would this Macbeth be? One might say what Hazlitt said of
Kean's acting when seen from the gallery: 'All you discover is an
abstraction of his defects, both of person, voice and manner.'
Of this actor's voice we knew beforehand that he has very little,
and that consequently the surge of passion in the soliloquies
must reach us not as a great tide, but in driblets. What we were
not quite prepared for was his failure in mask. Dodd was one of
Lamb's darling actors, but I doubt whether even Elia would
.have regarded that player's 'broad moony face' as suited to
Macbeth. Mr. Laughton in this part looked very much as we
fancy Dodd must have looked. At its best 'the wide champaign
of his chops' was expressive of Tartuffe; there were too many
moments when a fringe of ignominious whisker conjured up
perilous resemblance to Mr. Robey. Add that in such lines as
'Prithee, peace: I dare do all that may become a man' the actor
let creep into his voice the accents of elvish expostulation last
heard at Offenbach's Cnossus. Visually and aurally, then, the part
was not rendered at all; the heart and essence of Shakespearean
acting were not given because to give these is not in this player's
physical means.

But all physicians will tell the sufferer from cardiac disease that
his heart has a second line of resistance called compensation.
What compensations did Mr. Laughton's acting afford? First,
one may say a complete intellectual grasp of the character, of
which one felt that no nook or cranny had been left unexplored.
Everybody expected the Banquet Scene to be a tremendous
business, and Mr. Laughton did indeed fill it with the most
imaginative horror that I can remember, at the words 'Avaunt,
and quit my sight!' bouncing away from the ghost and landing
half-way up the staircase like an indiarubber cat. This was
followed by an exquisite essay in taking comfort; there was real

heartache in 'I am in blood stepped in so far', and 'Come, we'll to sleep' was conceived as lullaby, the sad pair rocking breast to breast. I have no space to tabulate Mr. Laughton's subtleties, such as the breathlessness of Macbeth's first entrance to his wife, and the feeling round for plausibility after the discovery of Duncan's murder. As against these must be set the fact that the scene of the apparitions failed, perhaps because Mr. Laughton chose not to see them, and preferred to throw himself into a hypnotic trance and babble like a medium at a spiritualist séance in the Cromwell Road. The 'To-morrow and to-morrow' speech found him bereft of any notions about it, and the 'sere and yellow leaf' passage went for nothing. This takes me back to Mr. Guthrie's pronouncement that the grandeur of the tragedy lies in the marred nobility of the chief actors. But. nobility must come out of your stage-player, and when Macbeth falls he must fall like Lucifer. Mr. Laughton was never within measurable distance of any kind of grandeur, and his performance beginning on the ground knew no heights from which to topple. And the heights of Macbeth are topless. Will this actor play the part better in, say, twenty years? Tentatively one says no, since on the intellectual side improvement is not needed, and the grand manner and miraculous organ are not likely to be attained. Told without sound and fury, the tragedy becomes a tale signifying nothing. If this means that Mr. Laughton is not a tragedian I cannot help it; he remains a great actor in another kind.

Miss Robson's forte is emotional hysteria, of which she has quite rightly perceived that there is no trace in Lady Macbeth. But has she found anything tremendous with which to replace it? Lady M. asks to be unsexed, and promptly gives a display of wifely solicitude and mothering which would qualify her at once for one of Sir James Barrie's plays. The justification is that the courage of Macbeth's lady is momentary and fleeting, owing to her having, when she drugged the grooms' posset, taken a couple on her own account. 'That which hath made them drunk hath made me bold.' Do not believe it! 'He that's coming must be provided for,' uttered earlier when she is stone-sober, is the key to this fiend in feminine guise. No, I am afraid I cannot regard Shakespeare's bloody-minded virago as anything other than a tragedy queen of the deepest possible dye. Lady Macbeth, as I imagine her, would regard Strindberg's harridans as mere softies, and here again it is largely a physical matter, this time of voice. That great inducting line, 'The raven himself is hoarse', tells us that the whole soliloquy must be croaked in the lowest tones known to the female register. And I insist that for 'O, never shall sun that morrow see!' the actress must find the tones that we are told Rachel used for: 'Soleil, je te viens voir pour la dernière fois!' If that morrow does see the sun it must be a blood-red disc climbing into a copper sky. Intellectually Miss Robson is beyond reproach. She has the mechanics of the part well in hand and perfectly conveys what we might call the lady's business side. In the essay from which I have already quoted Sir Arthur Quiller-Couch insists on this aspect of the character, which he illustrates by the story of the young lady whose father had been offered a bishopric. 'It was quite unexpected,' she wrote to a girl friend: 'Papa is even now in the library, asking for guidance. Dear Mama is upstairs, packing.' But Lady Macbeth requires more than strict attention to business and a high degree of plaintiveness, and I am not as yet convinced that this fiercely intelligent and finely emotional actress is entitled to be called a .tragédienne. If she is, then I submit that the tragedy is of Dryden's colour and not Shakespeare's.

First Nights: April 2, 1934

MACBETH
(The Old Vic)

MR. SWINLEY

Macbeth, for its boldness of sentiment, strength of versification, variety of passions and preternatural beings, deserves to be esteemed a first-rate tragedy, containing a number of beauties never exceeded, with many blemishes very censurable; dangerous in representation to weak minds; unintelligible to moderate conceptions in several places, upon perusal; therefore chiefly calculated for sound understanding, and established resolution of principles, either on the stage or in the study. — FRANCIS GENTLEMAN. 1770

FOR his production of my favourite tragedy Mr. Henry Cass has had recourse to that highbrow method which I most abhor, the window-cleaning school. Macbeth going to murder Duncan, and his Lady going to tidy up afterwards, move towards their design along a sill so precarious as to suggest the sidelong step of your artist in wash-leather. It is thought a good deal has dropped out of this play, notably Lady Macbeth's baby; and I suggest that among the losses is Lady Macbeth's cute notion in the matter of the royal bedroom. The housekeeping arrangements have been in her hands, Duncan has been 'in unusual pleasure', we are not told whether as a young man he was good at the rock-climbing, and there was always the chance that the combination of ledge and usquebaugh might do the trick, which would have saved his hosts any amount of trouble! But this revival has a graver fault. There can be no doubt that in this play Lady Macbeth is the king-pin, and that if for any reason the part is inadequately played this mighty drama comes asunder. It is all a matter of scale, of our old friend Relativity. Sir Thomas Browne has a passage about things which, possibly of importance in their own setting, can be so placed as to be of no moment, 'like to mice in Africa'. I do not pretend to have got the quotation correct, but it suggests what happens when a Goneril or a Lady Macbeth are physically insufficient. Hazlitt writes: 'A lady of the name of Barnes has appeared in Desdemona at this theatre. Her voice is powerful, her face pretty, but her person is too *petite* and undignified for tragedy. Her conception of the part is good, and she gives to some of the scenes considerable feeling and effect; but who shall represent the "divine Desdemona?"' This seems to me to apply quite perfectly to Miss Vivienne Bennett's Lady Macbeth. What actress of a round and dimpling countenance, of a height lacking the necessary inches, and with no holding in tragic mien or bearing — what shall a clever little player (who, by the way, is an exquisite Desdemona) make of the 'fiend-like queen'? Miss Bennett tried very hard, but it is or should be an axiom of acting, as of war and business, that to do one's best may be half-way to failure. The player probably knew she could not look the part. Could she make up the weight by diction and emphasis? This, alas, only made matters worse, for your authentic Lady Macbeth *is* the part so tremendously that she is relieved from the necessity of doing very much with it. Actually, of course, she must always be doing a great deal, but the impression on the spectator will be that the part is playing itself. Now we saw Miss Bennett striving to play the part, and every line of the part, and every word of every line, for all it and they were worth. Her delivery of: 'Thou'rt mad to say it!' would have put the castle staff wise long before the event. Then take the passage beginning: 'Come, thick night!' and ending: 'To cry, "Hold, hold!"' Lady Macbeth is telling Heaven not to interfere, whereas Miss Bennett, by shouting the last two words at the top of her voice, transferred the horror from Heaven to herself, as though she, Lady Macbeth, would prevent the murder. Again, in the passage about the milking babe, she put so much emphasis on the word 'brains' as to suggest a choice of injury to the child! The sleep-walking scene had little suggestion of somnambulism and none at all of poetry, Lady Macbeth's frenzied efforts to get rid of the spot being a highly realistic exposition of the difficulty of washing off a real defilement, like that familiar to golfers who use pitch. Whereas the stain is on the soul, so that the smear on the hand becomes merely a symbol. Towering falcons may in this play be killed by mousing owls, but not in the acting of it. What, in shrt, we saw was a very clever young actress flying — and flying very bravely — at a part of which she comprehended every word, but not one word of which suited her. To discourage Miss Bennett is the last thing I should want. To be a repertory actress must be to fail in some parts, since the actress is not born who can, in one and the same season, be wise, amazed, temperate, and furious, and play all leading women to all leading men. Ellen Terry wisely said: 'It is no use an actress wasting her nervous energy on a battle with her physical attributes. She had much better find a way of employing them as allies.' The passage occurs in a lecture on Lady Macbeth.

If Lear is the most difficult character to act, Macbeth is the most difficult to interpret. Everybody knows what to make of Lear, but the difficulty is only in the making, whereas Macbeth is sent on to the stage with the enormous handicap of not knowing what to make of himself. There are those infernal Witches hanging round the neck of, and tipping the wink to, one who has already broached this business of murder to himself, while, in addition to the self-prompting and the metaphysical aid, there is the egging-on of his spouse. To see in *Macbeth*, as some do, no more than a welter of savage lusts is to reduce the central figure to the melodramatic Saturday-night stature of *Richard III*. The great point about Macbeth is that his lust for power is not savage enough. What he would highly, that would he holily; would not play false, and yet would wrongly win. The difference between Macbeth and the members of the audience is not that he is a murderer, but that they are not poets. Extraordinary sympathy should exist between them, and if we are not immensely sorry for Macbeth his battle is lost. Mr. Swinley, making no attempt to act any of this, appeared to have hynotized himself into reciting it, now glumly, and now with show of animation, but always reciting. He made the oddest mistakes in the text. This Macbeth declared that present fears were *worse* than horrible imaginings, wanted to know who lay i' the *third* chamber, and said to the dagger: 'Come, let me *grasp* thee!' There was one awful moment, too, when Macbeth said: 'What's he . . .' perceptibly hesitated, and so made us fear that he was going to slip into: ' . . . that wishes so, my cousin Westmorland?' and so fall to discussion of military rather than Caesarean operations. Let us think these strange abuses of the text were but the initial fear that wants hard use. Not, of course, presuming to dictate, but I suggest to Mr. Swinley that he should set about discovering the humanity in Macbeth, leaving the inhumanity to take care of itself. Also he might advantageously remember that as a poet Macbeth towers head and shoulders above everybody else in the play, and, indeed, in any other of the plays. For Mr. Swinley is a fine tragedian, though this part may not become him. His Macbeth is at least as inoffensive as that of Macklin, of which performance His Honour Judge Parry once wrote that it 'had nothing about it to rouse the animosity of the theatre-goers, unless, indeed, it was his kilt'. And we reflect that as Judge Parry never saw Macklin, we have to leave it to His Honour.

Mr. William Devlin's Banquo was a beauty, and as I am in the constructive mood, let me suggest to Miss Baylis that Macbeth and Banquo should repeat the Romeo-Mercutio exchange-of-parts business. Mr. Devlin does not have to talk to tell you what he is thinking, and Banquo's face while Lady Macbeth was paying her false compliments to Duncan was, as they say, a study. Throughout this performance Banquo's royalty of nature was admirably suggested, though here again I fault the producer for depriving the actor of the three lines:

> And yet I would not sleep. Merciful powers,
> Restrain in me the cursed thoughts that nature
> Gives way to in repose!

Shakespeare was careful to prove, and Banquo should be allowed to echo, that Macbeth's friend is not a galumphing innocent like

Antonio the Merchant, but one whose royalty consists in knowing temptation and withstanding it! Mr. Cass follows the namby-pamby modern method of having no Ghost in the Banquet Scene, a denial which has always seemed to me to be complete nonsense. When Shakespeare, or somebody acting for him, wrote: 'The Ghost of Banquo enters and sits in Macbeth's place,' he presumably meant it, unless we are to hold that whoever put the play together did not know the meaning of ten of the simplest words in the language. In comparison it is a trifling matter that Macduff should be deprived of his bonnet, though again Malcolm presumably knows what he is saying with his: 'What, man! ne'er pull your hat upon your brow!' It is adding insult to injury to deprive Malcolm of the line just because Macduff isn't allowed headgear. Here I think the actors should take matters in their own hands, and that in future while Mr. Swinley lets in that 'clutch', Mr. Leo Genn should secure that bonnet. Mr. Genn played Macduff very well, though the part is actor-proof; Macduff can never be a Macduffer. Mr. Cecil Trouncer, taking a lamentable view of Duncan, presented him as something between a toastmaster at a City banquet and a boxing M.C. at the Albert Hall. After a week I still shudder at a wilful and conscientiously perverse interpretation. Perhaps the best thing in the production was the lighting. At least it was this which prevented me from murmuring at the end: 'Tout passe, tout lasse, tout Cass!'

More First Nights: December 3, 1935

MACBETH

MACBETH
(The Old Vic)

MR. OLIVIER

We have each our private ideal of Macbeth, Hamlet, Othello, Lear; we have all of us read of, if we have not seen, great performances of these parts; so that every actor who undertakes them has to pass through a triple ordeal, encountering, first, our imagination, kindled by Shakespeare; second, our idealized memory of performances which used to please our, perhaps unripe, judgment; third, our conceptions of the great actors of the past, gathered from the often extravagant panegyrics of contemporaries. — WILLIAM ARCHER

PERHAPS this is the place to say — and if it isn't I shall still say it! — that I have been more 'got at' over Mr. Olivier's performance than by any other in my recollection. Chelsea semaphored, 'Unable conceive Macbeth as gigolo'. Bloomsbury signalled, 'No use for Macbeth as mountebank'. A young gentleman in corduroy trousers and a velvet smoking-jacket opined to my face that Macbeth should not be like a retired Army colonel. Reflecting that what the young gentleman stood in need of was an active drill-sergeant, I proceeded to turn a deaf, but not altogether deaf, ear to another of the mincing brigade, who suggested that the new Macbeth shouted too loudly. I say 'not altogether deaf' because even the austerest critic is none the worse for knowing what is being said by the mob! I am persuaded that those monuments to incorruptibility, our judges, take a good keek at anonymous letters before they consign them to the wastepaper-basket. Now my mentors, though self-appointed, were not anonymous, and it so happens that I have the greatest respect for their opinions in the domains of art and music as well as drama. Nor did I get the impression that the plushy young gentleman was altogether a fool. Why, then, should a performance which interested me throughout and at times excited me greatly fail so completely with these others? Can it be that they were judging Mr. Olivier's performance by some preconceived standard to which this actor's physical means, even if he were Garrick and Kean rolled into one, would still not let him conform? Can it be that they were like a man going to the circus expecting to see lions and who, confronted with a cage of tigers, says: 'These lions are poor!' Or can it be that I was wrong?

Anyhow, I was sufficiently intrigued, as they say, to pay a second visit and sit the play out a second time. And sufficiently conscientious to consider whether one's rules for measuring performances in classic parts stand in need of revision. I look at it in this way. Every critic has his ideal Macbeth, Hamlet, Othello, Lear. But the attitude he must adopt is not that of a schoolmaster correcting schoolboy answers. A critic has not finished with Mr. Jones's Hamlet by allotting it, say, 65 marks out of a possible 100. If I am not being too nice in this matter, let me suggest that this arithmetical judgment may be the only practicable method of assessing a newcomer about whom the critic knows nothing more than the immediate impersonation. Hazlitt, writing about Kean on his first appearance as Shylock, was in a very different position from Hazlitt years later considering Kean's Lear, when the actor's virtues and limitations, mental as well as physical, had become well known to him. This is why when it comes to allotting marks for a performance the critic must take into account not only how much that performance falls short of the ideal, but by how much it exceeds, or fails to exceed, that which the critic could reasonably expect from previous performances by the same actor. *Of course* Mr. Olivier's Macbeth, now presented for the first time, is inadequate, ideally considered. And perhaps we may first glance at what has been said of the adequacy or inadequacy on the part of actors greater than Mr. Olivier pretends to be. First there is Garrick, about whom Francis Gentleman winds up a fulsome panegyric with the request to know 'who has heard Macbeth's speech, after receiving his death wound, uttered with the utmost agony of body and mind, but almost pities the expiring wretch though stained with crimes of the deepest dye?' One reflects that this speech, not to be found in Shakespeare, must have been uttered not only with the utmost of Garrick's bodily and mental pain, but at considerable cost of the great actor's invention as well! Quin 'could not be expected to exhibit the acute sensations of the character'. Barry 'made a lukewarm affair of Macbeth'. Powell 'dwindled into boyish whimpering'. So much for Francis Gentleman. According to Hazlitt, Kean, being deficient in the poetry of the character, 'did not look like a man who had encountered the Weird Sisters'. This critic greatly preferred Kemble's Macbeth, although 'his tones had occasionally a learned quaintness, like the colouring of Poussin'. Of Macready, Lewes said that 'though unsurpassable in some aspects, he wanted the heroic thew and sinew to represent the character as a whole', and that his Macbeth 'stole into the sleeping chamber of Duncan like a man going to purloin a purse, not like a warrior going to snatch a crown'. Henry Morley was so greatly overcome by, and wrote at such length of, Helen Faucit's Lady Macbeth that he dismissed Phelps's performance of her great partner as a 'rude, impulsive soldier', while a lesser critic of the 'forties complained that in the banquet scene 'dignity and kingly courtesy were wanting'. Irving, according to Ellen Terry, thought that his Macbeth, though universally discredited, was his finest performance, and of his last act she writes: 'He looked like a great famished wolf.' Of Bourchier's over-acting in the part Allan Monkhouse once said, if he did not write, that one left the theatre wondering whether murder could be as serious as all that came to!

Since it would seem that with the exception of Garrick a great Macbeth has never been in the calendar, it is reasonable to expect that the new one should be lacking in perfect adequacy. It is a part demanding great natural and physical gifts, to which Mr. Olivier at present can only oppose natural and physical short-comings. He does not look like coping with Russian bears, Hyrcan tigers, and rhinoceroses, whether armed or unarmed. His voice, which in the 'To-morrow and to-morrow' and the 'Sere and yellow leaf' speeches should vibrate like a 'cello, is of a pitch rather higher than the average. In other words, he is not a natural bass and has some difficulty in getting down to baritone. All the same, he brings off some magnificent vocal effects, and his verse-speaking has improved. Ideally, Macbeth might be likened to some oak magnificent in outer shell but lacking roots, and presently to be riven by the lightning of conscience. But Nature has not so endowed Mr. Olivier, who is forced to play the whole part nervously among the high-tossed branches. The whole performance, then, is a study in nerves, and this actor, largely by force of highly expressive play of feature, makes a notable conquest over what might so easily be monotony. He begins in a low key. We realize that Macbeth is rapt, as Banquo says, in something more than contemplation of the Witches' promises; his mind harks back to the earlier occasion when to his wife he tentatively broke the murderous enterprise. He hesitated then, and is not ready now. As the murder draws near this Macbeth's passion increases. Many actors play the 'dagger' speech with the aplomb of a concert-singer reeling off 'Hybreas the Cretan'; the speech as it is now rendered is shot with apprehension. The ascent and descent of the staircase are done superbly, the voice falling at the awed 'Amen' and rising to a magnificent resonance with the 'Sleep no more' speech, which has a Nordic, barbaric, and what I hope I may call a Sibelius-like ring of doom. I pass over the nicely calculated scene with the murderers to welcome the beautiful and intensely Shakespearean delivery of

> Light thickens; and the crow
> Makes wing to the rooky wood.

The banquet scene a little disappoints in the same way that Phelps disappointed. Macbeth, who has put on kingship, should be more royal, and I am inclined to think that the leap on to the table is too much in Hamlet's vein after the play scene. This brings us to the last act, which is the best of any of the Macbeths that I have seen. It is played at white heat of both imagination and energy, so that it becomes a molten whole. Here the actor gathers up all his forces and all his knowledge of what ought to be done. It is the reverse of 'all over bar the shouting'. Mr. Olivier, who has made enough noise, and some people think too much, now gives the part the finest edge of his brain. 'Liar and slave!' is uttered with a cold, Irvingesque malignity. If the voice, expressing Macbeth's melancholy, still cannot accomplish the 'cello, it achieves a noble viola. The fight at the end is grandly done, and when sword and dagger are gone Macbeth's final gesture, in which he would fight Macduff with his bare shield, shows that not even the poetry in which he has been enwrapped, nor all the metaphysical stuff with which he has embroidered his wife's death, has robbed this soldier of his first valour.

To sum up, this may not be the whole of Macbeth. Ideally considered, the performance lacks grandeur, and the actor should look to his gait, which smacks too much of the modern prize-ring. But the mental grasp is here, and so too is enough of the character to take one spectator out of the Waterloo Road and set him down on that dubious heath. Further, is it not a point that whereas a stripling can fly at Hamlet, Macbeth is a weighty business which requires the momentum of age? Mr. Olivier will probably play this part twice as well when he has twice his present years. Meanwhile he registers another step in a career of considerable achievement and increasing promise. Alas that he is insufficiently helped by his Lady Macbeth, about whom I shall echo what an earlier critic said about an earlier actress: 'Miss Laura Addison has a good conception of the part, draws a just outline of it, but is incapable of filling it up. She is a clever actress, with a very laudable intelligence of the character, but with natural powers inadequate to its just exhibition.' Where Mr. Olivier is admirably aided is by the production of M. Michel Saint-Denis, by Motley's scenery of dried-blood hue and consistency, and by the incidental music of M. Darius Milhaud. The perkiness of M. Milhaud's themes and the irrelevance of their toylike colouring suggest by audacity of contrast the time's form and pressure.   *The Amazing Theatre*: November 26, 1937

MACBETH
(Piccadilly)

MR. GIELGUD

SHAKESPEARE in this play set Mr. Gielgud, the actor, a problem which he proceeded to solve as nearly as it admitted of solution; Mr. Gielgud, the producer, wilfully, and with his eyes open, set himself another problem which he did not solve — the actress to lead with him. Walkley divided actresses into mouseys-pouseys and roguey-pogueys: I will never rank Lady Macbeth among the teenie-weenies. The first poser was the old difficulty of reconciling Ross's description of Macbeth as 'Bellona's bridegroom' with the hag-ridden neurotic. Mr. Gielgud failed here, as every Macbeth worth seeing must fail, Nature not having seen fit to endow cart-horses with the nervous system of thoroughbreds, or successful generals with a genius for the introspective. Heaven protect us from the Macbeth who strides on to the stage like Kitchener at Omdurman, and for the rest of the evening barks the poet's lines as though they were words of command in an Aldershot review. Mr. Gielgud did his audience at the Piccadilly the courtesy of pretence; he gave Macbeth at his first entry a swashing and martial outside, though low in tone, gaunt and sombre like an El Greco. Having discharged the formal reply to his sovereign, and with the gloriously delivered 'Stars, hide your fires', Mr. Gielgud dropped the warrior and bent up each corporal and intellectual agent to the terrible feat of interpreting the most poetic of all murderers. He spoke the verse beautifully throughout, and was, I thought, particularly fine in the Dagger soliloquy, and the 'Seeling night' and 'To-morrow' speeches. But to speak Macbeth beautifully is not to act him fully; the actor still fails who is no more than a philosopher turned poet. Mr. Gielgud was not thus content. His collapse immediately after the murder was a masterpiece of nerves well matched by the truly magnificent virtuosity of the Banquet Scene, where the actor went all out. Contrary to most Macbeths, with whom going all out means petering out, Mr. Gielgud went on to finer achievement in the immensely difficult Apparition Scene, and overtopped this by holding together those final fragments where, if anybody is in danger of going to pieces, it is Shakespeare. All of this shows the command by the actor of immense reserves of nervous force, to which one must add imaginative control. Too often the short-long speech about the 'yesting waves' is a mere gabble; Mr. Gielgud untied the winds very much as three nights previously we had heard Sibelius untie them in the Prelude to *The Tempest*. If not the whole of Macbeth, then 'a piece of him', as Horatio would say.

I think it is Goethe who maintains that the play ought to have been called *Lady Macbeth*. Which, of course, settles the lady's size. If that is not enough, there is our old friend the *optique du théâtre*, which in this case I should prefer to call *l'optique du sens commun*. There is no law of Nature which ordains that in real life murderesses shall not be little women and bad wives, and it can be plausibly argued that the soul of a Goneril is fittingly encased in the body of a Mowcher. On the stage such a Goneril would not look right, any more than a strapping Cordelia or a plain Juliet would look right. *And that is all there is to it.* Miss Ffrangcon-Davies is a delightful actress in comedy, whom we last saw as Gwendolen in Wilde's farce. But could she have swelled to the overpowering architecture of Gwendolen's Mamma? I think not. And if not Lady Bracknell, then a hundred times not Lady Macbeth. She does not fill the eye. Scorn is the deepest note in this actress's register; scorn accompanied by an expression of faint disgust. She can neither speak daggers nor look them. I am compelled to say of this Lady Macbeth that which, changing the pronouns, Lewes said of Macready's Thane: 'She was irritable where she should have been passionate, querulous where she should have been terrible.' In place of the master mind, the nagging spouse; so that one questioned whether the likes of 'er would have succeeded in putting it over the likes of 'im. More Shakespeareanly, 'Nought's had, all's spent' sums up a clever, well-thought-out, and always courageous tackling by a gifted actress who is not a tragédienne of a part which makes the maximum call on tragic implementation. Mr. Nicholas Hannen bestows upon Duncan the Maeterlinckian quality of sweetness in old age. Mr. Leon Quartermaine endows Banquo with a beautiful honesty, and Mr. Francis Lister gives Macduff his full pathos. Mr. George Woodbridge's Porter is allowed to indulge in caperings which hint that this play is the next to be taken in the balletomane's ravishing stride. If this is so, I suggest that whoever is interested should borrow Messrs. Ayrton and Minton's scenery and Mr. Walton's music, and get it over.

July 10, 1942

HAMLET

(Haymarket)

MR. BARRYMORE

MOODS may be of many kinds, and Hamlet undoubtedly had his fair-weather ones. *Au fond*, this young man was of an amiable, lively, and even sunny disposition. How, else, could Ophelia have drawn up that shining catalogue? Or how, if his Prince's heart had been otherwise, could the frank and manly·Horatio have won to it? But Shakespeare, who never hit the nail except on the head, has already settled this beyond any argument in that one-line epitaph. 'Noble' and 'sweet' are Horatio's adjectives, nothing being said about melancholy. Is not the case a plain one of transfusion, the dejection being Shakespeare's? Put it the other way round. Is there a single line of the Sonnets which might not have been penned by Hamlet in one or other of his moods? This is only to reiterate the old statement that Hamlet is Shakespeare himself — a commonplace, doubtless, but one to be borne in mind whenever an actor reissues the old, magnificent challenge. It is the familiar affair of dual superlatives — the glorious morning obscured by basest clouds, 'heavenly alchemy', and 'ugly wrack'. Can the actor essaying Hamlet give us both aspects — the sky of bluest blue and the sweeping storms of darkest pessimism? Can he compass the tenderness of the 'heart's core' speech, the filial piety, the polished courtesy and badinage, the sinister pre-occupation, the nosing after corruption, the ranting and mouth-ing? Can he, in a word, pour into this great part all the treasures of the richest of human minds? Has he the physical perfections, the romantic riches, to pour? But Hamlet's mind has ugliness also, and your actor must in his person exhibit these as well. Mr. Barrymore's Hamlet draws fewer tears than Robertson's, but it is nearer to Shakespeare's whole creation than any other I have seen. In fact, this *is* Hamlet, since you have but to scratch the god and the demon instantly appears.

What are Mr. Barrymore's qualifications? Well, first, a hand-some face, intellectual as to the brow, a trifle womanish in the lower part, after the manner of the paintings of Angelica Kauff-mann. Next an agreeable voice, touching nobility here and there, but lacking the organ-note and in emotion running too easily to the head-notes of the tenor. Add the purest diction, perfect enunciation, and unexampled clarity. Now note a slim figure and the general illusion of princeliness and youth. All these are informed — and here is the key — by intellectual capacity of a rare order and analytical power of extreme cogency.

How, with such gifts, does Shakespeare's poetry fare? A trifle ill is the answer. Mr. Barrymore has the finest possible sense of values in the case of single words. Take such a line as 'How weary, stale, flat, and unprofitable . . .' and note how it is built up of successive images which come into the mind before the word is coined to represent them. The actor never gabbles. But this good quality may have its corresponding defect, by which I do not mean want of pace alone, but of power to sweep the listener off his feet. Mr. Barrymore builds lines out of words, but he does not always weld the lines into the whole that a great speech must be. The first and third soliloquies are ratiocinative, the second — 'O, what a rogue and peasant slave am I!' — belongs surely to the domain of pure emotion. It is a cadenza, a piece of virtuosity, an exercise in what musicians call *rubato*. This is the speech in which Hamlet is to prepare the spectator for his 'Get-thee-to-a-nunnery' tirades, and Ophelia's 'blasted with ecstasy'. Mr. Barrymore blasted it with pure reason. You felt that he saw himself first as a rogue, then as a slave, who, moreover, must take on the attributes of a *peasant* slave. He made note one by one of all the aspects of a player who should simulate grief — the tears, distraction, and broken voice. But Hamlet is at white heat, or working up to it, and the debating method does not carry us away. It is possible that this achievement is not within this actor's scope, but I submit that a declamatory failure would here be better than expository success. The sails of the actor's voice having no knack of bellying, Mr. Barrymore attempts to get power by sudden gusts, choosing a single word for an explosion. Sometimes the choice is quite arbitrary, as in his refusal to take the King when he is 'fit and seasoned for his passage'. Passage is the word chosen here, and the violence is without meaning. Certain it is that Mr. Barrymore cannot cope with such words as 'this majestical roof fretted with golden fire'. His Hamlet has too much the *indoor* look, as the essayist remarked of Raphael's figures, and will find his images in his own brain. Such a one would not rack the heavens for a comparison. Sun and stars are not his concern, and the words, being perfunctory, are robbed of their just splendour.

But I have given too much space to fault-finding. The play-scene was immensely fine, its climax being a miracle of virtuosity, and the closet-scene was perfection. Much of the latter was spoken on Gertrude's breast, and the pathos was overpowering. And from here right on to the end I thought the performance magnificent. It gathered power, coherence, and cumulative effect; in short, we knew ourselves to be in the presence of a fine and powerful mind. But surely the savagery and tang of the end are lost unless the quarrel with Laertes takes place where Shakespeare explicitly directs that it shall take place. At the words 'This is I, Hamlet the Dane!' Hamlet *must* leap into the grave. This is a giant's conception, and the vaunt in 'the Dane' is to prepare us for the vault. The actor made amends with a duel in which he was half impish and half 'fey'. At the realization of Laertes' treachery we saw him gather up decision; he spitted the King with gusto, and in his own dying found felicity. The whole performance had a hundred little perceptivities and touches, and no perversities of ingenuity. Only once was Mr. Barrymore naughty, when, at the words 'crawling between heaven and earth', he indicated that the former was situated in Ophelia's hair.

The cast was brilliant almost throughout. Perfection is not too complete a word for Miss Constance Collier's Queen, admirably 'lived', yet low in key. Would Mr. Augustus John paint another 'Tragic Muse'? Here is his subject and his colour. Miss Fay Compton's Ophelia was fragrant, wistful, and had a child's importunacy, unmatched in my time. Mr. Courtenay Thorpe's anguishing Ghost was authentically from another world, and spoke a music rare in this. Mr. Malcolm Keen made a good King, Mr. Waring a fair Polonius, Mr. Ben Field a creditable grave-digger, and Mr. Shayle Gardner a cherubic Fortinbras. A word is due to the Osric of Mr. Frederick Cooper and the Bernardo of Mr. Roy Travers, tiny parts excellently played. But few lines are left for the setting of the American Mr. Robert Edmund Jones. I declare this to be the most beautiful thing I have ever seen on any stage. The vast arch at the back served as the battlements, and was hung with curtains for the indoor scenes, played on two platforms intersected by a flight of steps. Up these Ophelia had to make a final exit of great peril, achieved by Miss Compton with immense skill and nerve. But should not the churchyard scene of Mr. Norman Wilkinson have the melancholy of summer afternoons? The dark and the cold may be more accurate, but the mind is thereby frozen with horror, when it should melt with pity.

The Contemporary Theatre, 1925: February 19, 1925

HAMLET
(Court)

MR. PERCY

MR. PETER GODFREY's production is a nice compromise between the exiguous Elizabethan stage — platform, balcony, and cubby-hole — and the columnar, jigsaw arrangements beloved of Mr. Gordon Craig. Such a setting at once brings up the question: How exactly did Shakespeare see his plays when he was writing them? Did he visualize the battlements at Elsinore and in the mind's eye follow the Ghost round about the castle? Did he imagine one room in which Ophelia should walk, another to serve as theatre for the play, another for the Queen's closet? Did he think of some familiar churchyard for Ophelia's burial? Or did he uniquely consider the stage on which his play was to be performed and how he was going to get the best out of its three planes? Probably everybody will answer this question according to the way in which he reads his Shakespeare. The poet drew prodigies of virtue out of bare necessity, but that does not prove that necessity is virtue. The best argument for the simplified setting of Shakespeare is the saving of time and the preservation of continuity. But it is hard to believe that the revolving-stage, which a National Theatre would presumably possess, would hurt the play of *Hamlet* more than the consent wrung forcibly from us that Ophelia shall be buried in the middle of Gertrude's closet. Given the occasional revival of Shakespeare's plays by private, limited enterprise, there can be no doubt that the method adopted by Mr. Godfrey at the Court Theatre is the best. It asks a good deal, but then the practised Shakespearean playgoer is prepared to give a good deal. It is almost the case of the willing seller and the willing buyer. I think that possibly Mr. Godfrey goes too far in making the Ghost shed his ghostliness and in depriving Ophelia of her flowers and thus reducing her to that kind of pantomime whereby elderly music-hall comedians are wont to indicate how young ladies do their hair. Again I think that though most Hamlets are too much in the sun of the scene's dead-centre, it is a mistake to keep this one too much in the shade. The seating at the Court Theatre is admirable, yet from where I sat Hamlet, being round the corner, was invisible for quite considerable periods. For Mr. Godfrey's arrangement of the text there can be nothing but praise, the action gathering momentum through the Play, Recorders, and Closet Scenes, and taking the Worm and Emperor speech in its stride right up to 'My thoughts be bloody or be nothing worth' before we are given our one and only breather. But I must register one protest against cutting a single line in this, the finest of all the soliloquies, and another against making the Ghost in the Closet Scene so inaudible as to render his words incomprehensible to anybody who should not know them by heart.

Mr. Esmé Percy did not fail as Hamlet, because he is too good an actor to fail in anything from Puck to Lear. I have mentioned Puck because this Hamlet seemed very nearly as care-free. Writing of Fechter's Hamlet, the first thing that Lewes observes is that 'his aspect and bearing are such that the eye rests on him with delight; our sympathies are completely secured'. When Mr. Percy appeared our eye rested on him with astonishment, and our apprehensions were immediately aroused. Hamlet, as his mother reminded us and as Goethe insisted, was fat. But *pace* these authorities, we cannot consent that Hamlet should be cherubic to the point almost of being chubby. When Hamlet debates the question of being or not being, we ought to feel that the matter has been vexing his bosom ever since his father died. Mr. Percy made the speech a metaphysical exercise newly happened upon, and delivered it with undergraduate relish, and as though he were addressing the Oxford Union. He did not take up arms against his sea of troubles so much as bob up and down upon them like a cork. He had little pathos, hardly anything of the mournful grace that Hamlet should possess, and none of the tenderness which, when Forbes-Robertson played, wetted every eye. He was never fey or fore-doomed, never elegiac. At the words, 'What, frighted with false fire?' Hamlet should tower over the King. Mr. Percy was almost puny here; and when later he stood on a contraption which raised him a foot from the floor he was still, metaphorically speaking, inches shorter than Claudius. It may be argued that Kean was a little man. But then Kean, when it came to passion, was 'a terror for his size'. Mr. Percy, though vigorous, was never dæmoniac, and in this scene, in which Hamlet at last lets himself go, there must be dæmonism. It was unfortunate that he delivered the verse jerkily, with too little appreciation of its loveliness and a leaning to the manner of counsel making points in a brief. He had unnecessary emphases.

But there were undoubted compensations. All that the part has of irony was capitally brought out, and full value was allotted to the macabre. Mr. Percy gave a new turn to the words: 'Thou wretched, rash, intruding fool, farewell!' the intonation at the word 'fool' conveying Hamlet's exasperation at Polonius carrying his doltishness to the length of being his foolish self when he ought to have been Claudius. But we did not even hear the words: 'Is it the King?' When Sarah Bernhardt said: 'C'est le roi!' and stood, Mr. Maurice Baring tells us, transfixed like some apostrophe in black, the whole meaning of the play was concentrated in the rippling gleam of her sword. Mr. Percy did nothing here, but he delivered the 'Now might I do it pat' speech extremely finely, and was very fine also in the utter weariness which he showed at the words: 'Nay, an thou'lt mouth.' Be it said, too, that the actor stood up to Hamlet's intellectual side, and that though his performance lacked plastic beauty it never wanted gusto. Mr. Percy obviously delighted in being Hamlet; and indeed that delight must always be present, the condition of any respectable performance of this greatest of parts being that it should resemble Mr. Micawber's reading of his letter and be carried through 'with a mixture of the lowest spirits and the most intense enjoyment'.

I am afraid I thought Miss Miriam Lewes quite miscast as the Queen. One felt that Hell never mutinied in that matron's bones and that she could never have looked upon, let alone have been tempted by, 'the bloat King'. Mr. John Laurie's Claudius was not nearly bloat enough, and too light in texture. Miss Gabrielle Casartelli was a completely prosaic Ophelia who, in the Mad Scene, walked about the stage in full possession of her wits and the decent black of a nursery governess in a family which has just lost its master. Mr. Neil Porter had the voice but not the appearance for Horatio; Mr. Charles Macdona as Polonius had intonations a good three hundred years too modern; and Fortinbras, who should be vocally superb, gave his army semi-audible commands in a manner to suggest that he could not have led a choir. I think I rather liked the First Gravedigger of Mr. Wilfrid Lawson, but I am in no doubt whatever about the Laertes of Mr. Eric Portman. Laertes it was who, at his second appearance, and half out of his mind with excited grief, shocked us again into realization that we were witnessing the greatest of poetic tragedies.

Their Hour Upon the Stage: February 12, 1930

HAMLET

(Haymarket)

MR. AINLEY

THERE is a great deal in Hamlet that no stretch of imagination can call 'nice'; it is Horatio's job to have sounded his friend's heart and thrown away the worser part of it. Watching Mr. Tearle, whose eye never left Hamlet and whose voice throughout touched one stop only, that of some elder brother's tenderness, one could conjure up the gentle, unalloyed spirit which Hamlet might so easily have been. There are two glimpses of this. The first is in that great hymn to friendship beginning: 'Nay, do not think I flatter,' and ending: 'Something too much of this.' Hamlet knows that the even tenor of friendship is one of the paths he is never to tread, and in this moment spills the treasures which he can never spend. The second glimpse, though it is earlier in time,

is at the phrase: 'For every man hath business and desire, Su
as it is.' I take it that this is not contemptuous and still less meaningless, and that in this phrase Hamlet takes leave of the common
way of happiness. Hamlet, on Tuesday afternoon, 'threw away'
both passages. This brings me directly to what was fine in Mr.
Ainley's handsome performance and to one aspect of it which
was not fine at all — the fact that never, in my view, did the actor
suggest that he was not reciting and bringing to that reciting a
conscious magnificence. In place of an interpretation of Hamlet
we had a display of executive virtuosity and bravura declamation
which, instead of revealing the character, blinded us to it. The
quarrel, since it must be one, takes its rise in Mr. Ainley's excess
of superbity. Surely Hamlet should be to the spectator's eye that
which he seemed to the Court? Now throughout the play nobody
has any inkling that Hamlet is a flaming intellect, a high-powered
engine working at terrific pressure. Only Claudius, and even he
only towards the end, suspects that Hamlet is more than the
dreamer everybody takes him for. Whereas if the young man had
bestridden his world colossally everybody must have been 'put
wise' to the presence of an extremely remarkable young man.
Now consider Gertrude's curt summons to her closet and her
opening rebuke. Are not these any mother to any naughty little
boy? It is obvious that to everybody at court — for Ophelia's
evidence is *ex parte* — Hamlet is a quite unremarkable young man.
But Mr. Ainley is not unremarkable. He has commanding presence, handsome looks, fine gestures, and his famous organ voice.
This Hamlet could never have been too much i' the sun; he *was*
the sun. Obviously if there was a master-mind about the place
it was his. Mr. Ainley accentuated all these magnificences, and
throughout assumed a pose and a mental habit reminding one of
Mr. Max Beerbohm's Lord Byron shaking the dust of England
from his shoes. Or one might say that he was leoninity itself,
throwing off the soliloquies 'like dewdrops from the lion's mane'
and generally giving rhetoric an innings of three hundred not out.

Does this mean that the actor who essays Hamlet must not be
well-graced? It does not. Does it mean that the soliloquies shall

not receive their meed of purple? Again no. What it does mean is that display of the graces must not supplant the search after character, also that the purple patches must not be regarded as the building of which they are only the ornaments. In other words the actor who cannot help being a banquet to eye and ear must take more than ordinary care not to starve the mind. It was here that Mr. Ainley put us upon short commons. There is a fantasy by Mr. Milne in which, on a summer evening, the butler at a Sunningdale bungalow says to his master: 'Excuse me, sir, but there's a knight in armour at the front door.' His master replies: 'Show him in, Timms, and bring the whisky.' Mr. Ainley received the ghost with hardly more dismay, and at the words: 'Angels and ministers of grace defend us!' when his whole soul and mind should be flopping on the earth and many actors do in fact grovel — carefully arranged his sword before dropping to one graceful knee. In the 'To be or not to be' soliloquy we were conscious, not of Hamlet finding *for the first time* words to express long-surging speculation, but of Mr. Ainley performing a cadenza. At the phrase: 'The undiscover'd country from whose bourne No traveller returns,' the actor drew himself up and underlined the statement, the actual fact being that a very awkward traveller, his father's Ghost, *had* returned, and that that was what all the bother was about. Mr. Ainley took the least interest that I can remember in his trap to catch the King. Hamlet, having declared 'For I mine eyes will rivet to his face', did nothing of the sort, but engrossed himself with the players, and actually addressed the words 'Wormwood, wormwood' to, of all people, Ophelia! Rightly, a high-light was made of: 'Is it the king?' But Hamlet did not resolve the question, which he should do by showing on his face chagrin at gathering from the Queen's comparative indifference that it is not Claudius. Alternatively, if Hamlet is not to know the truth for another three lines the actor did not hold suspended in his face the excitement of his question. Having delivered the line, Mr. Ainley gave himself an 'easy' so as to get ready for: 'Leave wringing of your hands.' Both passages were finely said, but not linked together. Even simple little effects went astray. For example, the words: 'The air, look you,' were taken in the orator's stride when they should have been a parenthesis enabling the lower-witted courtiers to know what has been meant by 'canopy'. Perhaps the most noteworthy thing about this Hamlet was the complete absence of melancholy, for which some well-ordered rages and a recurring smile were a poor substitute. We were given no tenderness for anybody, and even the lovely lines to Laertes: 'What is the reason that you use me thus? I loved you ever,' were dry as a bone. Strange, too, that the 'Nay, an thou'lt mouth' speech, where any amount of ranting is called for, came poorly off. But the whole performance reminded one of a magnificent façade attached to no particular building, a procession of utmost stateliness from purple patch to purple patch without any presentation of that inner life which should knit these decorations together. There is probably no reason why Mr. Ainley should not make good the defects here signalized, and perhaps the best way to begin would be to forget that Hamlet is a star part. Mr. Ainley has all the attributes of the great actor, but should remember that some of the genius of great acting consists in taking care that those attributes do not get between the audience and the character. Perhaps, too, when Mr. Ainley next plays the part he will see to it that the unsympathetic half of Hamlet is restored, including the passage about 'the bloat king', which I have never before known to be omitted. On Tuesday afternoon the play was so cut as to render nearly all the latter half of the tragedy meaningless.

Miss Gwen Ffrangcon-Davies gave a lovely performance of Ophelia, as one little detail will show. At the end of the mad scene Ophelia came down-stage towards Laertes with recognition on her face. But before she could take shelter in her brother's arms her mind clouded again so that she found herself confronted by a stranger. And it was a stranger to whom she said: 'God be wi' you!' This was most touching, and if it be a part of tradition, why then Miss Ffrangcon-Davies re-created it so that it seemed new. As Polonius Mr. Herbert Waring was admirable, though he might possibly have gathered a little more wool; and as Laertes Mr. Colin Clive, good actor though he is, could not bridge the centuries. There were some glorious pieces of miscasting. Miss Irene Vanbrugh, normally my heart's delight, will forgive me if I say that one viewed her Queen more in sorrow than in anger. As for the King, Mr. Cedric Hardwicke will also, I hope, forgive the suggestion that when one wants to see Churdles Ash one visits another play. Last, I shall risk Mr. Thesiger's eternal displeasure by submitting that Osric is not the principal character in *Hamlet*. Alas that the tittering evoked by this over-mannered impersonation continued after the actor's exit and prevented us from paying any attention to Hamlet's lines about the fall of a sparrow, lines held by many to be of some beauty!

Their Hour Upon the Stage: April 22, 1930

HAMLET
(The Old Vic)

MR. GIELGUD

To clap into't roundly, the short version of *Hamlet* now presented at the Old Vic is the best abridgement I have ever seen of this over-long play. There used to be a nonsense tag about 'the higher, the fewer'. But nonsense may be the shortest cut to sense, and it is sober truth that the higher the quality of the thought the fewer the number of the words one can digest. I speak here for the normal playgoer of ordinary staying power. The pretence that all that is essential in *Hamlet* cannot be got into three and a half hours' steady going is the vilest cant. It was a convenient pretence in the old days when scenery had to be unrolled, processions unwound, and precious minutes wasted in tiptoeing at the end of the Nunnery scene down-stage to embrace in heartrending fashion the extremities of Ophelia's tresses. That this made nonsense of the King's 'Love! his affections do not that way tend', was never a deterrent; it was an affecting piece of business which made very fine sense for Hamlet when the actor was determined to present that character as a model of amiability, meet for maidenly approval at matinées. In these circumstances all the late middle of the play had to go, with the result that many generations of West End playgoers have never seen a Hamlet who was not a perfect little gentleman throughout.

Mr. Gielgud's Hamlet is as good as any reasonable person could desire. One says reasonable, because the part makes demands that are unreasonable. It demands every grace of body, mind, and heart, and the power of expressing intellectual and spiritual ugliness. Hamlet, the noble heart, sweet prince, and all the rest of it, must make us feel that Horatio, bidding flights of angels sing him to his rest, came near to saying the wrong thing. There was so much that is murky churned up in that tormented brain that the demons might have been asked to lend a hand, respectfully, at a distance. Hamlet must make us cry one minute and shudder the next, and the actor who goes a little way towards fulfilling both halves of the contract is always a better Hamlet than one who fulfils one half abundantly and the other not at all. Let it be said that though Mr. Gielgud has not quite enough pathos he knows where the occasions for pathos are, and marks the passages with the greatest sensibility. The inability to draw tears proceeds from a physical, not an intellectual lack, and is purely the affair of the larynx. Many abominable actors possess the gift in full measure, and I suggest to Mr. Gielgud that he must at once set about acquiring it. In the horrific he does better, though I think he should cut an uglier figure physically in Gertrude's closet and take some of the music out of his voice. The man is beside himself, and the voice should be beside itself also. What all this amounts to is merely that Mr. Gielgud has neither the pathos nor the dæmonism of Henry Irving; given his present machine, I do not see that he could play Hamlet better. It is at least an exploration into the character rather than an exploitation of the actor, and three-fourths of the one virtue is always better than the whole of the other vice. This Hamlet is noble in conception. It has been thought out in the study and is lived upon the stage, with the result that you feel that these things are happening to Hamlet for the first time, and that he is here and now creating words to express new-felt emotion. The performance is not actorish and the affair of repetition; this Hamlet will cease upon, and about, the midnight, and that will be the end of him. The whole part was spoken with the nicest intention, and I shall not quarrel with Mr. Gielgud because his intentions were not always mine. The words 'Get thee to a nunnery' were delivered at the first time of utterance, and before Hamlet perceives the eavesdroppers, with maximum pathos as though Hamlet would draw out of that refuge its power to heal as well as mortify. The Play scene and everything that follows were taken at a terrific speed and with the right kind of nervous energy. At the words: 'What, frighted with false fire?' the house was really excited, and with the genuine excitement of a crowd when a goal is scored in a Cup Final, or of the *dedans* at Queen's last week when in the tennis championship Baerlein made that miraculous, impossible scoop. From this the pace never slackened until the 'All occasions' soliloquy, when it was purposely slowed down to permit of one of the finest pieces of sheer exposition I have ever heard. Strangely enough, the rant over the grave did not quite come off, perhaps because the actor was tiring. This scene, like Othello's, 'Wash me in steep-down gulfs of liquid fire' demands hardly anything except noise, and, as I judge, Mr. Gielgud did not here quite fill the big theatre. But everything after this was admirable. It should be added that the verse was spoken throughout like verse, and the whole performance conceived in the key of poetry.

Mr. Harcourt Williams's production in the Elizabethan manner was excellent throughout, though, frankly, I did not like his Ghost, which was vocally too light in colour. Is it possible that Mr. Wolfit's King, made up after the manner of Velazquez's Philip IV, looked a little too like Vandyck's Charles I in a bad temper? Miss Martita Hunt gave a thoroughly satisfying performance as Gertrude and, if she be economically minded, may at any time play Mary Queen of Scots without change of costume or headdress. The early scenes of Miss Adèle Dixon's Ophelia were comparatively unmoving. But the later ones precipitated paroxysms, and it is not true that all the credit must be given to Shakespeare, since there have been Ophelias who have worn this rue with indifference. Mr. Brember Wills came into his own as Polonius, and a very good own it was. The Laertes of Mr. Francis James did very nicely; but the Horatio of Mr. Gyles Isham did not do at all, unless we are to suppose that that young gentleman had spent a recent Saturday morning rowing from Putney to Mortlake and would presently be taking the field against the Australians.

Their Hour Upon the Stage: May 5, 1930

HAMLET
(Haymarket)

MR. TEARLE

What man is there, now living, who can present before us all those changing and prismatic colours with which the character of Hamlet is invested? — MRS. CURDLE

MR. GODFREY TEARLE, taking up the part at two days' notice in consequence of Mr. Ainley's illness, certainly showed that after six years he had not lost the trick of it. There were one or two verbal slips. Probably at succeeding performances Mr. Tearle has not said: 'See what a grace was seated on this *face*!' and in the line 'To give the world assurance of a man' has not stopped at the word 'of' and begun an entirely meaningless sentence with the words 'a man'. He should certainly not have said, 'Hell itself breathes out Contagion to this *vile* world', since Hamlet leaves the vileness for granted. Civilization did not crumble when, in reply to Polonius's 'The actors are come hither, my lord!' Mr. Tearle said 'Buzz' *three* times, but he certainly showed *trop de zèle*. Hamlet's first soliloquy was going well until the passage:

A little month, or ere those shoes were old
With which she follow'd my poor father's body,
Like Niobe, all tears —

Here Mr. Tearle turned the second line into:

With which like Niobe she follow'd my poor father's body all
tears!

At this point, down, so to speak, came baby, cradle, and all!
But this actor is no Humpty-Dumpty, and Hamlet was soon
himself again.

The Closet scene was drastically cut and made to end with
Hamlet's —

So again, good night.
I must be cruel, only to be kind:
Thus bad begins, and worse remains behind.

This was unfortunate, for, except on the supposition that Shakespeare is indulging in a bit of nonsense — an unsafe supposition
in this grand and close-knit scene — Hamlet must mean something
by this couplet. He probably means that having to give his
mother a wigging is bad, but that having to kill his stepfather is
going to be worse. But surely it must be an aside, for in the full
scene the order of thought is as follows. Hamlet says, 'Once
more, good night!' and follows this by that bit about the blessings.
He next deals with Polonius's death: 'For this same lord', etc.,
etc., after which he again says good night. I suggest that our
couplet, which now follows, must be an aside, because Hamlet,
far from intending to hint to his mother that further trouble is
brewing, turns to her again with, 'One word more, good lady',
and advises her categorically against the King's questionings.
But no actor of flesh, blood and *amour-propre* can be expected
to end the biggest scene in the play with an aside, and since the
bit about Polonius was also cut we were treated to the spectacle
of Hamlet kneeling with a lump in his throat at the words —

And when you are desirous to be blest,
I'll blessing beg of you —

after which, half rising, he said: 'So again, good night!' and when he had completely got to his feet waved his arms in front of Gertrude and frightened the life out of her with his tale of worse. Worse for whom and in what way the poor wretch was not to hear, and one went into the foyer wondering whether Gertrude awake at night would be any happier than Lady Macbeth asleep. Mr. Tearle was not responsible for the cutting, and if the scene had to end nonsensically one agrees that the actor was right to do it grandiloquently.

Elsewhere Mr. Tearle avoids anything approaching bombast, the soliloquies being given without any hint of bravura, conversationally, as between members of the same club. 'Let's straighten this out!' Hamlet seems to say, looking after the retreating First Player and turning in his chair to ask fellow-members whether it is not monstrous, etc., etc. One lingers over these details from a natural reluctance to come to the point, which is that Mr. Tearle's performance, though noble and extremely moving, has almost nothing of Hamlet in it. His 'nighted colour' is the plainest assumption; not to set one's life 'at a pin's fee' bespeaks a sickness incredible in one obviously compact of healthful zests; the brag about the Nemean lion's nerve, so manifestly the vaunt of delicate physique, loses its meaning in this case, just as the later 'Out of my weakness and my melancholy' is the clearest of wilful mis-statements. But these are physical matters, and no actor is to be blamed because he cannot subtract a cubit from his stature. Most important of all, this Hamlet has no vacillation and knows nothing of subterfuge. There is never any real doubt in Hamlet's mind as to whether the Ghost is honest, 'grounds more relative than this' being the merest pretext for delay. This brings us to the 'Now might I do it pat' speech, wherein some critics, think wrongly, have seen a Renaissance malignity which would pursue vengeance into the next world. But Hamlet's play-trick having turned out only too successfully, he is now at his wits' end for further excuse, and this notion about 'a more horrid hent' is the very ticket. In either case poor Mr. Tearle is in a fearful difficulty. His appearance connotes all your Anglo-

Saxon indifference to, and contempt for, anything resembling quattro-cento subtlety, and as he has been a mountain of resolution from his first entrance, the pretence that we are looking at Shakespeare's Hamlet must at this point be abandoned. Now, Mr. Tearle as Horatio is streets better than any other actor one has ever seen in the part or could imagine. Everything about him breathes the loyalty, the burly-tender and 'faithful Dobbin' aspect of that character, and perhaps I can best describe Mr. Tearle's Hamlet by saying that he plays it like Horatio translated. The result is a masterpiece of contradiction. Hamlet wins every heart before he has got his first diffident sentence off his determined chest. But he has won by a forthrightness and simplicity which shut and bar the door against the mental sickness to come. *Mens sana in corpore sano* is an admirable motto, but not this character's device.

Mr. Malcolm Keen's King is one of the best I have ever seen, whereas the Queen of that delicious comédienne, Miss Irene Vanbrugh, is one of the least convincing. The cockneyism of her 'Good Hamlet, cast thy nighted colour *orf!*' settles that. Of Miss Fay Compton it is perhaps unnecessary to say that one actress only has exceeded the beauty and pathos of her Ophelia. Mr. Dennis Hoey's Horatio is a rather gaunt and occasionally forgetful garnisher of Hamlet's bosom; Mr. Herbert Waring as Polonius is almost too authentic a bore; while if Elsinore can be credited with a Young Men's Mutual Improvement Association, then Mr. Tristan Rawson's Laertes is obviously its perpetual President. That good actor, Mr. Robert Speaight, is in the unfortunate position of having too little thew and sinew for the First Player but too much for Osric, which parts he doubles. Mr. Tom Reynolds has great fun with the Gravedigger, and in the matter of stoups of liquor Mr. Norman Page fetches and carries with a will. Lastly, Mr. Baliol Holloway's Ghost delivers his speech as though he has nothing else with which to while away Eternity. Perhaps he is right.

First Nights: March 3, 1931

HAMLET
(New)

MR. GIELGUD

WHEN a piece of acting is as good as Mr. Gielgud's Hamlet is known to be, it becomes the critic's duty to say not how far it exceeds the lowest standard but by how much it falls short of the highest. He must, when the highest honours are at stake, 'find quarrel in a straw'. Roundly, then, this Hamlet, beginning where most leave off, is fine; yet by a curious perversity it is only half as fine as this perfectly graced actor could make it. Now gather, and surmise.

The soldiers have stopped marvelling, and the curtain has risen on the first Court scene. Their Majesties are already seated, in a setting of such rich, if sombre, magnificence that the house breaks into applause. The King has made his opening speech and is asking Laertes what he wants, and we have still not made up our minds which among the courtiers is Hamlet! Or would not be able to do so if we were strangers to the London theatre and did not know Mr. Gielgud. Can it be that they are going to play Hamlet without the Prince? No; for at last we spot him, as much withdrawn as the width of the stage permits. Is he a trifle too spectacularly in the shade, a thought too determined to be the unobserved of all observers? Is there too petulant a charm in the sweep of chin and throat, like Byron sitting for his portrait? There may be, but these things are immediately forgotten in the exquisite and touching delivery of the 'Seems, madam' speech and the 'Too, too solid flesh' soliloquy. When Mr. Gielgud played the part four years ago I suggested that while knowing when he ought to be pathetic he had not, in fact, much pathos. This has been remedied to a very remarkable degree, and the spectator must have a heart of stone not to be moved by Hamlet's obvious affection for his dead father, made manifest in the little 'Take him for all in all' colloquy with Horatio. Mr. Jack Hawkins plays very well here, being staggered at Hamlet's 'Methinks I see my father', a little disappointed to find that his news is no news, and not sorry to hear that Hamlet is talking only of his mind's eye. The scene on the platform is well done, though Hamlet omits the longish and rather dull speech about the 'mole of nature'. Something, of course, has to be cut, and this is a good bit to be rid of, except that its retention underlines a point which cannot be made too often in connection with this play. This is that Shakespeare is a writer, not of acute psychological treatises to be pored over by obtuse Germans, but of stage plays of which one part can be inconsistent with another, provided each passes muster at the moment of performance. Nobody can be more natural than Shakespeare when being natural is his cue; and nobody can do more violence to nature if unnaturalness is the more paying proposition. (For example, every reader of Shakespeare must have asked why Horatio does not tell Hamlet about Ophelia's death when he meets him at the railway-station, and every Shakespearean playgoer knows that the answer is to permit of the tragi-comic colloquy with the Grave-diggers and the revelation to Hamlet *in view of the audience*.) As for the 'mole of nature' speech, it is not conceivable that any human being, expecting at any moment to meet his father's ghost, could or would embark upon that long and involved tirade about the power of a single flaw to undermine a character. That Shakespeare violates nature here is due to one of two causes — either the itch for spilling moral beans, or the mere dramatic necessity for prolonging the suspense. Owlish professors blinking at the passage will see in it elucidation of Hamlet's character, whereas Shakespeare probably puts it in to keep Hamlet, Horatio, and Marcellus a little longer in the dark. But that is by the way.

In all that immediately follows the Ghost's speech Mr. Gielgud a little disappoints, as here almost all exponents have a little disappointed. Oddly enough, of all the Hamlets I have seen, Tree fell least short here because, being an actor-manager aesthetically unencumbered, he had a spotlight by which to see him working hysterically up to that astonishing, romantic cry: 'Hillo, ho, ho, boy! come, bird, come.' Mr. Gielgud has to do this in the dark on a staircase, so that the working-up can only be vocal, and the actor's voice despite its range and melodic outline is not quite up to this feat. A spectator who did not know the words: 'Come, bird, come', would not hear them. Nor do I think that this Hamlet makes quite enough — if indeed he says it — of the little speech ending 'for mine own poor part Look you, I'll go pray'. It was here that Forbes-Robertson made Hamlet suddenly perceive that he is a doomed man; in saying: 'For every man hath business and desire, such as it is', his Hamlet realized that whereas business and desire may be sorry things, it is his unhappiness that he must abstain from both. Mr. Gielgud's rendering of the 'fellow in the cellarage' is ineffective, and singularly little is made of the promise to put on an antic disposition. This is perhaps intentional because, except for one subsequent hurried disarrangement of hair and garments, there is never any question, so far as I can detect, of the Dane being either mad or pretending to be. He is not even mad north-north-west; whatever winds blow he remains a model of lucidity.

It is at this point that the spectator becomes aware of a fixed determination on the actor's part to make as little as possible of anything that can be called the orthodox 'acting' of the part, to throw away — in the actor's sense — everything except the highest of its poetry and the most sensitive of its philosophy. The result, strange to say, is not an enhancement but a diminishment of the character. Hamlet, interrupted in his reading by Polonius, should put on a mock solemnity whereby the old man does not know that he is being made fun of. Mr. Gielgud is cheeky here, so that we wonder that the old fellow does not resent the boyish impertinence. But then, in my view, all the play's urbanity is given insufficient value. Mr. Gielgud pulls himself together for the 'Rogue and peasant slave' soliloquy, which he delivers grandly, rendering it like the first movement of some tremendous concerto and so that the 'To be or not to be' speech, which follows almost immediately, has the tenderness of a Mozartian slow movement. The scene with Ophelia must always beat any actor who is not content to take it as music, unless, of course, he is prepared to accept Sir Arthur Quiller-Couch's contention that this is a jumble of Shakespeare's play and that earlier story in which the bait used by the King and Polonius to discover Hamlet's secret was not Ophelia but a courtesan. Nothing else that I know of, except the madness motive, explains Hamlet's: 'I never gave you aught', which occurs at the beginning of the scene before he realizes he is being watched. The confusion of the two texts justifies Hamlet's planting upon Ophelia the vices of the courtesan, always on the supposition that Shakespeare jumped at this chance of invective and wasn't going to discard it because of its inconsistency with Hamlet's knowledge of Ophelia's character. Anyhow, the madness and Sir Arthur's contention between them accomplish the trick of making the scene feasible. But the most fascinating speculations must not lure us out of playhouse logic. Since Mr. Gielgud jettisons all suggestion of madness and since not one playgoer in a thousand has read Sir Arthur's lectures, we come back willy-nilly to the scene played as sheer music. Our present Hamlet, realizing that this is one of the great things in the play, tackles it for all his vocal grace and physical and mental elegance are worth, and his pathos here is again extraordinary. This in the present version brings the first part of the play to an end. After 'throwing away' the Advice to the Players, perhaps on the score that it is hackneyed, Mr. Gielgud again commands the most of our admiration for the rapt beauty of his speech to Horatio: 'Nay, do not think I flatter'. Then follows some more deliberate underplaying, and so rapid and casual is the dialogue here that I cannot remember having heard about either 'hobby-horse' or 'miching mallecho'. And surely Hamlet's lightning 'The Mouse-trap' should be a dagger driven up to the hilt into the King's conscience? Whereas when Claudius asks: 'What do you call the play?' Hamlet makes so little of the reply that the King could conceivably not hear him.

The end of the Play Scene is given effectively and prestissimo, after which there is another lapse, the scene with the recorders being given too slowly and as a dialectical exercise instead of being the ground-swell of a storm which has still to subside. And frankly it is permissible to hold that the scene with the Queen could do with a little less intellectual passion and a little more of the other sort. Here Mr. Gielgud receives insufficient help from Miss Laura Cowie, and what should be an emotional duet becomes a cold lecture on moderation in second marriages. But perhaps the cooling off is again deliberate, since Mr. Gielgud has no intention of giving the magnificent postscript about the 'convocation of politic worms'. How any actor can omit this beats me utterly, since half of Hamlet is portrayed here. The player returns to his best self in the almost mathematical exposition of the 'How all occasions' soliloquy, though the omission of the scene with the King and the resulting joining up of two lots of moralizing make this over-nice debater a colder-blooded fellow than the real Hamlet of the full text. If the concluding scenes do not wholly satisfy it is because we feel the want of something, though it is difficult to say what. The impression we have by this time gathered is of a Hamlet who can fly into the most shattering of pets. He has accesses of grief, but they do not leave him moody, there is no melancholy in him, his mind has not the richness of its words, he is not fey or marked for death, and his talk of ripeness is academic and not the ultimate philosophy of a man who feels that his course is run. To sum up, this Hamlet's specific gravity is akin to Romeo's, and when he dies we are conscious of losing no more than a gay, gallant, romantic companion; we do not feel that part of ourselves has died with him. I hope that the foregoing is not an ungenerous estimate. If it is, it is because the actor so wantonly sacrifices the acting strength of the play to no discoverable purpose. If he would reconsider this and give to the prose passages that loving attention he has given to the poetry, one would modify one's attitude almost without knowing it. One would then say wholeheartedly that this is Mr. Gielgud's intensest fulfilment of himself, and not inquire too closely whether an Irving or a Forbes-Robertson had richer stores of magic upon which to draw. This Hamlet abounds in loveliness, but one feels

that the actor's treasury could yield more. It would be wrong
not to insist upon the wealth of beauty and accomplishment
contained in that half of the character which is fully explored.
Elsewhere it is as though Hamlet had taken his own advice to the
players too much to heart. And didn't the first dramatic critic
say something about considering 'some necessary question of the
play'? If Mr. Gielgud will reconsider the many necessary questions of this play he will make his performance the whole which
at present it is not.' The poetic half, having attained perfection,
should be left severely alone.

The ladies who call themselves Motley have provided some
enchanting scenery and dresses. Mr. Vosper's King is satisfying,
and would be even better if Nature had not made the player's
cheeks creaseless; this being so Mr. Vosper has to rely on his
voice, which he uses excellently. Mr. George Howe makes
Polonius a most engaging old fool; Mr. William Devlin's Ghost
is insufficiently ghostly though beautifully spoken; and Mr. Glen
Byam Shaw's Laertes looks like one of the naughty children whom
Struwwelpeter's tall Agrippa dipped into the inkpot. Laertes
and Ophelia are of the company of Shakespeare's golden lads
and lasses and should be played as such. The rest is silence,
including Ophelia, for whom in my opinion that charming little
actress, Miss Jessica Tandy, is quite pathetically miscast.

More First Nights: November 18, 1934

HAMLET
(The Old Vic)

MR. OLIVIER

BEFORE pronouncing whether an actor can act Hamlet, one has
first to decide whether he can act at all. If this is too sweeping let
me for 'at all' substitute 'poetic tragedy'. Has the young man a
feeling for poetry, and a sense of the tragic? And since everything

that an actor does must be conveyed through his physical means, this is equivalent to asking whether he has a distinguished and mobile countenance, a resonant voice, a noble bearing, a princely gait, and sufficient stature. An actor may be twin-souled with Shakespeare, but if he be plain, rasping, cringing, creeping, and dwarfish, he must confine himself to Thersites and Caliban. The back of an actor's mind is not nearly so important as the back of his head, always provided the man can act. For if a man can act, his performance, though misconception stands the part on its head, will still give pleasure of a kind. Whereas conception alone, however right, if the means to convey that conception be wanting, gives nothing.

Now consider Mr. Laurence Olivier in the frank, brutal, and altogether sensible way in which the old dramatic critics considered the old actors. What is the first thing G. H. Lewes tells us about Frederic Lemaître? 'Lemaître was very handsome. He had a wonderful eye, with large orbit, a delicate and sensitive mouth, a fine nose, a bold jaw, a figure singularly graceful, and a voice penetrating and sympathetic. He had great animal spirits, great daring, great fancy, and great energy of animal passion.' And what is the last thing that he perceives in him? It is this: 'A note of vulgarity, partly owing to his daring animal spirits, but mainly owing, I suspect, to an innate vulgarity of nature.' Apply these things to Mr. Olivier. Mr. Olivier has a well-turned head, a pleasing, youthful face, a magnificent voice of bow-string tautness and vibrancy marred by a few commonplace intonations which could easily be eliminated, good carriage, a springy, pantherine gait, and the requisite inches. Mr. Olivier, then, can act, since in addition to the foregoing he possesses the mimetic talent. Now we must ask: Can he act Hamlet? I have just used the word 'commonplace' because I wanted to avoid the word 'common'. I detect in Mr. Olivier none of the vulgarity which Lewes found in Lemaître. But I do observe a modern, jaunty off-handedness which is presumably a legacy from parts of the Beau Geste order. I do not refer here to the one quality in which Mr. Olivier's Hamlet excels any Hamlet of recent years

— its pulsating vitality and excitement. After Claudius has left at the end of the Play Scene this Hamlet acts literally all over the stage, his 'Why, let the stricken deer go weep' being accompanied by a tremendous leap from the perched-up throne on to the mimic stage below, and thence down to the footlights in an access of high hysteria. That is matter for the most compelling admiration. The jauntiness complained of occurs in the philosophic passages, which too often take on a note approaching pertness. This is due to, I will not say a fault, but a characteristic of Mr. Olivier's playing which prevents him from being Hamlet.

The same great critic whom we have been quoting has a significant passage about Charles Kean, which I would apply almost word for word to Mr. Olivier: 'The fluency of Shakespeare's movements, the subtle interpenetration of thought and emotion, the tangled web of motives, the mingling of the heroic with the familiar, the presence of constant verisimilitude under exceptional and exaggerated conditions, all demand great flexibility of conception and expression in the actor, great sympathy of imagination, nicety of observation, and variety of mimetic power. In these Charles Kean is wholly deficient. He has the power of coarse painting, of impressive representation when the image to be presented is a simple one; but he has no subtlety of sympathy, no nicety of observation, no variety of expression . . . It is because there is no presence of poetry in his acting that we all feel Charles Kean to be essentially a melodramatic actor. The unreality and unideality of a melodrama are alike suited to his means. If he attempt to portray real emotion he leaves us cold; if he attempt to indicate a subtle truth, it is done so clumsily and so completely from the outside conventional view that we are distressed'. Or you might put it that Mr. Olivier's Hamlet is the best performance of Hotspur that the present generation has seen. One more quotation from Lewes, and I have done with him. 'For myself', he writes, 'I confess to have the smallest possible pleasure in a French actor when he is *profond et rêveur*.' And for myself, I confess to the smallest possible pleasure in a Hamlet who is neither *rêveur* nor *profond*. Mr. Olivier's Hamlet is entirely without melancholy, and its lack of profundity may be gauged from his delivery of the line to Rosencrantz and Guildenstern:

I will not sort you with the rest of my servants; for, to speak to you like an honest man, I am most dreadfully attended.

Here Shakespeare has the grimmest of double meanings; Hamlet is referring either to the Ghost or to his antecedent 'I have bad dreams'. Mr. Olivier speaks the words as though Hamlet were complaining of the attendance in a service flat.

But let us take the performance in a little more detail. This Hamlet at the beginning of the play is puzzled. But it is rather the honest, frank perplexity of a modern young man at Oxford or Cambridge whose annoyance that his mother should have remarried with such indecent haste is not going to prevent him from helping himself that afternoon to a hundred of the best off the sister University's bowling. There should be more 'to' Hamlet than this, even at the outset. We ought to feel that even if there were no Ghost and no murder, Hamlet is still an invincible neurasthenic. We feel that Mr. Olivier's Hamlet has not in him anything 'which passeth show'. A little disappointed here, we seize at the skill with which this Hamlet receives Horatio's 'My lord, I think I saw him yesternight'. Hamlet hears this without taking it in, and this is the first of many bits of straightforward acting which Mr. Olivier does excellently. The scenes with the Ghost and immediately after are crammed with all that excitement which is to be the note of the performance, and provide the first occasion for the welcome letting-out of that too rarely heard thing, a voice up to the demands of high tragedy. And now follows the admonition to Horatio and Marcellus. It may be that here the actor has to choose between Forbes-Robertson's heartbreak in 'For every man hath business and desire' and the wild and whirling delivery here indicated; Forbes-Robertson was not wild and never whirled. Mr. Olivier is entitled to take 'Look you, I'll go pray' at immense speed. But he must not, I think, make so little of the 'antic disposition' passage. This is the point at which the actor must declare himself in the matter of Hamlet's madness. For myself I have no doubt that Hamlet was completely sane, and I have never been able to detect one single word in the entire part suggesting the contrary. Johnson ('It never does to neglect Johnson') says: 'Of the feigned madness of Hamlet there appears no adequate cause, for he does nothing which he might not have done with the reputation of sanity.' Some little time ago somebody said to me about the most *méchante langue* in London: 'Lady X —— is not intentionally witty; she speaks exactly what is in her mind, and this in an insincere age is wit!' Now, wit at a court is wit out of place, and hence madness. Hamlet in his teasing of Polonius is merely speaking his thoughts aloud, and this, together with his melancholy and neurasthenia, would at the court of Denmark easily pass for madness. The point is that Hamlet, while remaining as sane to us as he does to Horatio and Marcellus, must convey madness to the rest of the court. Mr. Olivier skates over the 'antic disposition' passage as quickly as possible, and the question of madness real or assumed is then dropped. But I must not be too long. The passages of which Mr. Olivier makes notably little are, first, the scenes with the players. It is incredible that he should be unconscious of the sheer word-beauty of 'this brave o'erhanging firmament, this majestical roof fretted with golden fire'. When Forbes-Robertson said this, Rosencrantz and Guildenstern were struck into a Michael-Angelesque dumbness. He disappoints, too, in the 'Get-thee-to-a-nunnery' Scene and in the Closet Scene. To conclude the tale of blame, Mr. Olivier does not speak poetry badly. He does not speak it at all.

Now for the good points. The soliloquies are delivered with remarkable cogency, and immense power and fire in the right places. I do not think I have ever heard the Fortinbras soliloquy better treated. The lines:

> I do not know
> Why yet I live to say 'this thing's to do',
> Sith I have cause, and will, and strength, and means,
> To do't . . .

are trumpet-moaned as though it has at last broken in on the young man that indecision is his bane. Up to that time Hamlet has been the one person in all Denmark likeliest to get his own way about anything from pitch-and-toss to slaughter. Of the Play Scene and all that follows I have already spoken. The rest is a jumble of the good and the insufficient. The Grave Scene lacks reflective emotion, and there is not enough banter in the little scene with Osric. On the other hand, the fencing with Laertes — a moving performance by Mr. Michael Redgrave — is done with real virtuosity, which fades before the Death Scene. Mr. Olivier just cannot say: 'Absent thee from felicity a while', and he will have to live some time yet before he knows how to die. To sum up, this is obviously a performance carefully thought out, consonant with itself, and taken at admirable speed. On the other hand, it is not Hamlet, but a brilliant performance of the part such as Stanhope in *Journey's End* might have put up in some rest-interval behind the lines.

The King will be better when Mr. Francis Sullivan plays him outside his robes instead of in them, and the Queen of Miss Dorothy Dix conveys the impression of not being in the play at all, but of looking in now and again to do a bit of acting. As Ophelia Miss Cherry Cottrell strikes me as being unripe. Mr. Torin Thatcher makes an inaudible Ghost, and Mr. Frederick Bennett's First Gravedigger is the one gloomy spot in the entire production. Horatio just won't do, and Fortinbras, instead of being dumpish and insignificant, should be played by Mr. Shayle Gardner clad in gold armour. On the other hand, Mr. Alec Guinness contrives to make a character out of Reynaldo, and Mr. George Howe continues to be the best Polonius anybody has seen.

More First Nights: January 5, 1937

HAMLET
(Lyceum)

G. H. Lewes never saw Garrick's Hamlet. But, basing himself on Fielding's description, he deduced that the great actor 'tried to be natural, without duly considering the kind of nature that was to be represented'. And, possibly, without considering his own. For in the delineation of natural passion there are two natures to be considered, that of the character, *and that of the actor*. Every dramatic critic knows this, because it is exactly this which every day of the week puts him into his most familiar difficulty. Mr. X proposes to play Hamlet, undeterred by a mean expression, a common voice, an awkward station, and an uncouth gait. In these days of emasculated criticism can the critic say that Mr. X, because of these defects, is debarred from playing Hamlet? No!

There is this to be said straightway for Mr. Gielgud's new Hamlet, that the actor has all the physical attributes required to make that prince princely. The more important question to ask is whether this gay and gracious player can be deemed to be Shakespeare's Hamlet. 'Gay?' queries the reader, and I repeat, 'gay'. The English stage at the present moment boasts two tragedians only among our younger actors — Mr. Gielgud, whose nature is sunny, and Mr. Olivier, whose nature is splenetic. 'How far', comes a second query, 'should the critic be influenced by the personality of an actor, since the essence of the business is for the actor to cloak his identity and to pretend to be somebody else?' The answer is that the finest pretending in the world cannot wholly override personality, and that in the classic rôles it is on his personality that the actor rides to success. Lewes wrote: 'I never saw Kean's Hamlet. He must have been puzzled what to do with many of the long speeches and quiet scenes, and could have had no sympathy with the character.' Now if it is legitimate to say: 'I saw Kean and know he could not have played Hamlet,' it is surely legitimate to say: 'I saw Irving and know that his Hamlet must have been the ideal representation of Shakespeare's character.' Are we going to write of Mr. Gielgud's Hamlet, as Montague wrote to Francis Dodd of Irving's, that it was 'all over faults but a regular globe of passion and romance with huge subterranean caverns and flames of fire inside it'? I think not, and for a reason to be found in Montague's definition of the play as a 'monstrous Gothic castle of a poem, with its baffled half-lights and glooms'. You felt that when Irving had discarded Hamlet the actor himself remained a vast Gothic cathedral of a man in whom Hamlet's thoughts might have welled up naturally. That they would not is not to the point; even if the Shavian interpretation of Irving as ignoramus doubled by mountebank had been correct, the *envelope* remained. And in acting the envelope is three-quarters of the communication. When a 'natural' Hamlet is playing, the melancholy is settled and the gaiety assumed. With Mr. Gielgud it is the other way about, and probably this is the reason that my impression of this brilliant performance does not outlast the moment of its brilliance. It is cometary. That was Hamlet, that was! And the sky is empty again.

Now let us take the performance in detail. Mr. Morgan has percipiently observed that the first soliloquy, 'O that this too too solid flesh would melt', was a little forced. I agree. One feels that, with the knowledge of all that is to come, the actor can afford, and is indeed under the obligation, to play himself in. The trouble is Shakespeare, who, with an eye like Bradman, is so confident of the century he is about to score that he can open his shoulders at the first ball. The recent Greek Hamlet spoke this soliloquy with his head against a pillar, so that it was a study in lassitude and distaste, making it the empty soil of Hamlet's mind in which the flowers and weeds are to grow in such profusion. But it is probable that any first-class Hamlet must be a give-and-take affair, that if the actor decides to avail himself of this, he must renounce that. For example, Mr. Gielgud treats the long

scene with the Ghost as an occasion for heartrending pathos, and
I have certainly never seen anguish more movingly presented.
But is anguish the point? What about that metaphysical awe on
which Lewes is so insistent here? Does not this Hamlet run counter
to his own advice? What about setting on some quantity of
thoughtful spectators to cry, though in the meantime some
necessary question of the play be then to be considered? The
spectator cannot listen to A properly if he is busy looking at B.
Besides, a piece should always be played as though the audience
were hearing it for the first time, if only for the reason that there
is always somebody in the audience hearing it for the first time.
The spectator's mind at this point should be with the Ghost on the
other side of the grave and not with Hamlet on this. Forbes-
Robertson at this point had the stage darkened so as to be himself
almost invisible. Mr. Gielgud might be well advised to draw up
a profit-and-loss account as to what should be retained and what
thrown away at this point. Forbes-Robertson was marvellously
effective after the Ghost had gone because he had done nothing
before. Mr. Gielgud is comparatively ineffective because he has
done so much.

In the second act (Shakespeare's) Mr. Gielgud is for a long
time at his best. 'What a piece of work is a man!' is like a jewel
hung on the air, the reception of the players is charming, and the
second major soliloquy, 'O, what a rogue and peasant slave am I!'
is given the honours of maximum virtuosity. Some grand playing
is forthcoming in Shakespeare's third act. 'To be, or not to be' is
introspection's very self; a definite one of the many possible meanings has been selected for the scene with Ophelia; and the advice
to the players is easy and urbane. Then suddenly, and some may
think unaccountably, the performance dries up in the play scene.
But I think not unaccountably, holding the fault to be not that
of Mr. Gielgud the actor but of Mr. Gielgud the producer. What
is the sense of setting the King and Queen with their backs to the
audience when the interest now centres in their faces? Take away
the royal target, and however well Hamlet aims interest must
go out of the marksmanship. And if bad begins, worse remains

behind. My colleague Mr. Darlington praises the actress entrusted with the Queen for making her 'a woman with senses but no mind, luscious as a lollipop and shallow as a puddle'. I have nothing with this criticism. I make nothing of a Gertrude who is the double of the Comtesse de Lage in *The Women*, expatiating on 'l'amour, but not lopsided l'amour'! But the point is not what any critic can make of such a character, but what Hamlet can make of it, and I say that he can make nothing. Like Lamb's Old Actor, Hamlet in the absence of any sentient partner in the Closet Scene is reduced to fighting with his own shadow, to 'seeing ghosts', and it so happens that in this particular play Shakespeare indicates with extreme precision when Hamlet should be seeing a ghost and when not!

The actor fails too, and fails handsomely, in the third scene of Shakespeare's fourth act. The sinister itch, the spleen that finds its images in the sun breeding maggots in a dead dog, and its most exquisite sensation in the doom of all living flesh — 'and now my Lady Worm's' — this instinct for rottenness and death — 'your worm is your only emperor for diet' — is as much a part of Hamlet, whether we like it or not, as the most urbane of his philosophy, the most flowerlike of his chivalry, the last of his tenderness. Here Hamlet should show himself as much intrigued by putrescence, material and moral, as any Baudelaire that was to come after; the terrible quality of his gusto at this point is something far beyond that pert scoring off his uncle which is all that Mr. Gielgud gives. But after this scene the actor makes magnificent recovery, sending us into the foyer in good fettle with his delivery, at once superb and passionate, of the fourth major soliloquy, 'How all occasions do inform against me!' Back in the theatre it is disconcerting to find the graveyard scene strangely ineffective, and short, as it were, of specific gravity. But the subsequent mouthing and ranting are well done, and there is a remarkable death-scene in which the man really dies as distinct from the star actor who desists. Now let it be said that all these are personal reactions — they cannot be anything else! — to a performance of great intelligence, abounding interest, increasing vigour. It is an immense advance upon the performance of five years ago, and in the process of advancement has shed nothing of its nobility and poetry. But although I admire this Hamlet greatly, I think it must not be called a great Hamlet until one defect is remedied. 'The world is out of joint,' cries Hamlet. 'O cursed spite, that ever I was born to set it right!' The mark of the great Hamlet is to make the spectator feel that the finger of the casting director, if not of Fate, has known exactly what it was about, and that here and nowhere else is the actor to set Hamlet's world right. When this Hamlet tells us that he is 'dreadfully attended' we do not believe him. Perhaps with the years Mr. Gielgud will acquire that moodiness which sat so naturally on Irving. But then Irving had no need of years. He was destined to play Hamlet from the cradle.

The Amazing Theatre: June 28, 1939

OTHELLO
(The Old Vic)

MR. HOLLOWAY

Othello takes longer than any other of the great plays to rear its head above the melodramatic ground. This being so, Mr. Andrew Leigh did well to run his first act right through to the shindy between Othello and his Ancient and the tragic-comic scene of the exchange of vows. This first act kept us in our seats for two hours. Paraphrasing another poet one might say two glad hours, and it seemed not an hour, of supreme and supernal— cinema. One may keep one's reverence for this mighty play and yet realize that the first half of it is the earliest of all the sheik-romances, in which incidentally Shakespeare out-Hulls Mrs. Hull. The early events have all the swiftness and striking quality of melodrama; as happenings they 'intrigue' us to the exclusion of tragic implication. Sitting through the first half of this play is

279

really sitting on the jury at Iago's subsequent trial and being invited by counsel to note when the poison was first administered, the increasing doses, the tell-tale symptoms. Othello's 'Now art thou my lieutenant' and Iago's 'I am your own for ever' mark the end of the case for the prosecution. It is then and then only that we, leaving the jury-box, have time to consider how magnanimous was the soul of the victim.

Bulwer's old title: 'What Will He Do With It?' must be in the mind of everybody who goes to see a new Othello. Will the actor give us a Moor over whose primitive savagery the Venetian blinds have been let down? Or shall we have a suave and polished dilettante kin to the modern Ethiop who for a fee of three hundred guineas entertains us in our drawing-rooms after dinner? Mr. Baliol Holloway chose the way of the magnificent savage, almost of the African in whose walk is the stealthy pad of the forest, ultimately 'going native', as indeed, it is indicated that he must. 'And when I love thee not, chaos is come again' indicates the doffing of the mask and veneer of civilization. Towards the end Mr. Holloway was in a 'terrible state o' chassis', and quite rightly it was the chassis, or chaos, of Mr. Robeson in *The Emperor Jones*. He ended, or all but ended, in a purely animal frenzy, interrupted for one unclouded moment at the words: 'My wife! my wife! what wife? I have no wife.' Mr. Holloway knows that when at last the truth dawns upon Othello the play is over and that the rest is pure coda. Quite rightly his magnanimity became pure recapitulation; it was here that he recovered something approaching the equanimity of the civilized mind, and his: 'I have another weapon in this chamber' had the calmness, almost the nonchalance of a man so absolute for death that he had put all living emotion behind him. This Othello had the naturalness, and the dignity, and the mind of a highly educated Moor, and not of a cultivated English gentleman who wakes up one morning to find that his skin has unexpectedly turned black. There was no pretence that, despite his complexion, his soul was Hamlet's. It wasn't; it was Othello's. Neither were his transports and his tendernesses for Desdemona quite those which we use on this side of the Mediterranean. He had no northerly consideration for her, and she had neither existence nor identity except in so far as she was his. This Othello was wounded, one felt, not only in his love, but in his *amour-propre* and most of all in his sense of property. Altogether it was a fine performance, full of light and shade and subtlety, and marred only by the absence of beauty in poetic diction, though one should add that the actor was in poor voice owing to an attack of influenza. Although Mr. Holloway has greatly improved in his phrasing, he still parses each line, and punctuates his speeches with invisible stops and a care that allows you to distinguish between colon and semi-colon. By way of compensation Mr. Holloway's gestures throughout were uniformly grand, and if the actor touched pathos not more than once he was often within hail of terror. There was considerable virtuosity in the death-scene, though I am not quite sure about that final attitude when he lay prone on the ground with arms outstretched like a Rugby footballer who has just scored a try. And I respectfully suggest that Mr. Holloway should not take his final call with the jauntiness of an All-Black who has just converted that try into the winning goal.

Let me briefly say of Mr. Neil Porter that he gave an admirable performance, admirably spoken. This Iago was obviously an intellectual, and refreshingly unlike the usual furtive dog-stealer who would not impose upon the most trustful old lady, not to mention an experienced man of affairs like Othello. Miss Gwynne Whitby avoided the mistake which is fatal to Desdemona — that of being arch from instep to eyebrows. She was extraordinarily simple and unaffected and consequently succeeded in being affecting. Many Desdemonas are so much the leading lady that you feel they have only to give Othello a good shaking to bring the silly fellow to his senses, and you are consequently annoyed that they have not enough wit to take the simple means of putting an end to his nonsense. Miss Whitby successfully avoided this snag also; she was in the toils from the beginning, and remained there. Miss Dorothy Massingham acted cleverly, of course, but I thought that she played Emilia above her station and that her voice was not sufficiently dark in colour; Emilia should be a contralto of Ada Crossley's deepest dye. Mr. Duncan Yarrow was inclined to prettify Cassio, and did not extract the full strength out of that personage. Mr. John Wyse, a rapidly improving actor, made a perfect noodle of Roderigo. Mr. John Garside's costumes and settings were handsome, and there was a scene of great enthusiasm at the end, husbands turning into the Waterloo Road with renewed confidence, and wives emerging with fresh cheer.

March 7, 1927

OTHELLO

(Arts)

MR. WILLARD

ONE might be asked of *Othello* as Lamb was asked about *Paradise Lost*, whether one would have it any longer. 'No-no,' stammered Charles, 'b-but I wouldn't have the m-m-moon any r-rounder!' The length of this play is of the heavenly order, and he is a poor playgoer who would shorten felicity. Yet we still have Shakespearean producers who, fearing that after three hours we shall grow faint, set that measure as the sea-mark of their utmost sail. There are, of course, lines in all of Shakespeare's plays which can be cut. But there are lines in *Othello* which are a part of inheritance. They are expected, and not to get them is like being set down to a banquet with, say, the bread missing. For example, lots of children have been advised by their parents never to mistake the cod's head for the salmon's tail, and upon inquiry have been told that when they grow older they would hear that advice given by a very wicked man in a very beautiful play called *Othello*. Well, they would not have heard it at the Arts Theatre. They would, in addition, have missed Othello's anthropophagi and Iago's 'super-subtle Venetian'. Some of the cutting was more than foolish. Of the famous passage:

282

IAGO My friend is dead, 'tis done at your request
But let her live.
OTHELLO *Damn her, lewd minx! O, damn her!*
Come, go with me apart; I will withdraw
To furnish me with some swift means of death
For the fair devil. Now art thou my lieutenant.
IAGO: *I am your own for ever.*

All the words in italics were cut. Then why should Othello exit
on: 'You are welcome, sir, to Cyprus' and be deprived of 'goats
and monkeys'? Why should Othello not have his: 'I will chop
her into messes' and 'I'll not expostulate with her lest her body
and beauty unprovide my mind again'? And what is the play of
Othello if we are not to have:

I had been happy if the general camp,
Pioneers and all, had tasted her sweet body,
So I had nothing known —

and:

O you mortal engines, whose rude throats
The immortal Jove's dread clamours counterfeit.

One is accustomed to having Iago's matter cut to ribbons, but
custom is no sanction, and so to treat Iago is to do the dramatist
utmost disservice. Shakespeare seems to have felt that Iago's
reason for hating the Moor — 'It is thought abroad that 'twixt my
sheets He has done my office' — was too slight a peg to hold Iago's
ensuing villainy, and so he reinforces it with the speech beginning:
'That Cassio loves her I do well believe it,' in which the additional
motive: 'Now, I do love her too; Not out of absolute lust, etc.', is
given. To omit this and other of this character's speeches or large
portions thereof is to do Shakespeare the further hurt that we
underrate him as a thinker, since Iago is the most metaphysical
villain of them all. The conclusion one is driven to is that if the
shortening cannot be done without these sacrifices we had better
be penned up in the theatre for another half-hour, for the most

jaded critic will admit that in the matter of penning there is all the difference between a world-masterpiece and the light comedy which should have been over before it started. Iago is as important to the play as Othello, unless we consent to a drama in which a noble booby is entrapped by a villain who is mindless as well as kindless. But Othello is no simpleton — for which see Coleridge — and his ensnaring must be done by a master and not a whipper-snapper of vice, and this again means a virtuoso in villainy running to two complexions, one for the people in the play, who are his dupes, and the other for his, Iago's use and ours.

This, again, connotes an actor not only subtle in mind but practised in the art of acting, and the Iago in the Arts Theatre production was a gentleman whose intellectual mastery of the character I never began to doubt, but who did not impress me as having been much on the stage. There is no slur here, for the player in question is a patron of the arts and an amateur in the highest sense, and this appearance was, as I understand it, strictly occasional. The result was to throw all responsibility on to Othello, and I shall say that Mr. Edmund Willard acquitted himself very, very well. Mr. Willard is a good, straightforward actor, who for years had been doing patient service as ebon executioners and the like. His Othello was still Masrur, but with a difference. It had dignity if not majesty, and if the scene of the epilepsy was underplayed it was doubtless through the excellent resolve not to run entirely to noise and violence, since we all know Mr. Willard's capacity to lift any roof, and he knew that we knew. The scene of awakening suspicion was excellently contrived, and the last act was a capital example of simple, manly pathos. It is a pleasure to add that he treated the verse with respect. Not the whole part, perhaps, but a brave shot.

Mr. George Skillan did not realize that Cassio's denials of drunkenness are not asseverations in front of a police sergeant, but expostulations before his own moral nature that the thing is impossible. Mr. Francis James, by not over-playing Roderigo, made him credible, which was creditable. Miss Lydia Sherwood did not fail as Desdemona, and, indeed, one would have defied her to, and Miss Clare Harris, as Emilia, grandly let fly at what, given its length, is probably the best part for an actress ever written. The mounting and the lighting were excellent, and the grouping and stage pictures were very well conceived. Apart from the cutting, a praiseworthy production.

November 4, 1931

OTHELLO
(Savoy)

MR. ROBESON

COMING away from the theatre on Monday evening a lady was heard to say that the performance had seemed to her to be exceedingly natural. Precisely. But according to whose nature? — that of Shakespeare's Moor or of the player who enacted him? It was always said of Peter Jackson, the famous Negro prize-fighter, that outside the ring he was the essence of the unassuming. But unassumingness has never knocked a man down, and Mr. Robeson's complete failure to cope with the essential part of Othello arose from the fact that he did not assume enough. It seems foolishly necessary to insist that there is no more reason to choose a negro to play Othello than to requisition a fat man for Falstaff. In fact, there is less reason; for while all fat men are alike in fatness there are enormous divergences of all sorts among men of the same colour. Mr. Robeson, as an extremely sensitive artist, must know the risk attending the assumption of assumingness by one of his race, and that that way Harlem lies. I suggest that he did not trust his powers *as an actor* sufficiently; he certainly did not take the risk, with the result that all that Othello ought to be throughout the first two acts he was not. 'Emperor, You'se gittin' mighty low!' was this actor's climax in Mr. O'Neill's play. 'General, you'se beginnin' mighty low!' summed up the first part of Mr. Robeson's Othello.

285

There are certain well-defined qualities which the great figures in Shakespeare must possess, or give up the ghost of those figures by being no more than their ghost. The first thing Othello must possess is majesty, a majesty compounded of pride of race ('I fetch my life and being From men of royal siege'), sovereign assurance ('Were it my cue to fight, I should have known it Without a prompter'), and self-command ('When I know that boasting is an honour,' etc.). These three points are made by Shakespeare at Othello's first entrance. But the scene also contains the extraordinarily significant line: 'Keep up your bright swords, for the dew will rust them.' This is a line to be felt, not argued about; and the feeling must be that it could only be uttered by a man of intellectual ascendancy. Writing of Salvini, the late W. T. Arnold has this passage: 'The actor who does not convey the higher elements of spiritual beauty in the character does not convey Shakespeare's Othello. Tried by this test, Salvini's Othello stands sovereignly high. Nothing can be nobler than his manner to Brabantio. One who has heard Salvini knows how the "Keep up your bright swords, for the dew will rust them," should be said, and has gained the true conception of the way to play the scene in which Othello breaks in upon Cassio's drunken brawl. These are scenes which must be played in the grand style or not at all, and Salvini is a master of the grand style.' Mr. Robeson, alas, failed not only to show mastery of the grand style, but also to indicate any idea of its existence! He said the line with a casualness which amounted almost to the meaningless. Then when he came to: 'Silence that dreadful bell,' the note was one of personal annoyance. It is true that the extremely significant 'It frights the isle From her propriety' could not be said because, with miraculous infelicity, it had been cut! One felt, however, that the line could not have come naturally from this Othello because his mind gave no indication of that passion for decorum which dictates it. It is a commonplace that Othello, to have won Desdemona and be credited with that military career, must be a man of fine physique. Kean, said Hazlitt, was not stately enough for Othello whom he played like a gipsy, and he goes on to talk about meridian suns, crown and turban, Eastern magnificence, and all the rest of it. In the physical aspect Mr. Robeson largely failed. Though in the mere matter of inches he towered above everybody else, it was a tower cringing. He walked with a stoop, his body sagged, his hands appeared to hang below his knees, and his whole bearing, gait, and diction were full of humility and apology: the inferiority-complex in a word. The great 'Farewell' speech was without pathos, for in it Othello said good-bye to things for which it was impossible that he could have cared. This was nigger Shakespeare.

And now I come to the point by which every Othello must stand or fall — the quality of his jealousy. It is a mistake to regard Shakespeare's play as though it were Leoncavallo's opera or a scenario for Emil Jannings drawn to bigger scale. The personal element in Othello's jealousy is exhausted in the third and fourth acts where, in his display of purely animal frenzy, Mr. Robeson was exceedingly fine. But in the fifth act the passion rises to the heights of philosophic conception, and Othello's pain gives place to the moral affrightment that such things can be. All the world knows Coleridge's 'Jealousy does not strike me as the point in Othello's passion; I take it to be rather an agony that the creature whom he had believed angelic . . . should be proved impure and worthless'. John Forster, echoing Coleridge, suggests that it is the loss not of Desdemona's love but of his belief in the purity of sex which opens beneath his feet 'a tremendous yawning grave'. This is the grave which, in Shakespeare, is always opening. It opens before Lear at his 'Let copulation thrive', before Hamlet at his 'Why wouldst thou be a breeder of sinners?' and is discovered by Shakespeare himself in the famous 'The expense of spirit' sonnet. Othello conceives Desdemona's death not as a murder but as a sacrifice, and kills her not out of passion but because her conduct has shaken the world from its propriety. The reason Mr. Robeson failed to be Othello was that he had none of this highly civilized quality. He was not 'being wrought, perplex'd in the extreme', but perplexed throughout. He was not like the base Indian who 'threw a pearl away richer than all his tribe'; he was that Indian. 'It is the cause, it is the cause, my soul; Let me not name it to you, you chaste stars!' is the phrase of a man familiar with the heavens. Throughout the play this Othello had his forehead bent to earth not only figuratively but literally.

But Mr. Robeson's performance had, to a quite amazing extent, the qualities of its defects. Though one may not have agreed with the plane, the performance on that plane was entirely consistent. The meeting with Desdemona after the victory had a most touching simplicity; the third and fourth acts were rendered with magnificent power, so that Othello ceased to be human and became a gibbering primeval man; and the last act achieved dignity and pathos. Nevertheless, I cannot agree that the passage beginning: 'Whip me, ye devils!' and ending: 'Wash me in steep-down gulfs of liquid fire!' should be *sighed* over Desdemona's body. Salvini always used to say that this was the one passage in which sound was more important than sense. The production did Mr. Robeson enormous disservice in the matter of the lighting which robbed his features of all expressiveness, and turned his face into a black, unintelligible mask. The scenery was by Mr. James Pryde, and a programme-note informed us that in order to retain the quality of Mr. Pryde's paintings no attempt had been made to light the scenes realistically. May I suggest that the first object of lighting in the theatre is not to flatter a scene-painter but to give enough light to see the actors by! Add the fact that nearly the whole of the play was produced up-stage and in remote corners, and we got the result that the tragedy appeared to be taking place not in our midst but in the next room. One word more. Mr. Robeson has a beautiful voice which he uses clearly and distinctly, but not beautifully, or rather, not in the way of Shakespearean beauty. Each line, as he delivers it, is a prose line made up of the rhythms and cross-currents of prose. One should not have expected anything else, for to ask any coloured actor, however great his qualities of mind and heart, to recite Shakespeare's blank verse at the first attempt is like asking an English player to jump at once into the silver stride of Racine. Apart from Miss Peggy Ashcroft's exquisite Desdemona and Miss Thorndike's workmanlike Emilia, the other

acting was for the most part on a dismal level. As Iago Mr.
Maurice Browne, whose enterprise we are to thank for this production, mis-cast himself. He trotted through the play like Jack
Point in a temper, some schoolboy whipping a top, some incom-
mensurate gnat. The text was shockingly manhandled to the
ruination of the verse and often of the meaning, Iago's motive
being reduced from the phantom that it is to the shadow of a
phantom. This was modesty on Mr. Browne's part, but it was
modesty in the wrong place.

Their Hour Upon the Stage: May 19, 1930

OTHELLO

(The Old Vic)

MR. WALTER

THE real performance of this play began when Emilia said, 'O
gull; O dolt!' and that was too late. It was also at this point that
Miss Edith Evans began to be Emilia, since in all the earlier scenes
she had been not Desdemona's woman but her governess, the
decayed chaperon superior to her charge. I take it that Emilia is
the wife of a man who married beneath him, and, Iago holding
the rank he does, something plebeian. That there is a grossness
about Emilia is proved by the relish with which she enters into
Desdemona's query as to the amount of dishonesty she would
commit to gain the world, and the slatternly gusto with which at
the end she falls to abusing Othello. Miss Evans delivered her
confession of potential venality with the nice malice of a cat invited
by an eighteenth-century poet to state its view about goldfish.
Again, her gait and the movements of her arms when she folded
Desdemona's dress, though constituting a dance first gracious and
then grave, did not, I take leave to think, belong to the character.
But with Emilia's first salvo or discharge of honest heart all other

criticism went by the board, and it was then that Miss Evans gave us the only real emotion of the afternoon.

Any performance of this play must stand or fall by its Othello, and if this is not right no sublimation that pedantry may fasten upon any other character in the play will compensate us. Now, there is only one question to be asked about any Othello: Has he temperament? We do not ask by this whether the actor correctly simulates the gestures and demeanour of passion, but whether he admits us to the presence of a man whose nature in quiescence is already full to its banks, and with whom any and every expression can only be an overflowing. In this sense Mr. Wilfrid Walter is as temperamental as an usher at a well-behaved public school, and his assumptions of temperament, though industrious and conscientious, leave us cold. It is, of course, largely a matter of nationality; every little pastry-cook in Italy washes him in steepdown gulfs of liquid fire each time his wife makes eyes at the apprentice. If this quality is not present the performance must fail, and it is only when one is satisfied about this that it is worth while asking whether the actor has the requisite looks and presence, nobility and power, the faculty to suggest moral grandeur, and the ability to deliver verse. Mr. Walter's Othello is at once careful and perfunctory. Take the passage:

> Cassio, I love thee;
> But never more be officer of mine.
> Look, if my gentle love be not rais'd up!
> I'll make thee an example.

There are four separate emotions here, Othello's regard for Cassio, his regret at the necessity for his dismissal, his annoyance that Desdemona should be waked, and the consequent savagery of 'I'll make thee an example'. Mr. Walter delivered this passage on one level tone, calling Cassio's attention to the fact that Desdemona had been roused as indifferently as if he had asked him to observe the weather. I am afraid, too, that this actor's delivery of verse is too modern for Shakespeare; at least his vowelsounds are those one hears on prize-giving day at a school in

Highgate. Mr. Walter must not take it amiss that one does not think he can play Othello. If this is not the most difficult part in the whole range of English drama it is still one which requires special qualification, the ability to suggest that passionate saturation the negation of which constitutes the English temper.

Now about Iago. The difficulty with this character is that Shakespeare having done an infeasible thing, we still insist upon the actor attempting that which Shakespeare made infeasible. The text gives two lame reasons for Iago's conduct, which have been supplemented by the critical explanation that Iago's diabolism, coming direct from the Devil and therefore outside human logic, is to be accepted as self-sufficient. We are, I understand, to have presently a fourth explanation, which will be of the Freudian order. But that can wait. The immediate point is that Shakespeare has insisted upon Iago having more brains, a finer subtlety, and a greater metaphysical itch than almost any other of his characters, and upon his hiding all these behind a mask of superlative honesty. Now to look like the flower and be the serpent under it is a part of feminine equipment, whereas the male actor who must achieve this can do so only by having one face for the characters in the play and another for the audience; in other words, he must have a virtuosity unpossessed by any player since Kean. Irving could look evil with one cheek and saintly with the other, but even that great actor could not compass the monster in the guise of *faux bonhomme*. Failing supreme virtuosity, what shall the actor attempt? Shall he contravene Shakespeare's instructions and so make us despise Othello for being too easily the dolt and gull? Or shall he stick to Shakespeare and present so singly honest a face that even the audience can read nothing else? Mr. Ralph Richardson chose the second course, and growing more and more honest as the play proceeded convinced us that he couldn't hurt a fly, which was very good Richardson but indifferent Shakespeare.

Except that it was on the young side Mr. Robert Harris's Cassio was well-intended; Mr. Robert Speaight made an excellent Roderigo until the end, when, harking back to his Fluellen, he fell into pribbles and prabbles; as Lodovico Mr. Richard Ainley made a good popinjay of the Duke's envoy, perfectly reproducing what we may suppose to have been the manner of the Venetian Foreign Office of the period. It will be kind to say that Desdemona is perhaps as much Miss Phyllis Thomas's part as it is that of any actress. I do not think, however, that she should say: 'Am I that name, Iago?' as though Iago had reminded her of a boring luncheon engagement that she was trying to get out of.

First Nights: March 9, 1932

OTHELLO

(St. James's)

MR. MILTON

Othello, above all other tragic personages, needs great physical qualities in the performer. — G. H. LEWES

A physically insignificant Othello is inconceivable. — W. T. ARNOLD

WILL received opinion do, or must I prove that the first condition of any Othello is that the actor shall be physically magnificent? I should not have thought this necessary if a colleague whose intellect I value highly had not asked me on going into the theatre why Othello should not have been a little man like Napoleon or Lord Roberts. There is no reason except our old friend, the *optique du théâtre*, by whose logic Romeo must be a good-looking stripling and Othello a magnificent animal. But since it is possible that Shakespeare never heard of the *optique du théâtre*, let us refer to the text and see what is to be gathered from that first entrance in which, as is this dramatist's way, the character is declared. Can all that talk beginning with 'royal siege' and rising to the climax of 'My parts, my title, and my perfect soul' be conceived as the crowing of a bantam? Nonsense! To be robbed of all that

292

is towering in Othello is like being fobbed off with a snub-nosed Romeo, though there is no reason *in life* why Romeo should not be as plain as Traddles. Is the reader worried about Desdemona's 'I saw Othello's visage in his mind?' Dear sir or madam, this is explanation, not apology! Just as Shakespeare calls our attention to the nobility of his blackamoor while our eyes are still taking in his physical splendour, so with equal care he repeats the pattern by giving Desdemona this line, since by it he endues her passion with a spiritual and poetic value and distinguishes it from your modern young woman's fancy for a jazz-drummer. Take away Othello's pride of body and Desdemona can only mean that while his dial, as she would say, is not up to much, his mentality is up to *The Waves* and D. H. Lawrence. Mr. Ernest Milton's physical limitations being what they are, Othello's famous line can only betray him, and we feel that this lover's *ultima ratio* ought to read: 'She had a *mind*, and chose me.'

Now how did under-sized Kean 'get away' with Othello? Compensation, says Lewes, was to be found in this actor's lion-like power and lion-like grace, 'and his eye! who can forget that eye?' But leonine is the last word one would use for Mr. Milton, who in place of the noble, perhaps vacant, and certainly slow, unblinking majesty of the King of Beasts exhibits the eager, nimble-witted watchfulness of one of the lesser and more apprehensive cats. I take it that the note of Othello is the sublimity of a great mind which is also a childish one, childish in its simplicity, trustfulness, and the inability to harbour suspicion. It is upon this open nature that Iago works, the only alternative being Othello's stupidity; and Othello is not stupid, only 'perplex'd i' th' extreme.' But guilelessness and the inability to perceive guile in others is the last quality to be conveyed by Mr. Milton, whose spirit is compact of umbrages, past, present and to come, and whose mind is quick with defences against attack from all quarters. It is this air of scenting injury which made this actor our only Henry IV (Pirandello), designated him for Death in Casella's play — an inevitable choice — and qualifies him for all that is morbid in Shakespeare — Hamlet, Richard II, King John. But

Othello is magnificently alive, and to sickly him with the pale cast of excessive thought is not to play him at all. The piece is a tragedy of disintegration, and that cannot be disintegrated which nerves have already pulled apart.

The result is that the slow awakening of Othello's jealousy goes by the board. Iago's 'That cuckold lives in bliss' would have fully awakened the husband of normal apprehension, though in Othello's case the mine is at this point only half-sprung. With Mr. Milton we cannot understand that the explosion does not occur at the first charge, and wonder that Iago is allowed to proceed with his 'Steal away so guilty-like,' 'No further harm,' and all those equivocations about for aught he knows and daring to be sworn. This mind, which obviously travels faster than its tormentor's, must have taken the alarm at the first whiff of jealous prompting, and we feel that the horrid mention of 'cuckold' must have ended the play there and then. The worst of that intellectual subtlety of which Mr. Milton is a master is that it cannot counterfeit slow-wittedness, and this being so the play's most ingenious scene is deprived of its excitement. Of Fechter's Othello it was said that 'even if the actor had been calm and simple in his gestures he could not have been dignified and impressive; nature had emphatically said No to such an effect. Voice and bearing would have failed him'. In the early part of the play Mr. Milton's bearing has immense dignity, and the speech to the Senate can seldom have been said better. Later on his bearing founders because too much is asked of it. Half of Othello lies in the actor's voice, and one has to say with regret that Mr. Milton's, besides being of insufficient volume, is distinguished for a quality which is the last that should go with Othello. Used conversationally this voice has light and shade and a certain music; whenever the actor must let it out rhetorically, and whenever there is any poetry to be mouthed, it soars into the treble, to become something between a moan and a whine, like the wind whistling among gibbets. Mr. T. S. Eliot has said of the speech beginning 'Behold, I have a weapon,' that here Othello is cheering himself up prior to the business of despatch, lashing himself into the requisite fury and rather like, I suggest, a nervous cricketer whistling his way to the wicket. Mr. Milton fails completely here, and the last four lines, of which Salvini said the sense should be drowned in noise, are lost in a frenzy of soundlessness. To compensate for this the actor attempts to convey the matter by jerking his body to and fro like a released Jack-in-the-Box whose wires are still quivering. It is this vocal inadequacy that turns Othello's rages into tantrums, and his fulminations about forty thousand lives and nine years a-killing into bagpipe dronings. I shall conclude this estimate by repeating what was said by an earlier critic of the German actor, Dessoir, in the part: 'I regard his performance as unsatisfactory, but as the performance of a highly intelligent actor struggling against natural deficiencies.'

Mr. Henry Oscar, cutting Iago according to his natural cloth, and realizing that diabolism cannot be got into round, smooth, boyish features, concentrates upon plausibility, leaving the motive for villainy very much where Shakespeare left it, that is in the dark. His plausibility, however, is complete, and has exactly that shade of contempt which goes with the inferiority complex. Miss Lydia Sherwood cannot overcome the initial difficulty of having to melt us with Desdemona's fragility of intellect while convincing us that she has enough strength of mind to choose a darkie. In the later parts she is more successful. Mr. Nicholas Hannen presents in Cassio the gentleman who, overcome by drink, remains a gentleman, and Mr. George Thirlwell as Roderigo avoids the fantastic, which I think is a mistake. Miss Athene Seyler makes Emilia a comfortable soubrette to have about the house, and Miss Flora Robson, equally unsuited as Bianca, achieves a little miracle. Since Miss Seyler is a first-class comédienne, and since Miss Robson could play all the hags in *Richard III* lumped together, it is obvious that the two should have changed rôles. Even so the piece would still have been run away with by Miss Robson and Mr. Oscar pounding neck and neck, with Mr. McKnight Kauffer's beautiful scenery half a length behind.

First Nights: April 4, 1932

OTHELLO

(The Old Vic)

MR. SOFAER

It is perhaps lawful to say that 'Othello' will always be a pretty good play so long as the Moor is played by a pretty good actor. Watching Mr. Abraham Sofaer the other night I could not get out of my mind a picture in words of an earlier player who produced upon a critic of his day the exact effect that Mr. Sofaer produced on me. When I got home I rummaged about, and in Leigh Hunt found this: 'It is in the acknowledgement of gesture and attitude, but more particularly in the variation of countenance in the adaptation of look to feeling, that the actor is best known. Mr. Pope, in his general style, has but two gestures, which follow each other in monotonous alternation, like the jerks of a toyshop harlequin: one is a mere extension of the arms, and is used on all occasions of candour, of acknowledgement, of remonstrance, and of explanation; the other, for occasions of vehemence or of grandeur, is an elevation of the arms, like the gesture of Raphael's St. Paul preaching at Athens, an action which becomes the more absurd on common occasions, from its real sublimity. If Mr. Pope, however, is confined to two expressions in his gesture, he has but two expressions in his look: a flat indifference, which is used on all sober occasions, and an angry frown, which is used on all impassioned ones. With these two looks he undertakes to represent all the passions, gentle as well as violent; he is like a quack who, with a phial in each hand, undertakes to perform every possible wonder, while the only thing to be wondered at is his cheating the mob.' Almost every word of this describes my view of Mr. Sofaer's performance. This Othello may be said to be acted in a mask because it is played with one set of features which never alters. Except for the movement of the lips in speaking, not a muscle in the actor's face is moved to differentiate between joy, tenderness, perplexity, and rage; the player has, as we say, no facial expression. The voice, though noble, is monotony itself, being, except for the differences of loud and soft the same throughout; the spectator who had no English would have difficulty in knowing what kind of passion the actor was in.

In the following passage:

> I know, Iago,
> Thy honesty and love doth mince this matter,
> Making it light to Cassio. Cassio, I love thee;
> But never more be officer of mine.
> Look, if my gentle love be not raised up!
> I'll make thee an example

there are four changes of voice. The sentence addressed to Iago is normal and civil. That addressed to Cassio shows deep emotion struggling with duty. That to Desdemona should be marked by great annoyance, and it is this vexation which causes Othello to turn and rend Cassio. Mr. Sofaer made hardly any difference between the tone of these four sentences. It is obvious that this part, more than any other in Shakespeare, requires physical attractiveness in the actor, who must not add other handicap to Othello beyond his colour. Mr. Sofaer has stature and presence, but, alas; 'Le voilà donc ce nez qui des traits de son maître a détruit l'harmonie!' This matters nothing at all in the case of your Bolingbrokes and Mortimers, but as Cyrano well knew, it bars the way to romantic passion. In the matter of gesture Mr. Sofaer is as limited as was Pope. He, also, has two gestures. The first is when in unimpassioned moments the arms are raised either full or half-cock like railway signals; the second is when in impassioned moments the fist is shaken on a level with the forehead.

All this is not to say that Mr. Sofaer's performance is not an understanding one; it is understanding in the sense that we are persuaded that Mr. Sofaer understands it. But the business of the player is summed up in the Witches': 'Show his eyes, and grieve his heart.' The player must wring our hearts by exhibiting something shocking to our eyes; this, and not interior thinking, is the whole business of acting. In the actor's sense Mr. Sofaer does nothing with the part except exhibit its dignity, which may or may not be the same thing as suggesting, as one of my colleagues does, that it is a performance 'masterly in the flowing urgency of its thought'. In my view a little less urgent thinking and a little more practical doing is what is wanted in the theatre, and I shall stand by my guns and say that the first demand to make of any player is that he shall show us not what he has thought in the study but what he can do on the stage. In other words he must be *theatrical* in the first sense of that word, and Mr. Sofaer's Othello is the last word in untheatricality. I conceive this actor as extremely valuable in performances where a cold northern dominance and austerity are the note; when the wind is southerly he has little to give us. In other words, he lacks that on which the whole nature of Othello is built — to wit, temperament. May I put it that Mr. Sofaer is a fine actor in a school of acting whose validity I deny, though conceding that it is all a matter of opinion? As Johnson remarked in *The Rambler*: 'In things which are not immediately subject to religious or moral consideration, it is dangerous to be too rigidly in the right.'

As Iago Mr. Maurice Evans acted from the moment he came on to the stage. And went on acting, in the sense that you may take pleasure in a pianist's finger-work apart from his intellectual conception of the composer's idea. This was a boyish, eager Iago, perhaps a little too light in colour, but vivid and full of variety, making you feel that his words were the coinage of an ecstasy now first minted, and not the measured delivery of something conned and pondered. The Desdemona of Miss Vivienne Bennett was exceedingly moving, despite a dimpling, dumpling countenance which suggests that domestic pathos and not high tragedy will be her better medium. Miss Mary Newcombe as Emilia was temperamentally much more Moorish than the Moor, though I thought her a trifle too ladylike; Emilia should be more tart, with the tartness of peasant stock which has been taken into a great lady's household. However, Miss Newcombe went after the part like a shark after a nigger's leg, and took huge and successful bites out of it to everybody's delectation. A brilliant performance of a part which every actress with brains knows to be a grand one.

More First Nights: January 21, 1935

OTHELLO
(The Old Vic)

MR. RICHARDSON

THE late W. T. Arnold once ventured to think that a Manchester audience knew how to distinguish Talbot's Michonnet, which had been first-rate, from his Théramène. Similarly, I venture to think that the Old Vic audience will not confound Mr. Ralph Richardson's Othello, which in my view is an almost total failure, with his many genuine and unchallengeable successes in parts of a different order. Let it be said straight away that the fault is not one of intelligence. I have no doubt that Mr. Richardson perceives everything that there is in the rôle; the difficulty is that he has not the physical means to put his perceptions into practice. I am to assure Mr. Richardson here that it is as painful for me to write this as it would be for him if he should read it. He is an actor for whom every playgoer must have unwavering respect. He has never appeared in an unworthy play, nor has he until now ever filled a part almost wholly inadequately. The pity of it is that his Othello begins and ends so well. I think I never heard the address to the Senate given with a quieter dignity; the actor makes this a river of speech full to the banks, urgent but without noise. Nor have I ever heard better delivery of the miraculously beautiful 'If it were now to die' speech. But all this was before Iago's poison had begun to work. The last act, too, is wonderfully fine if you can look upon Othello as arrived at that state when he is already dead, with the violences of life put behind him and nothing left save the pathos of the end. Therefore one would say that Mr. Richardson satisfies in the approach to, and the retreat from, passion. But when it comes to the point of passion, lo and behold and a thousand times alas, he has none!

Yet it is obvious that he feels the need for passion, since we see him striving after it. He is like a chauffeur at the starting-handle wrenching his arm off but getting no spark because the engine is cold. The truth is that Nature, which has showered upon this actor the kindly gifts of the comedian, has unkindly refused him any tragic facilities whatever. His voice has not a tragic note in its whole gamut, all the accents being those of sweetest reasonableness. He cannot blaze. He saws away at his nether lip with the enthusiasm of a Queen's Hall fiddler. But nothing happens. Worse still, the result is faintly comic. Mr. Richardson must forgive me if I say that his broad, moony countenance, rich in bemusement and twilight conception, irresistibly reminded me of something Montague wrote about another great comedian when he once appeared in pantomime as a negro sea-cook: 'Mr. Harry Tate, with his face blacked except a liberal margin round the mouth, to give enormity and expressiveness to that feature, and then convulsed with apprehension by a proposal that he should break into the captain's cabin and steal a chart from under the carpet, was a sight to rout the brood of cares. "What about my breathing arrangements?" he demanded, the vast lips and the emergent eyes convolving and rolling with horror.' Thus do the eyes of this Othello convolve and roll. The difficulty as between an extremely sensitive artist and, I hope, a not insensitive critic is that when the actor's aim is high enough both performance and criticism are touch-and-go. When this Othello said: 'Though I do prove her haggard,' or: 'I'll chop her into messes,' or anything else in this vein, one did not even begin to believe him. But suppose we try keeping this performance and changing the part? If it were feasible to stage *Green Pastures*, what other English actor could approach Mr. Richardson as De Lawd? And this without jot or tittle of alteration in his present make-up and present temper. Then I see him, too, as Tchehov's

Kuligin, frantic to overlook a wife's infidelity. 'On peut résister à tout hors la bienveillance,' said Rousseau. Which being translated means that it's all up with any Othello who has any truck with compunction! And Mr. Richardson is made of nothing else.

There is an old nursery-rhyme which, for the purpose of this article, runs:

> Jack Sprat could eat no fat;
> His wife would eat no lean!

I have pronounced Mr. Richardson to be incapable of playing Othello. I follow this up by saying that Mr. Laurence Olivier can play Iago, but won't. For obviously any actor who can make any kind of shot at Macbeth must carry enough guns for Iago. Why does Mr. Olivier, who has the guns, refuse to use them? Why does he turn down what in pre-Freud and pre-Jung days was a plain monster in favour of some super-subtle dilettante, looking upon the murder of another man's spirit not only as a fine art, but as a highly amusing one to boot? Perhaps 'monster' is not quite the right word. One of Hazlitt's finest essays is on the character of Iago, who, he declares, when he was a child killed flies for sport. The grown man is a mass of 'diseased intellectual activity, with an almost perfect indifference to moral good or evil, or rather with a preference for the latter, because it falls more in with his favourite propensity, gives greater zest to his thoughts and scope to his actions'. Again: 'His amusements, if they are amusements, are severe and saturnine — even his wit blisters . . . There is in all his conversation an inveterate misanthropy, a licentious keenness of perception, which is always sagacious of evil, and snuffs up the tainted scent of its quarry with rancorous delight. An exuberance of spleen is the essence of the character.' Mr. Olivier gives us the exuberance but omits the spleen, and before we condemn this utterly we are, I suggest, to remember that this was exactly the vein in which Edmund Kean conceived the character! Hazlitt argues very nicely about Kean's performance. He does not want whoever plays Iago to 'exhibit an assassin going to the place of execution'. And he goes on: 'But though we do not wish him to be represented as a monster, or a fiend, we see no reason why he should instantly be converted into a pattern of comic gaiety and good humour.' He complains that Kean 'abstracted the wit of the character', that it was 'too full of trim levity and epigrammatic conciseness'. And that in a nutshell must be our reproach against Mr. Olivier's otherwise clever and always admirably mimed performance. Thomas Rhymer in 1693 first suggested that the plot-mechanics of this play belong not to tragedy but to comedy, meaning that a mislaid handkerchief is too light a thing to support the tragic loading of that bed. I have sometimes played with the idea that this piece might easily have been a comedy with Othello breaking its back, as Shylock breaks that of *The Merchant*. In this event Mr. Olivier's Iago would be entirely praiseworthy. Actually it is as though a light tenor should be cast for the part of Mephistopheles in the opera. Facts, however, are stubborn things, and the truth is that neither Gounod nor Shakespeare thought of light tenors in connection with Mephistopheles and Iago.

And I am sure that Shakespeare did not think of Kensington and Shepherd Market in connection with Desdemona and Emilia. It is conceivable that Miss Curigwen Lewis is doing the best she can for the former. Whereas Miss Martita Hunt ought to know better than send that forthright peasant woman who is Emilia in mincing search of the elegances. There were two rays of light in the darkness. One was the excellent Roderigo of Mr. Stephen Murray; the other was the quite first-class scenery of Mr. Roger Furse.

February 8, 1938

OTHELLO
(The Old Vic)

MR. VALK

THE part of Othello annihilates pretentiousness, and shows quietism the door. It goes against the English grain, demanding *fougue* from a race famous for phlegm; chopping into messes — the Moor's way with wantons — is nòt what we call cricket. Over and over again this unique rôle has defeated the English actor constitutionally averse from sawing his nether lip. Kemble, 'dry and tearless — was going to begin, but nothing came of it'. Macready 'whined and whimpered'. Forester 'ludicrously incapable in gold lace and crimson cotton velvet like an old-fashioned pulpit'. Young 'left no recollection'. Phelps's performance 'was far from his best'. My beloved Irving 'resembled one of Fenimore Cooper's Mohawk braves wrapped in his blanket'. Wilson Barrett 'was like a temperance lecturer'. Forbes-Robertson 'did not harrow us, did not freeze the blood in our veins'. Paul Robeson was 'a cringing tower'. Wilfrid Walter was 'careful and perfunctory'. Abraham Sofaer 'lacked that on which the whole nature of Othello is built — temperament'. Ernest Milton 'gave the unsatisfying performance of a highly intelligent actor struggling against natural deficiencies'. That good comedian Ralph Richardson was 'an almost total failure'. That fine player Donald Wolfit 'wanted a banjo'. The few exceptions were Edmund Kean, 'the finest piece of acting in the world', and the too-little-remembered G. V. Brooke. In my day there have been Godfrey Tearle, always granting that Othello was a Spanish grandee in disguise, Edmund Willard, who made a brave shot and few mistakes, and Baliol Holloway. Authorities: Hazlitt, Leigh Hunt, Dutton Cook, Knight, Shaw, Grein, Agate.

Free of the English handicap, the Czech actor Mr. Frederick Valk struck at once the note of immense dignity. Rightly he declined to make points in Othello's 'round unvarnish'd tale', preferring to play himself in, and give us time to take stock of his physical qualifications. Had the actor a mobile and *expressive* countenance? Did the neck-muscles bespeak virility? Was the head properly set on the shoulders? And were these broad enough to come through the 'moving accidents by flood and field'? One has seen Othellos so reduced by slavery that, like Mesty in *Midshipman Easy*, they are only fit to 'boil de kettle for de young gentlemen'. Had the actor's voice that ringing tone which in this country has for so long been the monopoly of the telephone service? Mr. Valk's delivery of 'Keep up your bright swords' settled that point. Long before the landing in Cyprus, any playgoer with half an eye and half an ear must have been satisfied that here was an authentic tragedian. Very skilfully this fine player avoided the trap of too easily believing in Desdemona's guilt, and equally he resisted the temptation to overdo the epilepsy. The ravages eating into Othello's mind are more terrible still, and Mr. Valk went on to fulfil them completely. Remarkable throughout was the ground-swell of passion, which, when the storm intermitted, did not subside all at once. But an actor may do all this and yet not be Othello. An English bishop, visiting Anatolia, entered a café and seated himself at a table opposite a large blond man eating spaghetti. Affably he began, 'I hear you have been much troubled with massacres?' Waving his fork, the man replied, 'Monsieur, avec ce bras j'ai éventré six femmes et dix enfants!' This is Othello's vein — the return, once the veneer of civilization is discarded, to the simple-minded, natural butcher. The Moor is *au fond* child and savage; he is *not* a Don Diègue strayed out of Corneille after getting himself painted the wrong colour. Mr. Valk conveyed what should be conveyed in Titian-like gestures and with sufficient poetry. Sufficient provided the spectator did his share. Is the foreign actor essaying Shakespeare *thinking* Shakespeare's poetry? If the spectator is convinced of this, it becomes his duty to help the actor in the matter of flow and cadence. Mr. Valk obviously knew when Othello should be speaking poetry, and one spectator at least was willing to do the rest for him. His exits had a sweeping grandeur more satisfying than most English actors' entrances, and my one suggestion is that he should discover a volume of tone somewhere between *ff* and *pp*. This being found, I announce the best Othello since Salvini, 'king of them all by his birthright under Southern suns'.

I do not pretend to have seen Salvini, whose last performance of Othello in this country took place two years before I was born. Neither did I see Grasso, about whom I must be content to take Sir Max Beerbohm's view. 'To regard Signor Grasso as from the English standpoint a passable Othello—let alone a "superb" one — is possible only to people who cannot distinguish tragedy from "knockabout" . . . Strength Signor Grasso has. Dignity, a sense of beauty, intellect, he may have; but there is no sign of them . . . Let us not make fools of ourselves about his alleged Othello.' And there are other gaps. I did not see the Othellos of Benson, Bourchier, Hubert Carter, Lewis Waller, Oscar Asche, Tree, or Matheson Lang. The last-named may well have been a good Othello; the pity of it was that he preferred to stump the country with a hybrid called *Carnival*, in which, if I remember rightly, he went to a fancy dress ball dressed as the Moor. I also did not see Randle Ayrton, though, judging from his Ford, he must have been very fine. Last on my list of Othellos overlooked is John Laurie, of whom a brother critic wrote that it was 'an exciting presentation of a neurotic Arab'. This raises another point — the sixth sense of the dramatic critic, enabling him to reconstruct a past performance, or deduce a present one from what he already knows about a particular player. Of the last-named actor's Ferdinand in *The Duchess of Malfi* I wrote that 'Mr. Laurie, despite his ravings, writhings, reelings, never came near frightening me; one brushed him off the mind like a fly. This actor's voice is too light, and what he falls into is a pet rather than a rage; the harder he acts, the more peevish that pet comes'. I may be doing Mr. Laurie an injustice, but I do not believe that he can alter the timbre of his voice or keep peevishness away; on the other hand I can see he would be admirable as Iago. If my view be correct, then Laurie's Othello is ruled out, just as my sixth sense would rule out his immediate forerunners with the exception of Lang and Ayrton. I do not hold Valk's performance to be ideal. It is a good performance because it contains the three essential things: nobility, temperament, and that suggestion of being pole-axed for which Shakespeare's expression is 'perplex'd in the extreme'. All the other Othellos I have seen have failed in one or other of these essential qualifications, and to possess any two and lack the third is just not to be Othello. If an actor is not Othello, then no amount of beautiful verse-speaking can save him. If he is Othello, then in the case of an actor playing in a strange tongue — Salvini acted in his own — we must expect something less than perfect delivery of the verse. Valk's faults include insufficient pathos and excessive bulk. He is slow and German, the buffalo rather than the tiger. Not by any means an ideal Othello. But I repeat, all things considered, the best I have seen.

A foreign accent may well be conceded to the Moor; whether his Ancient should indulge in vowel-sounds reminiscent of the Waterloo Road is more questionable. And should he make-up to look like all Second Murderers rolled into one? And since Iago is Othello's standard-bearer and not his batman, must the actor not make it credible that he should come within the General's social circle? Mr. Bernard Miles satisfied me on none of these points. But it was a good performance, earthy yet mercurial. Did he make the Ancient credible? No, but neither did Shakespeare. There is a good deal to be said for the point of view that the play was written at white-heat, or thrown together in a hurry, which comes to the same thing. Shakespeare was never averse to dragging in a bit of what, in Elizabethan days, passed for psychology, and perhaps with the recollection of his rival Marlowe's Mephistophilis, vanity as well as artistry told him not to be satisfied with a round unvarnished villain. The result, as Mr. Shaw pointed out long ago, is a hopeless mess. Mr. Miles wisely made no attempt to clear up the mess, and was amusing throughout in the manner of a black-hearted Sam Weller. As Cassio, that promising actor Mr. Laurence Payne was a little over-weighted; but he tried hard and will presently do. Miss Hermione Hannen made Desdemona so fragile that one was afraid she would come apart. Miss Freda Jackson was not only extremely effective as Emilia but looked Italian to boot, and Miss Renee Ascherson will be better when Bianca stops shrieking like an express train entering a tunnel. Good scenery by Mr. Frederick Crooke, delightful music by Mr. Clifton Parker, first-class production by Mr. Julius Gellner, the interpretation with the fewest excuses to be made for it of any recent Shakespeare production, and a triumph for the Old Vic. The fashionables stopped away, it was quite like old times, and I thought I heard Baylis applauding.

July 25, 1942

INDEX

308

INDEX

INDEX

310

INDEX